D0295452

09

Black and Asian Athletes in British Sport and Society

Black and Asian Athletes in British Sport and Society

A Sporting Chance?

Patrick Ismond

First published 2003 by
PALGRAVE MACMILLAN
Houndmills, Basingstoke, Hampshire RG21 6XS and
175 Fifth Avenue, New York, N.Y. 10010
Companies and representatives throughout the world

PALGRAVE MACMILLAN is the global academic imprint of the Palgrave
Macmillan division of St. Martin's Press, LLC and of Palgrave Macmillan Ltd.
Macmillan® is a registered trademark in the United States, United Kingdom
and other countries. Palgrave is a registered trademark in the European
Union and other countries.

ISBN 0–333–92061–9 hardback

This book is printed on paper suitable for recycling and made from fully
managed and sustained forest sources.

A catalogue record for this book is available from the British Library.

Library of Congress Cataloging-in-Publication Data

Ismond, Patrick.
    Black and Asian athletes in British sport and society : a sporting
    chance? / Patrick Ismond.
        p.   cm.
    Includes bibliographical references and index.
    ISBN 0–333–92061–9
    1. Racism in sports—Great Britain.   2. Sex discrimination in
    sports—Great Britain.   3. Sports—Social aspects —Great Britain.
    4. Great Britain—Race relations   I. Title.

GV706.32.I84 2003
796'.089—dc21

                                                            2003041435

10   9   8   7   6   5   4   3   2   1
12   11   10   09   08   07   06   05   04   03

Printed and bound in Great Britain by
Antony Rowe Ltd, Chippenham and Eastbourne

To my family, and to the 'dorsal-finned Stobbider'

Contents

List of Figures	viii
Acknowledgements	ix
Notes on the Interviewees	x
Introduction: a Sporting Chance?	xiii
Part I 'Race' and Male Sport	**1**
1 Understanding 'Race' and Sport	3
2 British Minority Ethnic Groups, Sport and Society	23
3 Sporting Beginnings	55
4 Sport in the Later Years	91
Part II 'Race', Gender and Sport	**125**
5 Women and Sport	127
6 Interviews with Black and Asian Sportswomen	143
Conclusion	183
Bibliography	188
Index	197

List of Figures

3.1   Cyrille Regis (*Photo courtesy of Action Rewind
      Photography*)   56
3.2   Jason Gardener (*Photo courtesy of Mark Shearman*)   57
3.3   Garth Crooks (*Photo courtesy of BBC Press Office*)   58
3.4   Gurbinder Singh (*Photo courtesy of Darren Holloway*)   60
3.5   Chris Sanigar   61
3.6   Paul Hull (*Photo courtesy of Bristol United Press*)   63
3.7   David Lawrence (*Photo courtesy of Bristol United Press*) 72
3.8   Sean Viera   77
3.9   Martin Offiah (*Photo courtesy of Wigan Observer*)   82
3.10 Zia Haque   89
4.1   Viv Anderson (*Photo courtesy of Middlesbrough
      Football Club*)   112
6.1   Joice Maduaka, front (*Photo courtesy of Mark Shearman*) 144
6.2   Azmina Mitha, left   154
6.3   Ivy Alexander   164
6.4   Myra Barretto   174

Acknowledgements

Many people have helped me in my journey to finish this book. I thank the fifteen athletes for trusting me enough to share their honest, considered, and at times inspiring views about the issues raised here. Without their contributions, the study would be so much the less. Throughout the time it has taken me to produce this book, I was also fortunate to receive the intellectual and emotional support of friends, colleagues and associates. I thank Ellis Cashmore, John Solomos, Stuart Allan, Jo Haynes and Judith Ramsden for looking at and commenting on early drafts of chapters; and Terry Henry, Jason Pegg and Jo Hopkins for commenting on later chapters. In particular, my heartfelt thanks go to Mark Taylor, whose insights and suggestions about the entire manuscript helped to formulate my ideas. I also owe a debt of gratitude to Jon Garland, in his role as prepublication reviewer, for helpful comments on the manuscript. My task of researching historical information was made so much easier by extremely helpful librarians. You are too many to mention, but special thanks must go to Ann Collings at Leicester University. You saved me at the last. I thank Karen Brazier, formerly of Palgrave Macmillan, for showing faith in the project in the first place, and also Jennifer Nelson for her advice and support. I also thank the team-mates who have played inside, outside and upfront of me during many never-say-die football matches. This 'community' contains people who have cajoled and supported me through fireside conversations about the subject of racism and sport, and helped me to persevere with the project. They are my closest friends. A special thanks to Billy Clay, Frank D'Arcy and Joel Samuels. Of course, the final responsibility for what remains is mine.

My biggest personal debt is to Jo Hopkins, without whose understanding and support, this book would not have been completed.

Notes on the Interviewees

Ages and information are relevant to the time of interview.

Former élite professionals

Viv Anderson (44 years) became the first black footballer to play in a full international for England. He has won numerous domestic honours in the game, and at the time of interview was assistant coach at Middlesbrough FC.

Garth Crooks (41 years) enjoyed a successful football career before becoming a leading sports journalist and broadcaster.

Paul Hull (32 years) combined success in rugby union with a career in the Royal Air Force. He gained a number of full representative caps for England in the 1990s, whilst playing for Bristol Rugby Club. At the time of interview, he was employed in a corporate hospitality role for the club.

David Lawrence (35 years) enjoyed a distinguished career in first-class cricket, becoming the first British-born black man to represent England at international level. He owns and runs a number of businesses in the West of England.

Cyrille Regis (41 years) had a long and successful football career, and was one of the first black men to represent England at full international level. Until recently, he worked at West Bromwich Albion FC in a coaching and administrative capacity.

Chris Sanigar (46 years) had a long and successful career as an amateur boxer, before turning professional and becoming the number one contender for the British Light Welterweight title. He currently works as a boxing trainer and promoter.

Current élite professionals and semi-professionals

Jason Gardener (26 years) is one of Britain's top male sprinters. He is the European indoor 60 metre champion, and one of the very few British athletes to run 100 metres in under ten seconds. He regularly competes on the international circuit.

Joice Maduaka (27 years) is one of Britain's top women sprinters. In 1998, she was crowned British champion over 60 metres (indoors) and 100 metres. She regularly competes on the international circuit, and has run one of the fastest times ever recorded by a British woman over 100 metres.

Martin Offiah (35 years) is arguably the most well-known rugby league player the British game has ever produced. A former member of the England and Great Britain Lions teams, Offiah has broken many records in a prolific try-scoring career. He has also won the domestic games' most prestigious honours. He currently plays for a rugby union club in London.

Gurbinder Singh (23 years) is a British weightlifting champion who competes in the 105kg class. He has competed at various national championships and won a bronze medal at the 2002 Commonwealth Games.

Sean Viera (33 years) has been a world and European kickboxing champion three times, and won the British championship eight times. He is a martial arts instructor, runs a security firm, and is promotions manager for a jazz dance troupe.

Current serious amateurs

Ivy Alexander (43 years) plays competitive, amateur football in a women's Sunday league team. She is employed as a social worker.

Myra Barretto (36 years) plays tennis and netball to County standard, and has also swum competitively. She is a qualified primary school teacher.

Zia Haque (53 years) played county-level badminton and hockey whilst in the army. Haque continues to play badminton to county standard, and manages his own sports shop.

Azmina Mitha (21 years) is a qualified self-defence instructor in Ju-Jitsu, a Japanese form of martial art. She has worked for Awaz Utaoh (see Chapter 6) for two years, in a part-time capacity.

Introduction: a Sporting Chance?

The idea that the world's population groups can be divided into discrete categories, or 'races', each with their own physical and psychological attributes, has a long history. Nowadays, the term 'race' can still be heard in everyday discourse, but has generally been discredited by science and academia. However, the spirit of this classification lives on, even if the terminology has changed. Populist discourses now refer to 'cultural differences' existing between different ethnic groups; whilst there has been a renewed interest in genetics and heredity. These more recent discourses, and the priorities of some scientific research, contribute to perpetuating ingrained beliefs about black and Asian groups, and their relationship to sport (see 'A Note on Terminology' below).

The logic of 'cultural racism' stresses that cultural groups share the distinctiveness of 'races', but rejects claims about their biological foundations. It is the lifestyle patterns, customs and mores of different cultures, rather than their biological attributes, which ultimately causes problems in shared social contexts. On the one hand, minority ethnic groups in Britain have experienced a general degree of social mobility and integration in the last thirty years. This has led to a more sophisticated analysis of racism in society, and a recognition of Britain's *de facto* multiculturalism. On the other hand, the racist murder of black teenager Stephen Lawrence was a signal of how unresolved 'race' is, whilst dominant references to minority ethnic groups have emphasised important signs of incongruity, thereby endorsing the logic of cultural racism. Media discourses constantly remind us about unsustainable 'floods' of illegal immigrants and 'bogus' asylum-seekers, with their alien, threatening lifestyles. At the same time, Norman Tebbit's 'cricket test', and the former Conservative Party leader William Hague's reference to Britain as a 'foreign land' (2001), showed how the coded language of race is used to signify discourses about the state of the nation, and nationality. Equally, the failure of black boys in the British education system; the perceived shortcomings of the black family; and the haunting spectre of black 'criminality' and inner-city disturbances, are interpreted by the media as more entrenched signs of problematic 'difference'.

The levels of interest shown by black people for sport, and their spectacular success in it, strikingly counterpoise these references; confirming sport as a 'natural' antidote to black social exclusion and marginalisation. When measured by the same criteria, a 'profile' of

British Asian groups broadly suggests higher educational achievement, and 'positive' family/kinship systems. The lack of Asian sporting success at international level has cemented dominant ideas about Asian religions and cultures as alternative forms of social authority, and sport as a purely recreational pursuit.

Genetics research is in rude health, and further supports the belief that the characteristics of different population groups can be predetermined: or, at the very least, are fixed to some degree. The ontological feel of some much-publicised genetics research has fed the public imagination, and is reflected in projects as diverse as the cloning of sheep, and the isolation of genes for intelligence and criminality. Organised competitive sport, with its emphasis on the harnessing of physical strength and discipline, and the ability to make decisions under pressure, has always represented a means by which genetic (read as 'racial') attributes could be seen in practice. In this context, 'race realists' (cf. Back *et al.*, 2001) are seeking to establish that specific population groups possess certain innate 'advantages' over other groups. In other words, that sportsmen (for it is invariably men) are born and not made.

Whether black success in sports is due to 'natural' athletic gifts, or to a combination of social, cultural and biological factors, is at the heart of debates over 'race' and sport. These debates are held at a range of levels in sport and outside of it: from sport's grass roots, to its more formalised echelons; by the media, and by interested members of the general public. Discussions about the strengths and weaknesses of black, Asian and white athletes are routinely expressed as part of everyday discourse. Black athletes in Western Europe and the Americas have been spectacularly successful in disciplines requiring strength, agility, power and speed. This level of success, and their accompanying absence from sports coaching and management, have led to their 'natural' abilities being defined in predominantly 'physical' terms, while the success of white managers and coaches, and the eclipsing of white achievements in sports like basketball, American football and track athletics, has led to a strengthening of ideas about white mental acuity in sport. 'Commonsense' thinking on race and sport posits that white athletes work harder to achieve less spectacular results on the field, but demonstrate tactical and strategic aptitudes for the structure, control, team leadership and organisation of sport. These attributes also 'justify' white predominance in certain strategic roles within sport, and a black presence in positions where their physical attributes can be given free rein.

In Britain, a changing social climate, legislation and government-backed initiatives have helped to rid popular sports of more 'open' shows of racism. As a result, football in particular has experienced an increase in attending minority ethnic fans; albeit at the higher, élite levels where these measures have been most effective. The testimonies of black and Asian fans contained in such football publications as *Four-Four-Two* indicate that they feel less threatened by, and more included in, the rituals and meanings that are integral to sporting cultures. The issue of non-white people laying claim to British sporting institutions and values is important, given that the 'face' of British (particularly English) sport is increasingly multicultural. As the most obvious sign of a changing Britain, sport is also the focus for questions of national identity. These continue to surface, and reflect unease about the conjunction of Britishness with blackness and Asianness.

We are used to seeing a post-competition Denise Lewis, Arvind Parmar and Dwain Chambers (athletics, tennis, athletics respectively), drape themselves in the flags of Britain and St George. The spectacular achievements of élite black athletes, either as individuals or as part of a team, are interpreted as evidence that barriers based on race have dissolved, and that sport in particular is a meritocracy, largely free of discrimination. Even with more sophisticated discourses about the causes of racism, the success of the few can obscure the complex of reasons why (for instance) black and Asian athletes have largely failed to breach the highest barriers relating to management and coaching; or why an English-born cricketer of Asian origin is yet to play for the county of Yorkshire's first team; or why Asian women 'appear' (Parmar, 1995) to have no interest in sport at any level. The success of the few also comes at the price of increased intolerance of claims of racism, which affects participation at all levels. To be black or Asian *and* British is still an un-negotiated site of tension in sport, as elsewhere.

Referring to the concept of 'race', Husband (1987, p. 11) has suggested that: 'beneath its apparently simple reduction of complex individuals and societies to self-evidently basic units there is a highly complex body of emotive ideas'. He has argued that our belief in the existence of race lies in the concept's adaptability; its ability to not only make seemingly coherent sense out of contradictory and changed developments, but to exist at very abstract and specific levels. In sports such as football, black men have circumvented one-dimensional and long-standing ideas about their aptitude and temperament. But the ability of ideas about race to adapt, and to make sense of a lived reality, means that new race meanings emerge which both reify the concept, and mask uneven relations of power between different 'racial' groups. When black sprinters regularly run 100 metres in less than ten seconds, and white weightlifters invariably lift world-record amounts; when black athletes hold no records for swimming events, but exhibit a near-total dominance at the highest echelons of basketball; when quarter-backs in US football are predominantly white, in spite of a significant black presence in the sport; when black men appear to 'transcend' racial stereotypes in sports and thereby declare racism an outdated irrelevance; and when black sporting prowess does not translate to coaching and management, then popular understandings about sport and race are confirmed at a 'commonsense' level, and the real extent of 'progress' is obscured.

'Race' and sport in Britain

A substantial body of academic research on racism and sport has emanated from the US. This literature has examined the socio-economic and cultural factors shaping (predominantly) black access to, and experiences in, certain sports (see for example Chu and Seagrave, 1983; Omi, 1989; Greendorfer, 1992). By contrast, there is a relative 'silence' in the sociological literature on racism and sport in Britain. The sociology of 'race' and ethnicity has tended to examine discrimination in other spheres such as health, education, employment and housing. Historically, there has even been a dearth of writing in sports where minority ethnic men have had a presence to some degree, such as boxing and athletics; whilst the experiences of more recent sports stars have tended to be conveyed through the medium of individual biography. What follows is a partial and brief reference to sources on sport and 'race' in Britain (see also Chapters 1–6).

Cashmore's *Black Sportsmen* (1982) is a significant, pioneering attempt to examine the issue of racism and sport in Britain. *Black Sportsmen* sought to uncover the reasons why so many black men enter sport, and what their experiences of racism were across a range of different sporting contexts. But whilst providing a useful intervention, the study has been criticised for findings based on an atypical study of black male athletes competing in a narrow range of sports; and for its 'pathological' profile of the black family. It has also received some criticism for failing to fully account for class-related factors in explaining the different attitudes to sport between African-Caribbean, Asian and white groups. The edited collection of essays in Jarvie's *Sport, Racism, and Ethnicity* (1995) have more of an international than a British-based focus. Its British studies are presented as 'stand-alone' contributions, looking at the specific problems confronting (for example) Asian boys in an inner-city school, or élite black sportsmen. As such, the British studies do not engage in a comparative analysis of interviewee experiences. What the various contributions *do* share is the call for an analysis of racism to be grounded in relations of power, in specific social contexts. As Jarvie argues, research on sport, race and ethnicity often fails to differentiate between structural and individual change. Since it is perfectly possible to have individual mobility within a rigid stratification structure, this is one way in which dominant groups in society can secure broad consent for their ideas and actions from subordinated groups. For this reason, cultural and structural processes need to be considered in analysing the impact of racism.

Studies examining the relationship between sport and race in football have appeared in academic journals, or as detailed research monographs. For example, there is a significant and influential body of work produced by Leicester University's Football and Sociology of Sport centres (see for example Williams, 1992; Garland and Rowe, 1999; Bradbury, 2001). The complex ways in which race, nation and identity are articulated within contemporary football cultures are explored in *The Changing Face of Football* (Back *et al.*, 2001). This study represents a valuable contribution to the field, highlighting the continuing problem of institutionalised racism, and overt forms of racist abuse located within specific fan cultures. Importantly, the study employs a sophisticated theoretical framework to interpret the wealth of research data. A similar claim can be made about Carrington and McDonald's edited collection on racism and sport in Britain (2001), which draws on previous research material and a number of authorial voices. *Corner Flags and Corner Shops* (Bains and Johal, 1998) is helping to dispel ideas that Asian men totally lack interest in a sports career, instead detailing how their efforts are thwarted by racist structures and processes in sport. Relating specifically to cricket, recent studies have tended to focus on the collective difficulties faced by black and Asian players in local leagues, and have also helped to challenge popular ideas about British Asian groups and sport (see for example Searle, 1996; Long *et al.*, 1997; McDonald and Ugra, 1998). In the same vein, the formation of contemporary black and Asian male identities in sport has been explored by Fleming (1995, *a*, *b*) and by Werbner (1996).

An epistemology of feminist writing on sport has been overwhelmingly concerned with the experiences of white women. As a result, the specific priorities and concerns of black and Asian women in British sport have been obscured, and are under-researched areas of social enquiry. In recent years, this absence has been addressed through small-scale studies typically concerned with black and Asian women's experiences of sport as a leisure pursuit, in a community setting (see for example Carrington *et al.*, 1987; Verma and Darby, 1994; Parmar, 1995). These studies reveal that attempts to increase Asian women's participation in sport need to be more sensitive to concerns of religion and culture than they have been up to now. Theoretically and empirically, Hargreaves' *Sporting Females* (1994) is a notable analysis of aspects of life and culture which are intrinsic to the development of female sports. More directly, *Sporting Females* also includes interview and secondary source material about British black and Asian women, and their sporting experiences.

A sporting chance?

Black and Asian Athletes in British Sport and Society is intended to fill a gap in the existing literature on sport and race. It seeks to do so by integrating the testimonies of minority ethnic athletes with academic research and empirical data. *Black and Asian Athletes* aims to make a contribution to debates that recognise a greater complexity in the relationship between 'race' and sport. The study's sub-title reflects this aim, and challenges the notion that sport in Britain currently exists as a realm of equal opportunity, free of race and sex prejudice. Since racial ideologies and processes adapt to suit particular contexts and social formations, Gilroy has argued that it is more appropriate to talk of *racisms* rather than *racism* (1993). It is important therefore to look at personal biographies in sport, to see the different ways in which 'racism' is interpreted and experienced.

Black and Asian Athletes is an interview-based study containing the reflections of athletes of African-Caribbean and Asian origin, who participate across different sporting levels and contexts. It is one of the few UK-based studies to integrate an analysis of the responses of élite professionals with committed amateurs. The study includes six former 'élite'-level athletes, five current élite athletes, and four with a serious commitment to amateur sport. Following Hargreaves (1994, p. 2), 'sport' has been defined as: 'activities which are institutionalised, strictly organised and highly competitive, as well as those which are freely arranged, recreative and aesthetic'. Without such a broad definition, the significance and function of sport for Asian women, who are invisible in its professional and more formalised spheres, would be discounted.

Methodology

Although sport provides a good site to investigate complex ideas about race and racism, one main frustration concerned widening the interviewee-base of professional Asian sportsmen. Access to some élite Asian professionals was constrained by time, and mediated by intransigent agents who acted as 'gatekeepers'. The ones I spoke to informally claimed that a study of this nature was 'too (commercially) risky', and would possibly damage their athlete's careers.

Black and Asian Athletes has adopted a qualitative approach to the treatment of research data. Data was collected by the use of in-depth interviews by (semi-structured) questionnaire; and the added flexibility afforded by open-question formats made these the preferred instruments to elicit responses. The personal accounts of the respondents have been contextualised with reference to academic research on minority ethnic groups and sport, and a variety of other secondary sources. Newspapers, sports publications such as football 'fanzines' and anti-racist pamphlets, television sources and the internet are chief in this regard. I sought not only to highlight the ways that racism and sexism manifest themselves, but to make sense of these effects through theoretical explanation and the wider social environment.

As far as possible, respondents were chosen because of their special positions as black and Asian sportsmen and women who have participated at *different sporting levels*. This is particularly important. In common with Asian women, an Asian male sporting presence is overwhelmingly located at the amateur, recreational level. An exclusive analytical focus at the élite level would obscure the mix of factors accounting for why Asian men appear to organise their leisure time in ways which run contrary to mainstream sporting practices and institutions.

There is a fairly broad age-range of respondents (21 to 53 years). In places, this has facilitated a cross-generational analysis of how ideas, practices and processes which shape minority ethnic participation in sport are perpetuated, given new meanings, and defended. The study also examines these meanings across *different sporting contexts*. In this way, the perceptions and experiences of Azmina Mitha, a martial-arts and defence instructor working with Asian women in a local community centre, are just as significant to this study as those of footballer Garth Crooks, a former Tottenham Hotspur striker, and now respected television sports journalist; and Martin Offiah, a superstar of both rugby league and rugby union.

Over a period of three years (1999–2002), eleven men and four women have been interviewed for this study, and their accounts offered separately. The disparity in numbers between male and female respondents was motivated by the existing priorities of academic research, as well as its 'omissions'. Sport is primarily a male preserve in society, and the experiences of black and Asian men dominate the concerns of academic research on sport and racism. Given the constraints of space, the volume of men's research suggests a more cumulative, group-oriented approach to data analysis. But a more collective approach also means that a greater number of 'voices' are needed to avoid the risk of interviewee silences in key question areas.

Women's accounts were offered separately because the meanings and functions of sport for women have been significantly less explored in Britain (Hargreaves, 1994). Enormous struggles for race, *or* gender equality (but rarely both), and in other areas such as employment and health, have assumed priority; whilst sports feminism has been dominated by secondary sources, and has a white, middle-class character. As a key consequence, black and Asian women have faced a frustrating struggle to claim recognition and a more complex, encompassing identity within sport. By individualising their contributions, in the form of single interviews, I sought to provide the 'space' for each respondent to articulate the meanings that shape their personal relationships to sport. Within a relatively more flexible framework concerned with the impact of 'race' and gender, a greater proportion of quotation to narrative is an attempt to let the interviewees 'speak for themselves', whilst still recognising the need to clarify points in relation to broader themes. It can also be argued that there is a need for *extended* interviews, because we live in a 'soundbite' culture where considered views are marginalised or assumed away.

Structure of the book

In order to frame the active debates, and to provide a social and historical context, *Black and Asian Athletes* is divided into two main parts. In Part I, *Chapter 1* explores the ways in which a resurgence of ideas about genetics and heredity has contributed to sustaining and reproducing white privilege in sport. These ideas support the racist practices and processes that show themselves in some traditionally 'masculine' sports cultures. *Chapter 2* provides a social context to the men's interview chapters. It relates the sports racism experienced by black and Asian athletes over the last century, to wider social events and circumstances. Chapter 2 is not a comprehensive account of minority ethnic sporting involvement, or shaping social events. Instead, it emphasises how a shifting climate within British sport has reflected tensions over 'race', national identity and belonging outside of it. For this reason, the very presence and achievements of a number of this study's more well-known athletes, such as Viv Anderson and David Lawrence, have publicly challenged racist constructions of Englishness.

Black and Asian Athletes is interested in how (if at all) the interviewees identify and reflect on racism in sport. These perceptions are explored in *Chapter 3* and *Chapter 4*. Key sites for the expression of racialised ideas and practices have been recognised in current research, and shape the areas for enquiry used here. Starting with the athlete's early years, these factors include teacher expectations and stereotyping, the role of the family, and the influence of role models. As the athletes progress through the life course, the focus of concern is whether these, and other ideas and practices, have 'taken hold'. So, for example, to what extent has the athlete become locked into sports and sporting roles that supposedly reflect their 'natural' abilities, and been affected by other manifestations of racism? On the last point, the testimonies of David Lawrence and Sean Viera contribute to our knowledge about some sportsmen's reactions (during competition) to repressive political regimes such as apartheid. The conventions of media coverage are also critical to reproducing racism in sport. Chapter 4 is concerned with the interviewee's perception of the media's role in perpetuating racist practices and discourses.

The focus of this study turns to sportswomen in Part II. However understated, black and Asian men at least have an historical presence that can be traced in the literature. But *Chapter 5* argues that the historical contributions, and specific needs and concerns of minority ethnic women, have been obscured. Hence, it is useful to provide a necessary descriptive chapter on women and sport that also fleshes out the empirical reality of black and Asian experiences. The four, personal accounts of the sportswomen in Chapter 6 reflect both a need to explore the meanings and uses that black and Asian women gain from sport, and to address a limited academic focus on their participation. *Chapter 6* broadly follows the analytical themes of interview chapters in Part I, but also highlights how the significance attached to sport varies according to a person's individual biography. So for example, the testimony of Azmina Mitha conveys a sense of her early struggles to break free of patterns of behaviour deemed appropriate for an Asian woman, and her attempts to develop ways to encourage other Asian women to participate in sport. And the reflections of Ivy Alexander highlight the ways in which sexual orientation can impose very real constraints on sports' liberating potential, and the expression of self-identity.

Although the interviews are presented separately in Chapter 6, they are also analysed cumulatively in places. This is to highlight where concerns around similar issues elicit a cross-comparison of experiences and/or responses. Where appropriate, the research data is also analysed comparatively with the men's. It is not my intention to set the male interviewees up as the norm, thereby 'privileging' their accounts. Rather, the aim is to highlight where issues of 'race' supersede concerns over gender, social class, religion and so on.

A study of this size can only hope to make a small contribution to sociological debates on racism in sport, and our understanding of the uses and meanings that black and Asian groups gain from it. Although a number of testimonies of the famous and not-so-famous are combined in one study, their chosen sports are not fully representative of minority ethnic participation. A more complete account would also be gained from interview-based studies of other groups. In this regard, little research has been done on the small Chinese, Iranian and Turkish groups in Britain. There is a need for more extensive research on black and Asian women and sport. Large-scale studies of the ways that different Asian religions and social classes approach and relate to sport would also enhance an epistemology of race and sport in Britain. *Black and Asian Athletes* has a definite 'English' focus. More work could be done on the ways that black and Asian groups in Wales, Scotland and Ireland experience racism, and negotiate questions of identity and belonging in sport. In short, an increasingly developed body of literature can provide the basis for comparative, multilayered analyses of minority ethnic groups and sport, in specific social contexts.

A note on terminology

This study acknowledges the complexity of debates surrounding terminology. Although there is no necessary relationship between the two concepts, minority **racial** groups are more commonly referred to as minority **ethnic** groups. In Britain, this tends to mean peoples of **African-Caribbean** and **Asian** origin. The terms 'Asian' and **South Asian** also have a restricted usage in this context, generally referring to people originating from the Indian sub-continent, as well as those political refugees from Kenya, Uganda and Malawi, who are descendants from India and East Africa. And due to the struggles for ethnic self-identity that took place in the 1980s, the term 'black' now has a more specific usage. Increasingly, it generally refers to peoples of African-Caribbean rather than Asian origin. In line with everyday discourse in Britain, the term **black** will be used interchangeably with *African-Caribbean* in this study. Similarly, *Asian* groups will also be referred to as *South Asians*. This study also recognises the contested nature of the term 'mixed-race' (see for example Alibhai-Brown, 2001). In the cases of the two mixed-race respondents, Jason Gardener and Myra Barretto, 'black' and 'Asian' are used (respectively) because both describe themselves in these terms, and because both claim to strongly identify with this part of their identities.

Part I
'Race' and Male Sport

1
Understanding 'Race' and Sport

Sociology can't explain it. My heart says 'no', but my head says 'yes'. I have to believe that we blacks have something that gives us an edge. I want to hear from the scientists.

Arthur Ashe

My eyesight was just a gift of my race . . . The message from my eye to the brain, and from thence to the muscles, is flashed with a rapidity that has no equal amongst Englishmen.

K. S. Ranjitsinhji

Introduction

This chapter has two main, related aims. The first is to show why the resurgence of ideas about biological determinism contribute to perpetuating an invisible and powerful position of white privilege in sport. The second is to show how certain traditions, practices and ideas, existing in such sports as football, cricket and rugby, can disadvantage minority ethnic groups, and thereby maintain existing relations of power. These ideas and processes are based on commonsense understandings of 'races' as real categories.

The 'level playing field'?

To watch an international football match (what about Argentina versus England in the 1998 World Cup, or Germany versus Cameroon in the 2002 World Cup?); or to watch the final of the 100 metres at the Olympic Games; or to watch a Wimbledon tennis final, is to appreciate that modern-day sporting contests are 'war by any other name'. Such meetings embody a level of legalised aggression and competitiveness that captures the public imagination. They also contain the compelling elements of established stage plays – success and heartache, pathos and high drama, luck and emotion – that to varying degrees constitute our social lives. However, the 'theatre' that sport provides would be diminished if the arena were not thought of as a forum where, under egalitarian conditions, competitors succeeded through a combination of hard work, endeavour, talent, self-sacrifice and discipline. In fact, this popular understanding of the characteristics and ingredients of modern-day sport is so pervasive that an array of sporting terms are still used as metaphors for fairness in other areas of life. A 'level playing field', 'playing the game', 'a sporting chance' (the sub-title of this book): each has been invoked in struggles for economic, political and social rights.

This question of 'fairness' is significant when considering the history of racism and sport in the US: a country that has produced a large and influential body of research on the subject. Although it is commonplace to see black competitors in international events today, their participation was not a feature of sports contests throughout the twentieth century. At various points, particularly in the period to the 1940s, the imposition of a 'colour line' effectively barred black people from competing for championship honours against white opponents in such sports as horseracing, boxing, basketball and baseball. The progressive eradication of these 'Jim Crow' laws, as they were known, was influenced by a combination of playing structure and philosophy; a shrewd awareness of the financial advantages of ending exclusionary policies; and the self-motivation of disadvantaged groups and individuals (see Ashe, 1988; Coakley, 1994). And although (as in society as a whole) desegregation did not (and still does not) mean true racial integration, increasing numbers of African-American males followed their white, working-class peers into professional sport.

A select few have enjoyed spectacular success, both in financial terms, and as revered national and international sporting icons. Their achievements, and the high numbers of African-Americans entering sport, led to suggestions that involvement could provide a social and cultural solution to the 'problem' of disaffected black youth. So much so that, by the 1960s, sport was championed as a key agent in promoting racial assimilation and integration (Carrington, 1986). The 1960s represented a turbulent time in American race relations. With uprisings for civil rights taking place in a number of the inner-cities, sport took on an almost messianic role. In other words, sport had been invested with an immense social function for black people; and the more obvious removal of barriers to participation enhanced its status as a sphere of equal opportunity, and for achievable aims. More recently, the resurgence of ideas about different races has helped to refocus sport as a contemporary social solution to the West's 'race problems'.

The importance of 'race'

By the 1970s, African-American sportspersons had a growing presence in such sports as basketball, baseball, boxing and American football. In order to explain this increase, 'scientific' investigation was harnessed to a more populist line of enquiry.

In 1971, Martin Kane published an article with the basic premise that physical features distinct to the 'Negro race' (*sic*) – such as 'longer limbs', 'narrower hips', 'greater arm circumference' and 'double-jointedness' (1971, p. 75) were key to explaining its advantages over other 'races' in sport. Kane's thesis was criticised at the time for its flawed methodological approach, and false assumptions inherent to his argument: not least, the validation of 'races' as meaningful categories (Edwards, 1973; Cashmore, 1982; see below). Nonetheless, Kane's article was well-received by sections of the media and some sports commentators, and contributed to the exploration of 'race' differences as an area of renewed scientific enquiry. Kane's research findings arguably gave public voice to the private views of a number of sports fans and 'expert' commentators that had been largely confined to the club house, the local pub and informal discussion. Emphasising genetics and biology seemed the 'natural', 'commonsense' start-point from which to explain black predominance and unmatched levels of performance. And in the intervening absence of a coherent and equally compelling body of counter-enquiry (Fleming, 2001), the 'biologist' view has made a massive resurgence in sport, as in other areas of life.

The idea that the world's human populations can be divided into separate, distinct biological groups has been discredited in scientific circles. Research in the 1970s, for example, suggested that genetic variation *among* European, African and Asian populations was minuscule compared to differences *between* individuals within those populations. And as Kohn explains, these differences between members of any one population group are so great that no common assumptions can be drawn about the innate capacities of a 'race'. He states that: 'Africa encompasses the greatest variability in its human populations. To take visible characteristics alone, the tallest and the shortest people on Earth are found there; as are people with the thickest and the thinnest lips' (1996, p. 82).

DNA studies published in the 1980s indicated that the human species emerged less than 100,000 years ago: insufficient time for significant physical or mental differences among the 'races' to have evolved (see also Rose *et al.*, 1984). Nonetheless, Kane's text is just part of a long continuum of past and present works re-enforcing a popular, almost sacrosanct understanding that 'races' *do* in fact exist, and that they are subspecies with distinct physical constitutions and mental capacities.

'Races' are popularly understood to provide the basis for a very real type of relationship in shared social contexts (Mason, 1996). Husband's reference to race as a 'social fact' of British life (1987), highlighted that racial differences are regarded as problematic; consistently leading to levels of inequality, discrimination and social exclusion experienced by non-white groups, across a range of institutional spheres. Gilroy (1993) has emphasised the 'plasticity' of this societal racism. He argues for an analysis of racism that takes account of historical relations of subordination; and of how particular ideologies owe their existence to deep-rooted issues of power. Since these ideologies and processes survive and adapt to suit particular social formations, it is more appropriate to talk of *racisms* rather than *racism*. There is a voluminous academic literature in this area (see for example Smith, 1977; Brown, 1984; Husband, 1987; Solomos and Back, 1996; Skellington, 1996).

Genetics, and 'race'

Today, a search to identify the specific characteristics possessed by different (racial) groups is part of a seemingly inexhaustible agenda of genetics research. Crucially the pace of, and investment in, this research, and its attempts to answer fundamental questions about human life, have made sociological and scientific rejections of 'race' somehow seem invalid, and out-of-date.

Heidi Mirza (2000, p. 301) further develops this point about genetics as a popular discourse, stating that:

> We live in a climate when the public love affair with genetic determinism: easy, televisable, reportable, bizarre almost paranormal explanations, seize the public imagination. We like to hear the anecdotal tales of the Minnesota Study of twins, who though genetically similar, but raised apart, end up sharing the same habit of flushing the toilet before as well as after using it . . . It would seem that this new age of gene science appears to be able to accommodate a new popular version of biological determinism. Our physical visible differences have become popular public spectacle.

Breakthroughs in the mapping of human DNA underpin the research's broad social significance; and have been spoken of in the same breath as the invention of the wheel, and landings on the moon. The recent decoding of chromosome 22, for instance, offers the key to improving the way that conditions such as schizophrenia and congenital heart disease are treated, if not their eradication. Scientists claim to have identified a 'criminal gene' present in persistent offenders; and an 'irrational gene' in violent North Americans (shaped, apparently, like a .38 calibre handgun! (Klam, 2000)). More directly, the isolation of genes for intelligence revitalises interest in the 1960s work of Eysenck (1971). The essence of his findings was that African-Americans had a lower innate intellect than their white counterparts. Genetic pre-determination can be read as a grand narrative of the past and the present; ennobling ideas on social order, and the very nature of being.

Against this background, it is not surprising that ideas on race still underpin informal belief systems on the strengths and limitations of black sportsmen and sportswomen. To such an extent that, to capture the spirit of Stuart Hall's famous quote on race and class, 'self-evident' truths are the mode in which sporting opinions are lived. These 'truths' still crop up frequently among sports 'experts', coaches, media pundits and 'knowledgeable' members of the public (Cashmore, 1982; Back *et al.*, 2001; Hill, 2001). They refer predominantly to black rather than Asian men; and to men rather than women; a fact also reflected in the volume and priorities of academic research (Birrell, 1989; Jarvie, 1995). However, the explicit meanings of race discourses have been masked by an increasingly more 'hyper-sensitive' vocabulary.

In the current climate, investigating the role of race in human sport performance is highly sensitive for a number of reasons. Sport scientists have seemingly been reluctant to raise the hypothesis that evolution has given peoples of African ancestry an athletic edge, to avoid the view consistently accompanying it: that an inverse correlation exists between athletic prowess and cerebral function. As the sportswriter Frank Deford stated on a US television programme in the 1980s: 'people feel if you say blacks are better athletically, you're saying they're dumber'. Nonetheless, these ideas have been endorsed by prominent figures in US sports, such as Al Campanis, and Jimmy 'the Greek' Snyder, and illustrate the real level at which they are given substance. In 1987, Campanis, the former Vice-President for Player Personnel, Los Angeles Dodgers, stated that African Americans 'may not have some of the necessities to be . . . a field manager or perhaps a general manager', but instead were 'gifted with great musculature . . . [and] . . . fleet[ness] of foot'.

Whilst writing this, I cannot help but wonder about the myriad ways that Campanis allowed his convictions to influence his senior decision-making role. I imagined the team talk telling black players to play their 'natural' game and to do what comes easily. I could imagine the lack of sympathy and castigation of a black player who, although he may look as if he's 'given his all', is probably being 'too relaxed' in his attitude. Finally, I could imagine the physical discarding of coaching applications from black players, and other more subtle means of dissuasion.

In 1988, Jimmy 'the Greek' Snyder suggested that African-American males made good 'ball carriers' in US football because their slave ances-tors were bred to have big strong thighs, and that this trait had been inherited (both cited in Small, 1994, p. 102). This view was popularly endorsed by the mainstream media. The media gave less credence to the view that millions of African-Americans not fitting Snyder's racial stereotype had been discounted; or that the control that white slave-masters exercised over the sexual behaviour of their black slaves had been exaggerated.

To some, binary divisions that separate whites, with their capacity for enhanced thought and intellect, from blacks, with their physical prowess, are fundamental to understanding racial differences. Not only do these ideas form the basis for 'explaining' the absence or lack of 'progress' of black people in sports coaching and management; but also the positions they occupy in team sports (Chapter 4). Whether black people are naturally better at sports than white people due to their genetic make-up is therefore not only an enduring, but a highly emo-tive issue. One of its subtexts is that black people are closer to beasts and animals than they are to the rest of humanity. The following extract is from a *New York Times* report on the African-American Joe Louis, before a boxing fight in the 1930s:

> the magnificent animal . . . he eats. He sleeps. He fights . . . Is he all instinct, all animal? Or have a hundred million years left a fold upon his brain? I see in this colored man something so cold, so hard, so cruel that I wonder as to his bravery. Courage in the animal is desperation. Courage in the human is something incalculable and divine.
>
> (cited in Coakley, 1994, p. 244)

This is a blatant enunciation. But compare the unalloyed bestiality of the above, with the inferences in an extract written some seventy years later, and concerning boxer Mike Tyson's preparation for an impending fight:

Great fighters feed off their apprehension. Tyson is at his most deadly when his animal instinct senses danger. The prospect of a powerful foe disturbs him into preparing rigorously, focuses him on his prey and excites his lust for battle.

(Powell, 2002, p. 88)

Currently, anxiety over the meanings and usage of 'race' research has led to the masking of racial inferences by a more polite language of ethnic and/or cultural 'difference' (Gilroy, 1993). In the context of mediated sport, there has been a shift away from references to 'race', and towards discourses which have helped to reinforce the idea that black success is due to 'natural' athletic gifts (Jackson, 1989; Staples and Jones, 1985; Cole and Denny, 1994; Chapter 4).

'Black is best': Jon Entine and *Taboo*

Referring to the scientific search for a relationship between 'race' and sports performance, Coakley (1994, p. 246) remarked:

It seems strange to think that a single genetic trait or even a combination of traits could explain the successes or failures of a genetically diversified group of athletes from many areas around the world across a range of different sports requiring different physical abilities and characteristics. But racial ideology has set some people out on a quest for such a trait.

Jon Entine's book, *Taboo: why black athletes dominate sports and why we're afraid to talk about it* (2000), is an influential tome that has reactivated debate about the effects of genetics and heredity on sports performance. The title is an arresting statement, with a frustrated desire to 'get at the real truth' as its subtext. In the West, it is notable that the word taboo, like its phonic relation voodoo, can be associated with a lack of scientific rigour, and a certain amount of melodrama and hyperbole. The book itself is an easy read: an accessible antidote to detailed, opposing scientific data, and sociocultural analysis.

Entine prefers the term 'population' to 'race', and acknowledges significant genetic variability between black groups in different parts of Africa. Nonetheless, he proceeds to construct a case for considering the 'innate' aptitudes of black African people, or peoples of African origin. In so doing, Entine simply reaffirms both the notion and the 'naturalness' of races as indelible categories.

Entine argues his case with 'scientific' evidence of black sporting prowess, and a plethora of supporting statistical facts. Black performance is examined in the professional sports of American football, baseball, track and field, and basketball. At first sight, the data is compelling. We are informed that the last white man to hold the world's record in the 100-metre sprint, the German runner Armin Hary, ran a 10.2 second race in 1960. Furthermore, Entine states that: 'the best time by a white 100 metre runner is 10 seconds, which ranks well below two hundred on the all time list' (p. 34). We are also informed that the East African runners, especially Kenyans from the Great Rift Valley, are just as dominant in the distance events in men's races. Since 1964, Kenyans have won forty-five Olympic medals, including fifteen gold. It is a record 'exceeded by only the sprint-rich United States, with a population ten times larger' (p. 39).

As well as making claims about the African ancestry of male world record holders in sprints, the middle distances and marathons, Entine also emphasises that differences between athletes of East and West African heritage could arise and be maintained over time. In short, differences *between* black population groups explain specific aptitudes in particular running events: and these differences point inexorably to a mix of genetics, biology and ancestry that makes black people generally better at sports. And now that they have equal access to previously restricted sports, their 'difference engines' (to use an old computing term) mean that peoples of European and Asian origin will never be able to compete on an equal footing again. The significance of Entine's arguments for black people themselves are touched upon by the former tennis player Arthur Ashe, in a televised interview. 'Sociology can't explain it', he claimed. 'My heart says "no", but my head says "yes". I have to believe that we blacks have something that gives us an edge. I want to hear from the scientists' (cited in Entine, 2000, p. 80). And although a sporting identity is more closely associated with black people, the Indian cricketer K. S. Ranjitsinhji (Chapter 2), writing in the 1920s, showed that these ideas have a wider significance.

The imperatives of a slave economy were seen to have their part to play in explaining black sports performance. Entine details that black slaves, brought from Africa to the US, were bred to become strong, fast, agile, and powerful enough to do whatever physical labour was required by their owners. There is no conclusive body of evidence to confirm the idea that such genetic characteristics are passed down through generations (in fact, there is considerable scientific *opposition* to this view). Nonetheless, it is argued that because of this breeding, highly specialised features involving physical prowess became dominant in this black population group. Again, the validity of this view is less significant than its place in the popular imagination.

Entine's book devotes less space to an analysis of the social and cultural factors which act as barriers to progress in sport and other spheres; and to acknowledging the dangers of an analysis based on a fairly limited repertoire of sports. This is not surprising, given his enthusiasm for the idea of black sporting prowess. But perhaps anticipating the criticism that his 'scientific' analysis reinforces existing racial stereotypes, he is careful to state that genetic difference does not equal inferiority or superiority. In fact he goes further, suggesting that athletic superiority is really a function of high intellect. Most glaringly, Entine does not produce an equivalently developed treatise to explain the successes and failures of white athletes, even though their performances in certain sports should, a priori, require exploration. This omission is not unusual. Although black sportsmen and their performances have generally been subject to minute, detailed examination, as Coakley (1994, p. 245) notes:

> there have been no studies looking for a weight-lifting gene among Bulgarian men, or a swimming gene among East German women, or a cross-country skiing gene among Scandinavians, or a volleyball jumping gene among Californians who hang out on beaches. There have been no claims that Canadians owe their success in hockey to naturally strong ankle joints, or instinctive eye-hand-foot coordination, or an innate tendency not to sweat so they can retain body heat in cold weather. Nobody has looked for or used genetic explanations for the successes of athletes packaged in white skin.

Implicit in Coakley's observation is an imbalance symptomatic of uneven power relations: and exemplifying the pattern for research to be done *on* the powerless *by* the powerful. Indeed, this question of power relations leads Small to pointedly ask: 'Where are all the "graceful", "lithe" African-Caribbean gymnasts? Apparently beating their heads against the wall of racialised ideologies and discrimination trying to get education and employment to put them into positions where they can enter such sports' (1994, p. 105).

Although most of Entine's book is devoted to explaining male supremacy in sport, a short section centres on female athletes. Entine argues that women have historically had far fewer opportunities than men to participate in sport; and that there is insufficient documentation to make meaningful comparisons between black and white female athletes. I would suggest that this is because the superficial evidence in women's sport is less compelling. Referring to athletes' use of performance-enhancing drugs, Entine makes an unsubstantiated claim that 'the magnitude of the problem is anyone's guess' (pp. 321/2). This cannot escape the fact that in the last ten years, world, commonwealth, European and Olympic athletics finals, at a range of distances from 100 through to 10,000 metres, have been contested (and won) by ethnically diverse women from Eastern Europe, Western Europe, Africa and the Americas. These statistics challenge the 'commonsense' basis that gives the black male and sport theories such currency. And whilst Entine accepts that racial and gender bias have impeded black women in sport, he does not consider the impact of stereotypes concerning their more overt physicality, and dominant roles in the family (see for example Hargreaves, 1994; Lovell, 1995; also Part II).

Hoberman's book (*Darwin's Athletes: how sport damaged black America and preserved the myth of race*, 1997) is a further and notable example of the ways in which 'polemical and unsubstantiated' arguments are made about race and sport (Carrington and McDonald, 2001*a*, p. 10). Hoberman asserts that historical racism is a prime factor structuring the sporting and other experiences of black and white people in American life. Sport is particularly affected by these racist processes, since it is seen to heavily prescribe stereotyped roles. For instance, black people as athletes but not coaches, and the positional and occupational segregation occurring in multiracial sports (Chapter 4). Hoberman sets out to prove that African-American athletic excellence in sports derives from a pathological male dominated culture, which is inflicted with a 'sports fixation' that has always prized success in sports above all else. However in doing so, he has arguably diminished the triumphs of African-American female competitors, whose achievements do not sit entirely comfortably in his framework.

The normalisation of whiteness

For some, a more complex and cautious picture of *agency* (or the freedom to act purposefully) contrasts with a belief about black athletes' 'inexorable' sporting progress. The academic research supporting this view is less 'populist' and sanguine. It emphasises the ways in which sport, in spite of the success enjoyed by a few, can create the illusion, or 'myth' (see below), of a level playing-field of opportunities. Instead, far greater numbers of black and Asian people embarking on sports careers may encounter racist economic and social systems, and the likelihood of a professional dead end (Edwards, 1984; Majors, 1990; Small, 1994; Jarvie, 1995; Marqusee, 1995*b*). Attempts to uncover the varied, complex ways that sport becomes idealised are important to the sociological literature on minority ethnic groups in this area.

Through his concept of 'myth' (1957), the social theorist Roland Barthes provides one way of understanding how sport can become so invested with optimism and a sense of 'naturalness'. An underlying message of Barthes' myth was that there was no distinction between the signifier (a word or sign that triggers the concept of an object) and the signified (the mental concept triggered by the signifier). We need look no further than English football to provide a potent illustration of this. The signifier is the physical presence and success of black footballers in England's premier league, and on international duty; whilst the signified is a presumed 'level playing-field' of opportunities for realising 'natural' sporting ability, and the breaking down of racial barriers. Sport then represents a rarefied sphere of meritocracy, with a black presence at the highest levels in sharp and striking contrast to other areas of social and cultural life. Similarly, the absence of British Asians from the professional game signifies their lack of interest in football as a career, and their limited aptitude for this sport specifically, and sport in general.

Identifying the ways that white identity is normalised in sports is central to deconstructing this myth. *Whiteness* is defined as an invisible, but pervasive and powerful position of normative race privilege (Frankenberg, 1993); and is concerned with understanding how culture racialises practices and norms. In this regard, Sivanandan (1977) noted that although the structure of white racism was built on economic exploitation it was, crucially, 'defined culturally'. Problematising white identity is a fundamental project, in Coco Fusco's view, since ignoring this would have the effect of redoubling its *hegemony* (see below) by naturalising it (in hooks, 1989). Roediger goes further, suggesting that demystifying and exposing whiteness is more important than problematising the concept of 'race' (1994, p. 12).

While Barthes understood myth as being infused with ideological messages of control, the political activist Gramsci envisaged the means by which this control was achieved. In this regard, Gramsci's concept of 'hegemony' (1971) is also an important tool to understand whiteness in sports. His ideas for interpreting a wide range of elements of popular culture have influenced research into minority ethnic groups and sport; with modern sporting developments emphasising their continuing value. Gramsci understood hegemony as a complex, cultural and ideological means by which dominant groups in society secured broad consent for their ideas and actions from subordinated groups, even as the latter's interests were being compromised. His concept has been adapted by theorists to provide useful insights explaining the idiosyncrasies of freedom and constraint in sport. In this way, Hargreaves (1994, p. 22) claims that the concept has been used by theorists to:

> explain . . . the ways in which dominant meanings and interests which are inherited from past traditions engender opposition and have to be defended, while new meanings are constantly being worked out and struggled for . . . Hegemonic configurations of power are understood to be part of a continual process of change which incorporates negotiation and accommodation . . .

How significant are Hargreaves' 'dominant meanings and interests . . . inherited from past traditions'? In sport, a naturalised position of advantage is maintained through the operation of established, *informal* codes of behaviour, which black and Asian sportsmen are expected to adhere to. These codes are ingrained in the fabric of some white-centred player and supporter cultures, and relate particularly to team sports. If black sportsmen disrupt the codes within which they are expected to work, refusing to 'play by the rules' as it were, the sporting and social consequences could be acute. One of the most basic rules that black and Asian sportsmen are expected to abide by is to not mention an important consequence of 'difference' in Britain: racism. 'Normalcy' means not 'making an issue' out of race. Either explicitly, as a political position relating to wider societal relations; or in terms of a public discourse that implicates the culture and practices of a sports team, club or organisation. Not only do they risk alienation from their team-mates and the disapproval of their clubs' hierarchy and supporters, but transgression challenges the terms on which race and nationhood are defined. As Carrington (2000, p. 34) states:

> Blacks, and black athletes in particular, will be rewarded if they subscribe to the view that racism is non-existent within British society, or at least that it is a minor aberration, or better still if they avoid the issue altogether. But the athlete who highlights racism, or even dares to *suggest* that racism *might* be a factor within contemporary British life is immediately labelled as being paranoid, over-sensitive, bitter, ungrateful and troublesome. This ultimately affects how easily they are accepted [and defined, by the British media and public] as British.

Whiteness rules

Football, and to a lesser extent rugby league, are key sites for the construction of whiteness in sport. Despite the growing presence of minority ethnic players in the professional and amateur ranks, these sports have retained their most obvious sense of whiteness in terms of their player and supporting cultures. For example, Spracklen (2001) has shown how a normative identity construction in rugby league is northern, white, heterosexual, working-class and male, with black and Asian involvement as conditional and subject to negotiation. As a consequence, certain patterns of interaction have developed between white and non-white players which see racial 'difference' as something that should be acculturated to the white norm.

These patterns are certainly critical at the level of player/team-mate interaction. Dave Hill's study of the impact of black footballer John Barnes on football in Liverpool showed how, as part of building the team 'ethic', processes of inclusion and exclusion rely on racial 'banter': which is seen as an acceptable way of making race an issue. These processes operate routinely on the training ground, the field of play and the social environments surrounding the game, and mean that black players can regularly find themselves on the receiving end of racist 'jokes'. A black player's willingness to accept these jokes, and thereby to sanction often-established patterns of interaction in a team, is crucial to their acceptance as part of it, and their progression. Hill (2001, pp. 177–8) outlined Barnes' strategy for acceptance, and abidance by the normative code to which black sportsmen were expected to operate:

> At Liverpool, Barnes had his strategy worked out. On his first day at the training ground he sat at a bench with a couple of his new team-mates. Cups of tea were put before the two established players. Barnes looked up at the woman who brought them. He said: 'What am I, black or something?' Everyone fell about . . . 25 years of unbroken habit demanded that you had to conform or go under. Barnes pre-empted his own initiation. He gave permission for his team-mates to, for better or worse, relate to him in the traditional Liverpool way. I'm black. It's a joke. Everyone relax . . . After that, there were lots and lots of jokes.

Barnes showed 'character' by conforming to a white, male, working-class-coded norm of behaviour that is central to football culture (Hill, 2001. See also KIO/FURD, 2001a). Barnes' position was unique in that he was the first black footballer signed for Liverpool Football Club from another club, and the only black player to be playing consistently for the club at that time. It is reasonable to assume, then, that team-mates' interactions would alter in character and significance, depending on the number and status of black players. A less conformist 'survival strategy' has involved black players grouping together with other black players, forming 'friendships and social networks that are sometimes represented as cliques, sitting outside the clubs' normative white "centre"' (Back *et al.*, 2001, p. 151). However, the existence of these sub-groups helps to reinforce a perception of exclusivity from the (white) team and ethic. In contrast, the former footballer Ian Wright conveys a sense of the ways in which the presence of prominent black players at London's Crystal Palace club challenged these norms; thereby creating 'new meanings' in sport (Hargreaves, see above). As one of the established black players at the club in the 1980s, Wright helped to redefine the parameters of inclusion and banter. Referring to the club's purchase of two new (white) players, Geoff Thomas and John Pemberton, Wright stated that:

> Geoff and 'Pembo' were both northerners so they were mocked for their dopey accents, especially by Andy [Gray] and I who were brought up together in the same part of south London with Tony Finnegan. Brighty may have been from Stoke, but he was now an honorary Londoner so he got off lightly, but Geoff and Pembo got some serious abuse. Geoff handled it well – he had a quick, dry sense of humour and could give as good as he got – but Pembo was a different matter. He was so easy to wind up and had a temper that snapped after just a couple of minutes.
>
> (1996, p. 75)

But if professional football teams have gradually changed their racial compositions, the same cannot be said of the terraces. An overwhelming number, some 99 per cent, of spectators at live games are white, and this group is predominantly male (KIO/FURD, 2001*b*). A white, male imbalance has had the effect of perpetuating cultures of exclusion, and creating a popular understanding that the 'problem' of race has been imported with the minority ethnic groups themselves. In their study of the complex ways in which 'sectarianism' interfaces with racism and national identity in Scottish football, Dimeo and Finn (2001) highlighted how the very presence of minority ethnic supporters and players in this environ was perceived as the cause of ensuing racial problems. The subtext of this 'no problem until *they* got here' perspective is, again, that minority ethnic groups have to adjust to existing structures, accepting the abuse that is an unfortunate feature of stadium matches.

Abiding by the norms of the game also means that when black and Asian footballers receive racist abuse from supporters on the terraces, they should not react to it. Rather, they should show more 'character' by not complaining, by accepting racist chanting as 'part of the game', and by letting their footballing skills 'do the talking' for them. This strategy translates as 'hitting your oppressors where it hurts them the most', and is cited as the most effective counter to racism by a number of high-profile sportsmen (Chapter 4). The Manchester United manager, Sir Alex Ferguson, had this to say on the subject of racist abuse, when interviewed for an anti-racism football magazine:

> I remember when we were playing at Wembley, one of the Oldham players called Paul Ince a black so and so, and he reacted and got a second yellow card. I said to him 'Why do you get upset with that? You call me a Scots bastard.' He said 'But you're not a race.' It's how you look on being called names. Sometimes I think you've got to say, forget it. Plenty of English people down here call me a Scottish bastard. But when the prejudice stops people getting a job, puts them out of a job, or stops them getting a place on the team because of their colour, that is prejudice, *that is real racism to me.*
>
> (KIO/FURD, 2001*b*, p. 8, my emphasis)

Sir Alex Ferguson is one of the most highly respected and influential managers in the British game. His testimony reveals something about the normalisation of race privilege; and the ways that sports cultures can become divorced from the ferocity and impact of their race discourses. The code within which Ferguson operates downgrades the use of such common racial epithets as 'coon', 'monkey', 'nigger' and 'jungle bunny' to the status of petty 'name calling'. It fails (or perhaps, refuses) to recognise how the weight of historical meaning attached to words like 'nigger' may impose a qualitatively different level of psychological strain on black players: one that is not comparable to abusing someone who is white and may also be bald, or freckly-faced, or Scottish, or knock-kneed, or a combination of these things. Ferguson also failed to recognise the link between the structural and vernacular forms of racism, and the subtle ways in which institutionalised discrimination operates. And if a player sometimes 'over-reacts' to racist abuse (or, indeed, takes offence to racist 'jokes') as it is plain to Ferguson that Ince has done, it is *he* who is perceived to be at fault. In this regard, a very common reference for black 'transgressors' is that they have a 'chip on their shoulder'; a term popularised by (black) track athlete Derek Redmond concerning his then-colleague, Linford Christie.

Perhaps the extent of this strain can be gauged by a useful yardstick: the 'Cantona affair'. In 1995, the then Manchester United footballer Eric Cantona reacted to the taunts of an opposing team's fan by launching himself (feet first) at the spectator, before exchanging punches with him. Cantona, unbound by the code that governs black reaction, snapped under a level of provocation which the vast majority of professional black footballers endure with depressing frequency. In any case, the acceptance of racially marked terms of inclusion in playing and supporting cultures creates a vicious circle. If black players don't complain about racism which they feel oversteps personal boundaries of acceptability, they are simply legitimating this dimension of white-centred sports culture. And when the possibility of substantial reward is considered alongside the intense effort and focus required to be an élite sportsman, the tendency to conformity (an inherent part of the 'team' ethic) is exacerbated. Nonetheless, a number of high-profile black footballers, such as Ian Wright, Stan Collymore, and Nathan Blake, have publicly drawn attention to incidents of racial abuse at the hands of other players, supporters and even their national team managers. But in so doing, they have strained the bounds of a tightly scripted behavioural code that has resulted in their assessment of racism being nullified by denial. Again, Sir Alex Ferguson's reaction to a 'racial' incident involving his team's goalkeeper, but this time with former Arsenal footballer Ian Wright, is instructive. During a tense and highly competitive game, Wright accused the former Manchester United goalkeeper of calling him a 'black bastard'; a claim the goalkeeper strenuously denied. In a subsequent interview, Ferguson claimed that:

> In the spur of the moment, I think, Peter Schmeichel must have said something, as the camera showed. But I don't think that Peter Schmeichel could ever be classed as a racist. Ever. I have never known him to say anything.
>
> (KIO/FURD, 2001*b*, p. 9)

Denial by the game's senior figures of a real 'problem' with racism is also reflected in the way that perpetrators are classified, and by television's treatment of abuse towards black players. Despite the best efforts of organisations and initiatives aimed at challenging racism on the football terraces, the game still has a significant problem with chanting and other forms of abuse. Although this abuse varies in extent and intensity, depending on the stadium (see for example, Nichols, 1998; Brown and Chaudhary, 2000), it is consistently classified in the following way: as the actions of a small, 'mindless' minority (usually referred to as 'hooligans'), who are hell-bent on causing trouble, and are not 'real' fans. For this reason, Back and associates (2001) have argued that the classic stereotype of a shaven-headed, xenophobic racist hooligan not only obscures the complex of racist views held by 'ordinary' fans, but also deflects attention from more subtle institutional practices.

Racist comments and gestures have been a feature of live games since the first black players tentatively plied their trade. With the onset of sophisticated technical equipment, these comments and gestures have been increasingly discernible to the broadcast public. Previously, television has largely refused to acknowledge the racist nature of these chants and, in so doing, can be said to have trivialised their impact on the recipients (see also Chapter 2). For instance, during the European football championships in 1988, a section of the British crowd subjected the Dutch defender Ruud Gullit to an audible litany of racist name calling, and monkey noises. 'Gullit getting some good-natured barracking when he gets possession', stated the commentator. Recently however, the levels and intensity of racist abuse directed at black players in Europe has resulted in condemnation in the British media, and from the players themselves. In the latter regard, England players Emile Heskey, Kieron Dyer and Ashley Cole have complained about extensive racist abuse whilst playing in a European Championship qualifying game against Slovakia in Bratislava (October 2002). Significantly, the media's vociferous support for these players, and condemnation of fans racism in Europe, has arguably sidestepped the persisting nature of the problem amongst British fans (see for example Chaudhary, 2002). Whiteness is strengthened through viewpoints that discount the existence and significance of racism.

A disproportionate number of black men continue to make a career out of sport, and therefore encounter and attempt to negotiate these informal codes. By contrast, British Asians are significantly less represented among the ranks of professional and semi-professional sportsmen. Sport is understood to be less of a career option for Asian groups in Britain (Chapter 2). But this should not detract from the impact of racism for those individuals and groups hoping to join formalised and more integrated playing structures.

Whiteness and recreational sport

British Asians are overwhelmingly concentrated among the recreational ranks in sport (Williams, 2001). This concentration is principally in sports like cricket and football but also, to a lesser degree, in hockey, weightlifting and squash. For British Asians, *whiteness* functions both within recreational sport, and at the level of dissuasion from a professional career.

Research into Asian groups and their relationship to sport certainly indicates a will to formally participate at all levels (Verma and Derby, 1994; Bains and Johal, 1998). However, the limited professional involvement of British Asian athletes has skewed the focus of a number of (small-scale) studies towards issues of involvement for Asian communities, particularly where they constitute a significant sector of the local population (Carrington *et al.*, 1987; BYRT, 1988; Fleming, 1995*a*, 1995*b*). These studies have found that meanings and practices, which operate at a variety of levels, lead to Asian men's exclusion from mainstream sport. For instance, the verbal abuse suffered by black professional sportsmen (Chapters 2, 4), can be an integral part of sporting relations for Asian players in recreational cricket. According to Carrington and McDonald (2001*b*) verbal abuse, or 'sledging', is directed primarily at Asian players by their opponents, rather than the spectators who patronise this level of cricket. The authors also suggest that league officials may simply ignore such instances of verbal abuse.

At a more overt level, research has also highlighted incidents of physical attack and intimidation against Asian players in 'mixed' leagues of white and non-white sports teams. Some Asian football teams have suffered horrific racial abuse, whilst there are reports that in cricket, a number of white teams have preferred to move to less prestigious leagues for reasons of race (see for example Lindsey, 1997, 1999). The authors of one study concluded that, 'the "whiteness" of English cricket ensures the continued subordination, marginalisation and disadvantage' of black and Asian cricket through the retention of an exclusive and insular identity (Carrington and McDonald, 2001*b*, p. 64. See also Westwood, 1990; Long *et al.*, 1997; McDonald and Ugra, 1998). In addition, there is evidence of biased umpiring decisions based more on stereotyped ideas about Asians, than the actual rules of the game; excessive bureaucracy institutionalising the segregation of Asian clubs from official leagues; and 'nagging' feelings by Asian players of antipathy towards them when joining white clubs. Curiously enough, some Asian players believe they are ostracised by regional white clubs because of their 'over-competitiveness' and 'aggression' (Duncan, 1998; George, 1998). There is some irony here, given popular stereotypes about the frailty of Asian males!

Facing exclusion from established local league structures because of the resistance of white players and officials, Asian sportsmen have resorted to actively creating their own all-Asian leagues and clubs. These local initiatives have bucked a trend of general decline amongst black and white teams by increasing in number. But although the clubs may fulfil a vital social and cultural function for Asian youth (Williams, 2001), they are not part of the infrastructure that professional sport relies on for access to talented young sportsmen. For the aspiring professional, the Leicester Asian Sports Initiative is one of the few schemes which seeks to provide increasing opportunities for young Asian football players to join a professional club's school of excellence (see also Chapter 2). It is not surprising then, that British-Asian footballers who have honed their skills in the vast network of all-Asian leagues have not made an impact on the premier league: and, by extension, have not received recognition to play for the national team. But perhaps the consequences for Asian sports careers of separateness are most noticeable in Yorkshire cricket. It is curious that despite a concentration and predominance of Asian groups in Yorkshire, of thriving Asian leagues and a professed interest of Asian players to play for the county's first team (Williams, 2001), no *Yorkshire-born* black or Asian player is yet to have this honour bestowed on them. And in common with other, non-white groups, a general perception of hostility at sports stadia explains their low physical presence, and accounts for a significant second-hand following by satellite television coverage.

Playing recreational sport in all-Asian clubs is, as indicated above, bound to a desire to retain distinctive cultural identities, and homeland ties. A distinctive Asian identity can certainly seem implausible in the context of professional sport, and further emphasises its exclusionary whiteness. For instance, writing about the impact of particular Asian footballers on the Scottish game, Johal (2001) feasibly suggests that these 'mixed-race' sportsmen have had their ethnicities 'forsaken' in their quest for 'socio-cultural alignment'. Using the example of the Anglo-Asian footballer Ricky Heppolate, he claims that:

> [He] is a very apposite illustration of how football welcomes those who can fit into accepted convention of what it is to be British and what it takes to be a footballer. He speaks no sub-continental language, only English, he does not practice or adhere to any of the

religions of that region, was raised in a very 'white' environment with little South Asian influence and has no 'emotional attachment to the country of his birth [India]'.

(2001, p. 159)

For Johal, Anglo-Asian sportsmen were not regarded as having an Asian identity; and were therefore lost as symbols to challenge ingrained ideas about Asian peoples and sport. And in the current climate, it is feasible that Islamaphobia in Britain has contributed to a 'siege mentality' among Asian groups that exacerbates their feelings of separateness (see also Chapter 2).

Concluding remarks

This chapter has examined the significance of ideas about 'race' for black and Asian sports participation. The science of genetic pre-determinism has pervaded the popular realm, fuelled by 'commonsense' understandings about specific racial aptitudes and differences. It is from the strength of this relationship that Entine is able to write so determinedly about black advantage in sport. By avoiding a detailed critique of white sporting aptitudes (a white gene debate), and by giving limited weight to arguments rejecting genetic inheritance, he has reinforced uneven relations of power in this area. Hegemonic ideas and practices in sport naturalise whiteness, and obscure the means by which the 'myth' of race disadvantages certain minority ethnic groups.

Black and Asian sportsmen needed to find ways to negotiate racialised ideas and practices in order to carve a niche, however small, in their chosen sports. The following chapter will show how 'race' has shaped their sporting experiences in Britain over the last one hundred years.

2
British Minority Ethnic Groups, Sport and Society

Sportsmen interviewed for this study will have their names printed in italics.

Introduction

Chapter 2 aims to show how a shifting climate within British sport over the last century has reflected tensions over 'race', nation and belonging outside of it. In so doing, it will highlight the prevalence of ideas about culture and biology as signifiers of 'difference', and their very real consequences for minority ethnic participation.

It is beyond the scope of this chapter to provide a detailed, comprehensive account of minority ethnic involvement in British sport. The reader could consult Garland and Rowe (2001) for instance, for an account of the early contributions and experiences of black footballers. Instead, this chapter will make limited reference to a range of sports (such as athletics, cricket, boxing and football) in which British black and Asian sportsmen have succeeded as professionals and semi-professionals, and in which they been engaged as amateurs. Football, for one, is the most played sport in the world, and the most keenly watched. Unlike other sports which have a significant minority ethnic involvement, it has been co-opted as a site for the virulent articulation of racism and nationalism, and white identity constructions. And cricket, as well as being popular among British Asian groups, provides a powerful focus for anxieties about national decline. With both sports therefore, it is easier to examine the ways in which minority ethnic involvement has been shaped by racist reactions to a growing non-white presence in society. There is a strong emphasis on *overt* hostility in this chapter. By this, I mean verbal and/or physical abuse that has a racial dimension. Other practices are given life through a system of meanings and values, and impose their own constraints which are more subtle and subjective, and therefore less easy to detect. Overt hostility, and more subtle racist practices are important elements of white hegemony in sport, and the latter will be explored through interview testimonies in later chapters.

In crucial ways, the experiences of black and Asian groups participating in mainstream sport have been qualitatively similar. But British Asian sportsmen have a far more limited historical presence, a fact reflected in the dearth of available secondary material. Although the absence of Asians in British sport has traditionally been explained in cultural terms (see below), ideas about race still operate in ways which obstruct Asian efforts to carve out a sports career. The sports participation of Asian groups has been catalogued separately to emphasise this relative absence, as well as the effects of racialised ideas and practices.

Given the overall aims of the chapter, I have felt it useful to refer briefly to the ways in which the behaviour and demeanour of high-profile (and therefore more easily recognisable) sportsmen such as Frank Bruno (boxing) and Linford Christie (athletics) have captured the cultural *Zeitgeist*. By this, I mean the spirit of the times reflecting the tensions and contradictions of being a non-white, British sportsman.

African-Caribbean men and British sport

1889 to 1951

Black and Asian involvement in professional football is generally associated with the period from the 1960s, but can actually be traced back to the genesis of the modern game in the latter part of the nineteenth century. Until recently, their contributions have been marginalised or ignored. In the first quarter of the twentieth century, two notable Egyptians played for English football clubs. Hussein Hegazi played for one season at Millwall, 1912/13, whilst Tewfik 'toothpick' Abdullah plied his trade for first division side Derby County in the 1920s. However, accounts of the exploits of Arthur Wharton and Walter Tull were perhaps the most glaring omissions from the annals of British sporting history. In 1889, as goalkeeper for Preston North End (also known as the Invincibles, and a founder-member of the Football Association), Wharton became Britain's first black professional league player. He also gained national recognition as a 100 yards world record holder, and outstanding county cricketer. Wharton's successes were achieved against a backdrop of colonial expansion, and the increasing popularity of natural selection theories which warned against the genetic contamination of the superior 'Nordic' race; and regarded non-white peoples as intellectually, physically and morally inferior to white people. In spite of his aforementioned and other distinctions, Wharton died penniless, and recognition of his achievements had to wait for almost a century (Vasili, 1998). It is these same racial strictures that make the career of Walter Tull seem all the more remarkable.

Tull was the first black outfield professional to play in the English League, turning out for a number of high-profile clubs. According to Vasili, a promising career at Tottenham Hotspur (a.k.a. Spurs) came to an abrupt end because of the racial sensitivities of the time:

> After a game at Bristol City on 9 October 1909 Tull was racially abused by a section of the home supporters. The headline of one match report ran 'Problem of the Colour Prejudice' . . . Spurs . . . dropped him to the reserves and unloaded him the following season . . . Because the directors didn't want the abuse Tull was getting to unsettle the team.
>
> (cited in KIO/FURD, 2001*b*, p. 3)

With the onset of the First World War, Tull became the first black combat officer in the British army. The respect and affection he must have gained, first as a footballer, and then a footsoldier, meant that he circumvented the rigid codes on 'race' and theories of natural selection that had hampered the career aspirations of so many minority ethnic servicemen. At a time when Military Law excluded 'negroes' from exercising 'actual command' as officers, Tull graduated as an officer cadet in 1917. Then, as a second lieutenant, he lost his life leading his troops into battle on main-land Europe (Askwith, 1998). A measure of his popularity and the effect he had on his peers (Tull was posthumously recommended for the Military Cross) can be gained from the following questions. Askwith asks: 'Why did Tull's (white) men risk heavy machine-gun fire in their efforts to retrieve his body? Why did Tull's superior officers risk the wrath of an establish-ment that considered "Negroes" scarcely human by recommending him for a commission?' (p. 6).

By the end of the war, the growing non-white populations which had settled in former slave ports such as Liverpool, Cardiff and Bristol faced a number of 'anti-black' riots and confrontations (Fryer, 1991). Considerable social hostility to a non-white presence was also reflected in the sporting arena. In the 1930s, the footballers Jack Leslie and John Parris ran the gauntlet of abuse from their own and opposing team mates and fans. This period was one of mass spectatorship, with fans standing in close proximity to the pitch. It is therefore easy to imagine that the hostility to a black and Asian presence would have felt intense and unremitting. But it would be wrong to suggest that black footballers were totally unwelcome in British sport at this time. In 1938, Parris became the first black player to appear in a home national side, representing Wales. Furthermore, the literature does highlight a more 'favourable' reaction to black sportsmen in other fields such as athletics and cricket.

By way of background, cricket was firmly associated with the former British Empire, and was widely adopted in colonies in the West Indies, and in India and Pakistan. With the eventual mass participation of black Caribbeans in the game, cricket became a symbol of Caribbean racial unity, and resistance to the iniquities of colonialism. In Britain, a black presence in the prestigious first-class county game was rare before the end of the Second World War. One notable exception at the turn of the century was C. A. Ollivierre, a black cricketer who played for the West Indian tourists in 1900, stayed in England, and played 110 matches for Derbyshire as an amateur between 1901 and 1907 (Williams, 2001). In certain instances, social class could usurp 'race' as a signifier of difference. This partly explains why assumptions of innate white supremacy may have limited the presence of black cricketers at the county level, but did not preclude the impact and influence held by a number of high-status Indian cricketers at the same level (see below).

It was not until the late 1920s however, that a small number of black Caribbean players came to Britain as *professionals* to play in the well-regarded local Lancashire leagues. Learie Constantine and George Headley were both employed in this capacity, and made perhaps the greatest impact on the British public and the game. Constantine helped his club to win numerous honours, and the 'novelty' of a black man playing lavish, crowd pleasing cricket won him many admirers. When Constantine walked down the pavilion steps, Haworth wrote, 'the whole crowd rose in a buzz of excitement', and when he made a good score, 'he performed antics. He would play balls through his legs, go down the wicket and volley them, hook off-breaks, and run desperate singles. Everybody loved him.' (1986, p. 29, see also Hill, 1995). Constantine drew crowds in their tens of thousands, and was credited as being solely responsible for his club's high gate receipts. Evidence in the inter-war years of spectator antipathy towards black and Asian cricketers is scarce, but Williams (2001) provides some indication of racial hostility from their white colleagues. In 1931, the Derbyshire and

England professional Bill Storer claimed that he 'believed in England for the English and was not enamoured of importations, especially of the ebony hue' (cited in Williams, 2001, p. 22). Storer's concerns pre-dated current debates over race and belonging; at a time when the notion of a non-white symbol for the nation was barely credible.

Over a decade later, Constantine's established fame and popularity still could not insulate him from the baser iniquities of racism. In 1943, he was refused accommodation at the Imperial Hotel in Russell Square, because of his colour. As he had already paid a deposit on his room, Constantine sued the hotel for being in breach of contract. His standing with the public was such that, when he won his case, he received hundreds of letters of support and congratulations (Howat, 1975).

Black involvement in athletics and boxing also characterised their sports participation in the inter-war years. In athletics, migrants such as the popular Guyanese sprinters Harry Edward and Jack London achieved notable success at Amateur Athletics Association (AAA) meetings. London represented Britain at the 1928 Olympics, and equalled a world record in the semi-finals of the 100 yards sprint (see also Watman, 1968). In fact, black people initially made most inroads in the sport of professional boxing, which remained a key area because of the opportunities for financial reward (Cashmore, 1982). But in spite of this earning potential, the vast majority of black boxers based in Britain were unable to challenge for a British title for two reasons. Firstly, a ban prevented non-white boxers from doing so, and secondly, sportsmen from overseas needed to fulfil a ten-year residency requirement. In 1948, the British Boxing Board of Control (BBBC) removed the first of the aforementioned stipulations preventing British-based boxers challenging for a national title. In the same year, British-born Dick Turpin became the first black champion to be recognised by the Board when he won the British middleweight title. Inspired by his older brother's exploits, younger brother Randolph Turpin became the first black British-born world champion, when he beat Sugar Ray Robinson for the middleweight title in 1951.

1951 to 1971

At the same time, a paucity of home-grown soccer talent led to a growing instability in football's transfer market, as many clubs cast their nets outside Britain in a search for less expensive players. Since Britain had extensively spread the game to colonised areas in Africa, India and the West Indies, the post-war migration of labour from these areas increased the numbers of non British-born black and Asian players playing in

England (Vasili, 1998). In any event, here was a ready and willing market. In common with migrants answering calls from the National Health Service, transport, and the textile and service industries to rebuild Britain's economy, potential sportsmen shared a general optimism about the chance to escape from depressed Caribbean economies. The Caribbean was riven with social and political strife (Phillips and Phillips, 1998), and the rewards and possibilities available in the 'Mother Country' seemed enticing. Not only had these commonwealth peoples fought on the side of the Allies in the war, their homelands were steeped in the mores and culture of England. By extension, they felt 'more British than the British'.

Giles Heron, who played for Celtic between 1951 and 1952, and the Jamaican Lloyd Lindbergh 'Lindy' Delaphena were outstanding and, in terms of a black presence, still singular talents on British football's domestic stages. In spite of more open shows of colour prejudice, which included verbal abuse and physical threats from other players and some fans, Heron was generally regarded as a favourite (Cosgrove, 1991). The 'mixed' reactions to both Heron, and to Delaphena at Portsmouth, illustrated the contradictory ways in which *whiteness* could manifest itself. Making his debut for Doncaster Rovers in 1955, the 'Yorkshire born and bred' Charlie Williams also developed a rapport with the fans: and this eased his transition from footballer, to popular comedian and television presenter.

Stereotypes about the limited abilities of minority ethnic sportsmen may have constituted a less 'overt' form of racism than verbal (and sometimes physical) assault: but these stereotypes had an arguably more profound impact on their careers. In 1953 the English national football team had suffered its first defeat on home soil, in a game against Hungary (the score was 6–3, and Nandor Hidegkuti scored a hat trick). Defeat precipitated a soul-searching over playing tactics that reverberated throughout the football 'community' for years afterwards and, I believe, would have contributed to the strengthening of these racial stereotypes. By the late 1950s, both black *and* white players were struggling to find a place in the game's changing tactical culture, and hone the skills necessary to deal with evolving ideas about formation and ball retention. But it was the perceived limitations of individual black players which may have provided the binding, 'commonsense' framework that has vestiges even today. In the midst of this footballing evolution, the fact that *one* black player was a 'glory hunter who disliked hard graft', was unable to 'ride a tackle' through lack of 'commitment' and had 'no head for tactics' had far-reaching implications. Writing anecdotally, I have spoken to a number of my father's black friends who sought to play professional football during the 1950s. In their view, coaches, fans and white players alike used these individual assessments as a kind of crude genetic blueprint for all black players. Future generations of black players were also to have their careers stymied by stereotypical assessments of aptitude and ability (Chapter 4).

Williams' success, then, did not signal a 'new dawn' of sporting and wider social acceptance of minority ethnic groups in Britain; and the fate of Albert Johanneson was a jolting reminder of how painful and slow this process was going to be. The South African-born Johanneson proved to be an outstanding player for Leeds United in the 1960s. At a time when black players were still rare enough to have a novelty value, Johanneson's engaging manner and popularity did not prevent him from regularly receiving racist abuse (in the forms of verbal insults and written correspondence) from his own and opposing 'fans', and opposing players. In waging these racial assaults, British football fans appropriated popular culture as part of their armoury. As Hill (2001, p. 13) notes:

In 1964, a British-made movie called *Zulu* went on general release, detailing the resistance of British troops to a bunch of African 'savages'. That season, Johanneson turned out for Leeds against Everton at Goodison Park. The Merseyside fans, taking their cue from the film, bombarded Johanneson with their version of Zulu chants and plenty of nasty remarks. There is a famous clock at one end of the Goodison ground, whose face carries a selection of adverts. After the game, one of the Leeds players remarked that Johanneson could have recited every word of the copywriter's text, so anxiously had he willed the hands to tick round to the final whistle.

One year later (1965), Johanneson was to become the first black player to play in a Football Association (FA) cup final. Nonetheless, his achievements in club annals were marginalised. Ultimately, his career came to be characterised by exhausting and fruitless attempts to gain the recognition and rewards of his less talented peers.

Johanneson tentatively plied his trade at a time of acute anxiety over the meaning and consequences of non-white immigration. For the first time in Britain, post-war migration had established a collective black presence; in numbers approaching 200,000 by the 1960s. This 'critical mass' of black people prompted the Jamaican poet Louise Bennett to famously call the process of migration 'colonisation in reverse'. In response, and from its first incarnation in 1962, successive Commonwealth Immigration

Acts aimed to control 'coloured' settlement, thereby defining black and Asian peoples as a social problem; a threat and a burden, whose numbers should be limited. The erosion of civil liberties that resulted directly from this parliamentary consensus (Ben-Tovim and Gabriel, 1987) contributed to a climate in which overt racist attacks flourished. This was not so long after the Notting Hill 'race' riots in 1958, during which black carpenter Kelso Cochrane had been stabbed to death. 'Colour bars' in employment and housing were commonplace. The initials NBI (no blacks or Irish), surreptitiously inserted at the top right-hand corner of job application forms, were a subtle way of discouraging black and Irish people from even applying. Support for extreme right-wing organisations and policies grew; exploiting white, working-class fears of competition for jobs, housing, and anxious perceptions about Britain's fading character and stature. In 1964, the district of Smethwick in Birmingham became one of the first significant venues for a successful, overtly racist, political campaign. The victory achieved by a local politician, Peter Griffiths, was all the more remarkable because it came at the expense of a senior Cabinet Minister in a 'safe' seat, and on the back of the slogan: 'If you want a nigger for a neighbour, vote Labour' (Brown, 1999). In 1968, the Conservative MP Enoch Powell's now notorious 'rivers of blood' speech warned that Britain must be 'mad, literally mad' to be 'stoking up its own funeral pyre' by not facing up to its 'race problem'. The Commonwealth Immigrants Act passed in the same year reflected the apocalyptic tenor of Powell's words, and was condemned as 'racist, inhuman and degrading' by the European Human Rights Commission in Strasbourg. For some, ever stricter immigration controls were not enough: the repatriation of immigrants already settled in the UK was the only answer. The long hot summers of race riots in the US further focused British minds to the troublesome, alien presence in their midst and the failure, in practice, of a multiracial society. That racist abuse was directed towards black sportsmen, particularly footballers, by white supporters and some white players, was as depressing as it was inevitable.

In the same year, events surrounding a proposed cricket tour to South Africa further illustrated the significance of 'race' and racism. Basil D'Oliveira, a 'Cape Coloured' born and raised in South Africa, was selected by England for a tour of his homeland. His selection placed him at the centre of disputes concerning whether England should play cricket against a South African team selected on racial grounds, and therefore a potent symbol of the country's racist apartheid regime. The tour was eventually cancelled, since D'Oliveira's presence in the party was deemed 'unacceptable' to the South African government.

From the 1970s to the 1990s

Faced with the prospect of other, more limited, career options, black athletes continued to 'go about the business' of sport, achieving a number of unprecedented 'firsts'. In 1972, Clive Sullivan became the first black sportsperson to captain a national side when he lead the Great Britain rugby league team to victory in the World Cup of that year. In 1975, Bunny Johnson became the first black boxer to become heavyweight champion of Britain; whilst in the same year, John Conteh became world light-heavyweight champion. Perhaps most notable of all, *Viv Anderson* became the first black footballer to win a full international cap for England in 1978. And in 1980, the conspicuously successful athlete Daley Thompson won an Olympic Gold medal and also went on to claim the world decathlon record; whilst Roland Butcher became the first black man to play cricket for England at test level. Black people were also making inroads in the sport of rugby union. James 'Darkie' Peters had become the first black man to represent England at international level, winning six caps between 1906 and 1908. But a sustained black involvement in the sport is generally associated with the period from the late 1970s onwards. Andrew Harriman's international success was to be repeated by Chris Oti, Jeremy Guscott, Victor Ubogu and *Paul Hull* among others. Perhaps most notably, Guscott was regarded as arguably the most gifted rugby union player the English game had ever produced.

Like other black sportsmen before and since, Sullivan, Conteh and Anderson were conspicuous symbols of a British society which, although *de facto* multicultural, was not at ease with that identity. When the Jamaican-born Bunny Sterling became British middleweight champion in 1970, he recalled the litany of racial threats and intimidation indicative of wider society's unease about the notion of a black man holding a British title (see Cashmore, 1982). A decade later, the presence of British and world middleweight champion Alan Minter further symbolised that the meaning of a boxing match transcended mere supremacy in the ring, and became instead a proxy for issues of race and nationality. Before a televised defence against black American Marvin Hagler, the shouts of Minter's fans made it clear that he must never let a black man (presumably of any nationality) take his title.

As well as *Anderson* (above), football in the 1970s and 1980s witnessed the playing success of such luminaries as Clyde Best at West Ham United; and Brendan Batson, *Cyrille Regis* and Laurie Cunningham at West Bromwich Albion. The latter were imaginatively known as 'The Three Degrees' (after a well-known female music trio)! And by the early 1980s,

Justin Fashanu emerged as one of football's most high-profile players. These dedicated, hard-working players were popular among their 'home' supporters, but 'encountered torrents of abuse, hate letters and threats as they ran the gauntlet every Saturday at places such as West Ham, Liverpool and Manchester United' (Back *et al.*, 2001, p. x). The hard-fought success of these individuals left them in no doubt that a level playing-field of opportunities in sport was simply a 'myth' (Chapter 1).

Challenges to terrace racism were sporadic, and tended to be instigated by supporters groups anxious to counter the presence of far-right extremist organisations at matches. Although support for far-right parties collapsed following the 1979 General Election (Garland and Rowe, 2001), their strength prior to that time explained the continued absence of minority ethnic supporters across the country (but see for example Bains, 1997). One of my earliest secondary school memories is of the racist *British Bulldog* magazine being sold on the streets of Shepherds Bush in West London, near the site of Queens Park Rangers' football stadium. Reading the publication, it seemed to me that it tried to goad fans into competing for the title of the 'most racist ground in Britain'. But in spite of this, football and other sports still provided inspiration for aspiring black players already inured to the harsh realities of racism, with its more severe limiting of opportunities in other areas of life. The psychological strain that racism placed on black subject formations could be gauged by the popularity at this time of Rastafarianism: a religious movement seen as a vital source of emotional and cultural support.

The 1980s seemed to exacerbate these tensions over the precise terms of 'belonging', or who does or does not have the right to call themselves British. In 1979, then Prime Minister Margaret Thatcher had warned that the good nature and tolerance of British people would be stretched if the country were 'swamped' by too many people of a 'different culture'. Press coverage of black people at the time interpreted this cultural equation in ways which supported Thatcher's prognosis. If black people were portrayed in the press at all in this period, it was almost exclusively on the back pages for their sporting achievements, or on the front pages for their alleged criminal activities (see for example Searle, 1987; Dijk, 1991). And then Hall and colleagues (1978) showed how the crime of 'mugging' had been racialised as a specifically *black* crime, and was linked to British capitalism and the decline of the nation state. A number of inner-city uprisings by black (and white) youth at the start of the decade precipitated a 'moral panic' centring around this continued perception that black people posed a threat to British culture and to the 'British way of life'; and further intensified the search for a solution to the 'race problem'. Norman Tebbit, the former Conservative party chairman, had a simple answer. At a 1981 party conference, he summed up the feelings of the delegates, coining a phrase that has passed into common use. To a rapturous ovation, Tebbit declared that: 'My father grew up during the 1930s, when times were hard. He didn't riot. He *got on his bike* and looked for work and he kept looking until he found it!' And in 1982, figures released (and widely publicised) by the Metropolitan Police Force further contributed to the racialising of crime by suggesting that the vast majority of street crime in the capital was committed by young black men.

In some 'ethnically diverse' areas, educational authority adoption of multicultural and anti-racist teaching strategies was a direct response to the sidelining of predominantly 'West Indian' (to use terminology common for the time) children in British schools: a problem identified years earlier by Coard (1971) among others. Broadly speaking, these strategies aimed to recognise the contribution and diversity of different ethnic groups, and thereby challenge the eurocentrism seen by some to be at the heart of West Indian underachievement (see for example Rattansi, 1993). However, attempts to move towards a more inclusive model of education were met with some disdain, hostility, and lack of sympathy; and were subject to confusion and misinterpretation. Whilst multiculturalism was variously attacked as misguided by some white teachers, the right-wing press dismissed anti-racism as the diabolical brainchild of 'loony left' London councils attempting to undermine British culture and values (Honeyford, 1984, 1988; Murray, 1986). As part of a general assault by central government, stringent local government spending cuts affected equality issues, as concerns of race were pushed further down the agenda.

For West Indian boys in particular, one consequence of the afore-mentioned unrest was the social endorsement of sport as a mainstream solution to their aggressiveness, 'attitude' problems, and educational shortcomings (Chapter 3). Sport was all the more compelling given the increasing and spectacular success of black athletes; and a failure to appreciate that resorting to crime may be rooted in class circumstances, rather than 'pathological' black cultures. In short, popular beliefs about the sporting prowess of black men existed alongside fears about their 'criminal tendencies': with each as a 'signifier' (cf. Barthes) of biology and culture. When the popular boxer Frank Bruno appeared on Terry Wogan's television talk show in the 1980s, he echoed the sentiments of other black sportsmen before him, by claiming that sport had 'saved him' from a life of crime. But he also implied that a life of crime was 'common' for black men growing up in London at the time (see also Cashmore's interview with boxer Maurice Hope. 1982). The importance of this perspective for reinforcing ideas about black pathology is emphasised by Carrington. Bruno reinforces *whiteness* by confirming: 'an underlying narrative of dysfunctional black male on the verge of crime and delinquency . . . as a result of weak Black family structures without strong male figures' (2000, p. 134).

The overt racism experienced by black players in football's domestic game has already been mentioned, and became more intense on the international stage. The game was increasingly being used as a site for reclaiming and articulating a virulent, xenophobic nationalism. Prime Minister Margaret Thatcher regarded the violence perpetrated by the country's football fans as the 'English Disease'. This reached its unfortunate nadir in 1985, when confrontations between sections of the Liverpool and Juventus crowds led to the death of 39 Italian supporters at the Heysel stadium in Brussels. A foundation stone of English xenophobia claimed nationhood as an exclusively white preserve so that when, in 1978 (above), *Viv Anderson* had become the first black player to represent England at full international level, he found himself the target of a sustained and co-ordinated hate campaign. More notoriously, *Cyrille Regis* had a similar reaction from racist fans when playing for England. When he first made the England football squad in the 1980s 'he was sent a bullet through the post. The next one, the accompanying note informed him, would be delivered via his kneecap on the Wembley turf. Needless to say "Big Cyrille" wore protective knee pads on his England debut!' (Vasili, cited in KIO/FURD, 2001*b*, p. 3). The brilliantly creative footballer John Barnes had an early international career blighted by hostility from some white fans, which was partly fuelled by successive managers failing to maximise his talent. But a fine performance was no guarantee of fans' acceptance. Like the Regis incident above, what follows is an oft-cited but still exemplary anecdote of the time. Hill recalls how Barnes' 'wonder goal' against Brazil in a four-sided South American tournament in 1984 was greeted by white supporters, encountered when the players were travelling back to England:

'They were quite well behaved for a while', remembers one of the travelling reporters, 'but there was a free bar on the plane. They got progressively more pissed, and then they started getting abusive.' The prime target for the England supporters' malice was Ted Croker [the then Football Association secretary]. The core of their complaint was the composition of the England playing squad. 'They were shouting down the plane, "You fucking wanker. You prefer sambos to us." They just kept on. It was relentless.' John Barnes' goal against Brazil in Rio had sparked perhaps the most celebrated England victory since they won the World Cup 20 years before. Now he was obliged to sit there with two black colleagues, Viv Anderson and Mark Chamberlain, and impotently soak up the sound of naked racial hatred from the men who were supposed to be cheering him on.

(2001, p. 89)

The cumulative effect of racist practices embedded in the national culture, and rooted in the culture of public and private agencies (such as employment, housing, the police and the judiciary), was a number of further uprisings. These were of such a level and intensity that, along with the royal marriage of Prince Charles and Diana Spencer, they have almost come to define the entire 1980s. As Britain's newest 'underclass', physical protest seemed the only resort for a sector of society increasingly frustrated with conditions of social and economic deprivation, and political alienation. In response, right-wing politicians, the police and the mainstream media confessed confusion and vociferously condemned the uprisings as the activities of lawless youth motivated by greed and alien cultural values (see for example Murdock, 1984; Keith, 1993).

The treatment of minority ethnic sportsmen continued to highlight a link between the 'text' of racist reaction at stadia, and the 'context' of social, economic and political life. In the late 1980s, Britain experienced a period of slump precipitating mass unemployment, and creating conditions of deprivation conducive to the rise of racial intolerance and discrimination. So that, although there was an increased involvement and acceptance of black footballers and boxers, and of black athletes and rugby players, their performances were still accompanied by crude racist baiting. In the sport of rugby league, Ellery Hanley was regarded as its most recognisable name, whilst *Martin Offiah* was seen as its rising star. Nonetheless, the game's gritty atmosphere, with its overt racist abuse, provided an equally stern (non-playing) test for these individuals (see Chapter 4).

England's black cricketers fared little better in this more 'gentlemanly' of sports. Supporters at Yorkshire Cricket Club's Headingley ground in Leeds subjected *David 'Syd' Lawrence* to a barrage of racist chanting and threats of physical attack which continued when he made his test debut for England in 1988. Despite the parlous state of English cricket, with its need for a 'saviour', he was given a mixed reception. Furthermore, in test matches against the West Indies, Lawrence indicated that his place in the national side provided a lived contradiction both for white English supporters, and black British-born supporters of the opposition. That the latter group emphatically supported the West Indies seemed, he felt, to be more about a political resistance to racism in British society, than a physical connection to the lands of their forebears (Chapter 4).

In the volatile, 'passionate' atmosphere of the football stadium, the obvious and high levels of racist abuse directed at black football players were also audible to the British television public. I have vivid memories of watching BBC1's highlights programme *Match of the Day*. I often thought that the abuse must have been very loud indeed because, despite their best efforts, the programme editors failed to muffle the sounds of racist chanting. There seemed a widespread assumption that talking about it made the problem worse, and that if it was ignored, it would simply go away. In short, the broadcast media's 'code of silence' on this issue was consistently adhered to by studio commentators, and helped to define racist abuse as an aberration in the game. The freelance journalist Dave Hill has produced a highly readable biography of the ex-Liverpool and England footballer John Barnes. In 1987, during televised evening highlights of a 'local derby' between Liverpool (Barnes' team) and Everton, Hill notes that:

> the spectator noise . . . rose to a crescendo when the action involved John Barnes. Every time the Liverpool winger got the ball he was loudly and vehemently booed . . . Photographers stationed along the goal line were astonished by the violence of the language directed at him, clearly audible to the players at the edge of the field. Barnes took corner kicks in a hail of spit. Meanwhile, a substantial section of Everton's fans assailed Liverpool's new hero with chants, prepared specially for the occasion . . . the relentless repetition of a distortion of the home team's name: 'Niggerpool, Niggerpool, Niggerpool'.
>
> (2001, p. 184)

By the late 1980s, there was as yet no official, government action to deal with or address the problem of minority ethnic supporters deterred from going to matches by the racist reactions of white supporters. This is not to say that the overt racism characteristic of the time went totally unopposed. Chanting, and the sale of racist literature at football matches, were increasingly being challenged by low-profile anti-fascist groups and organisations, and by proactive fan groups adopting their own initiatives. Not all fan organisations were sympathetic to these initiatives. Indeed, anti-racism in football in this period was 'largely instigated by grassroots fans organisations, who were often acting in the face of active opposition of the clubs themselves' (Garland and Rowe, 2001, p. 46). Nonetheless, the Football Supporters Association (an independent, national campaigning body) was formed in 1985, with an express aim to put the development of anti-racist strategies high on its agenda. And organisations like Leeds Fans United Against Racism and Fascism, formed in 1987, worked tirelessly to remove racism from the terraces; whilst sympathetic sections of the press gave various local campaigns wide coverage (see also Back *et al.*, 2001).

A search for 'respect'

It seems relevant to briefly reflect that a number of the most prominent black sportsmen adopted personas reflecting the insecurity that came with being black in Britain, and which bred a 'defensiveness' in public situations. Both Linford Christie (athletics) and Ellery Hanley (rugby league) were perceived as sportsmen with 'chips on their shoulders'. Hanley felt that both his treatment by journalists, and media coverage, were intrusive, uncompromising and racist in tone. As a result, he refused all media interviews for almost the entire 1980s. To use rugby parlance, this was a strange and awkward 'stand-off'. As well as being a regular winner of rugby league's 'Man of Steel' award, Hanley enjoyed exalted status as the sport's national team captain, and was generally regarded as one of the best players that either code (league or union) had ever seen. Christie's defensiveness, and continued search for 'respect' were (in part) based on the ways in which his fame had failed to insulate him from the iniquities faced by 'ordinary' black people living in Britain. Christie regularly and bitterly complained about the 'numerous' times he was stopped and searched whilst driving his car, or stopped on the street under suspicion of carrying illegal drugs. The lewder imperatives of tabloid journalism were an affront to the sensitivities of black sportsmen, and simply exacerbated these feelings. When Christie won the 100 metre sprint title at the 1992 Olympic Games, regarded as the 'blue riband' event, British tabloid newspaper headlines devoted a part of the coverage to the size and movement of his genitalia (Chapter 4).

From the 1990s to the present day

This chapter has referred particularly to the problem of overt racism in football. In the last decade, the existence and impact of legislative measures, combined with a climate of social change, have helped to reduce incidents of chanting and threatening behaviour at top sports stadia. Change has been symptomatic of recognition at an official level of 'problems' in the sport; and a shifting climate within sport has reflected broader struggles for ethnic identity outside of it. Change has also been influenced by a growing black presence. A survey of 92 League Clubs conducted in 1990 showed that 12 per cent of players were black (KIO/FURD, 2001b).

Although the 1991 Football (Offences) Act had made racist chanting at football matches an offence, the first significant attempt to eliminate racism from football grounds came when the Commission for Racial Equality (CRE) combined with the Professional Footballer's Association (PFA) to address the problem. The resultant Let's Kick Racism out of Football (LKR) campaign was launched at the start of the 1993/94 season. Supported by the game's governing bodies, some (but not all) supporters organisations and local authority representatives, it works to challenge racism at all levels of the game. By 1995, the campaign was publicly endorsed by all but one (York City) of 92 professional clubs existing in England and Wales at the time; and had enlisted the support of a number of high-profile players (principally Les Ferdinand, John Barnes, Ryan Giggs, Andy Cole and Eric Cantona. See AGARI, 1996). The campaign also stimulated a number of regional anti-racist initiatives, most notably Football Unites Racism Divides (Sheffield), Show Racism the Red Card (North East of England) and the Leicester Asian Sports Initiative (see below; see also Garland and Rowe, 2001, for a detailed discussion of these initiatives). Further progress to eliminate racism at football matches came with an amendment to Section 3 of the 1991 Football (Offences) Act. This amendment, enshrined in the Football (Offences and Disorder) Act 1999, now made racist chanting by a single individual (previously, two or more individuals had to utter words or sounds in concert) an offence. Crucially, and due in part to the influence of the LKR campaign, the FA made an official apology to black players and supporters for not addressing the issue of overt racism when the problem was at its zenith in the 1970s and 1980s. Equally significant, the media has increasingly acknowledged and condemned the racist dimension to fans' taunting of black players. In a marked shift, the period from the mid-1990s onwards has seen more media articles condemning racist chanting and abuse (see for example Harris, 2002).

It could be argued that the increasing commodification of sport is a 'driver' for the types of legislative measures, and the media's recognition of the problem as mentioned above. Strong commercial forces are endorsing sports' status as a commodity, resulting in the drive for a 'media product' that is more palatable and acceptable to sponsors and to advertisers. So that whilst initiatives to eliminate racism from the terraces are a central part of this commodification process, their effects are skewed towards the highest levels of sport. This 'top heavy' emphasis is supported by evidence suggesting that more acute problems of overt racism have simply been driven into the less policed domain of lower league football (Jones, 2002). As a member of a local amateur league football team I have unfortunate, first-hand experience of a phenomenon which both my friends and I believe, perversely, has *increased* since the sport has sought to 'clean up its act'. The LKR campaign has been 'unevenly developed' amongst football clubs, with some instituting more extensive programmes than others. This further reinforces a suspicion about the tokenistic nature of responses from some clubs (Garland and Rowe, 2001). In addition, a failure by the Football Association to condemn the sinister element to English fans' derision of black players at recent (October 2002) international matches, instead focusing on the activities of other country's fans, highlights the 'cosmetic' feel of this push for change (Chaudhary, 2002).

Statistics on minority ethnic attendance provide an important litmus test of the 'genuineness' and efficacy of these strategies. In spite of commercial influences, and the laudable anti-racist initiatives above, live football still fails to attract a representative proportion of black and Asian supporters. The high cost of attending matches may be prohibitive. But it is more likely that the absence of minority ethnic groups reflects a fear that legislative change is one thing, whilst cultural change is altogether different. In short, black and Asian supporters may have residual anxieties about the reality of a genuine shift in the attitudes and behaviour of white spectators. These anxieties may reflect their knowledge of the ways in which football is co-opted by some white groups; and their negative experiences in other areas of social life. According to a recent study (Jones, 2002), low attendance may be explained not by an absence of will on the part of minority ethnic groups, but by a strong perception that white supporters continue to racially abuse black and Asian players at sports grounds. In spite of improved circumstances at matches, the pessimism shared by black and Asian supporters about feeling unwelcome and unsafe is supported by Kick It Out, the organisation which runs the LKR campaign. Racist taunts are still a consistent and frequent feature of live football, even though the English Premier League attracts a growing contingent of foreign players. According to their organisation however, fewer than 40 people a year are successfully prosecuted for racist chanting (KIO/FURD, 2001*b*).

Although a perception of personal risk is seen to be less acute in some other sports, the absence of minority ethnic spectators is an issue affecting *all* sports. The following comments are specific to the ethnic mix of spectators at a football match, but have a wider resonance for sport and issues of national identity:

> The line separating the field from stadium had become a contact zone separating two faces of England. On the pitch the fact of cultural diversity was only too evident. Nevertheless, the social composition of the stands pointed to the ways in which white Englishness remained unaffected by the cultural diversity that increasingly defined what it meant to live in England.
>
> (Back *et al.*, 2001, p. xi)

The precautions a dedicated black football supporter feels that he has to make to attend live matches speaks volumes about the threat posed by manifestations of white Englishness. His enthusiasm and love for the game are tempered by the reality of an ever-present physical threat that keeps other black supporters away: that is, unless they are prepared to engage in an exercise of military precision. Billy 'the bee' Grant writes:

> After a five year break from international duty . . . I was back on the scene . . . For Euro 96 I had tickets for all games. What an atmosphere! What a change! Then I hit the France 98 qualifiers, France 98 finals, Euro 2000 qualifiers and then Euro 2000 finals. Before I knew it I was in the top 55 of the England supporters club. Me, a black supporter! Incredibly I have never been involved in any trouble at an England away game. We've managed to avoid trouble because of meticulous planning: what plane to get, where we will stay before the match, where we will stay after the match, what we'll wear.
>
> (cited in KIO/FURD, 2001*b*, p. 11)

To watch a football game involving club sides on the continent of Europe, and which includes black players, is to recognise the relative progress that English football has made in this regard. In the last few years, there have been a number of complaints to the Union of European Football Associations (UEFA) regarding the appearance of swastikas at stadia, burning effigies of black players, and the high levels of racist abuse directed at them. These countries have been much slower to institute similar deterrents at football grounds. In February 1999, not long after Kevin Campbell had signed for Turkish team Trabzonspor, the club manager remarked that: 'We bought a cannibal who believes he is a forward.' And in February 2001, the President of Italian club Verona claimed that he would not consider buying Patrick M'bomba (Africa's player of the year) because it might lead to an increase in racism at the club (KIO/FURD, 2001*b*). This admission constitutes official, tacit recognition that the game acts as a platform for grosser displays of racist aggression. Equally notable is that the scenario is strangely reminiscent of that faced by Walter Tull, almost a century earlier (see above).

Cricket and 'race'

Cricket's value to this study is less about the dynamics of crowd reaction, and how these may be a reflection of societal attitudes; and more concerned with the way the game itself is powerfully evocative of 'Englishness'. As Malcolm (1997) notes, although soccer is regarded as the national game of England, cricket is quintessentially the 'English' game. Whilst Maguire and Stead (1996, p. 17) have claimed that 'Cricket reflects and reinforces the tendency in English culture and identity to hark back to past glories. The "golden age" of cricket is at the high point of Empire.' As such, cricket is a prime barometer reflecting concern over England's diminishing role as a world superpower, and as a site of contested national identities. The 1990s were to provide potent illustrations of how a cricketing metaphor was harnessed to reactivate these concerns, and of how playing the game could function as a proxy for belonging.

In 1990, the Conservative MP and former cabinet minister Norman Tebbit questioned whether those black and Asian peoples coming to live and work in Britain should be compelled to 'take the cricket test'. This loosely translated as a trial of allegiance at test matches, where their loudest cheers should be reserved for England, rather than for teams representing their country of origin, such as the West Indies and Pakistan. Fundamentally, Tebbit's enquiry (and professed scepticism as to a lack of will on their part) was more than a simple challenge of black and Asian sporting loyalty. In truth, it should be properly interpreted as part of a wider public discourse aimed at contracting the limits of British identity: a debate which, as we have seen, has been a consistent feature of race relations since black and Asian peoples have had a significant presence in Britain.

Tebbit used a cricketing metaphor to obliquely raise this question of race, identity and belonging. Robert Henderson's article, appearing in the prestigious sports almanac *Wisden Cricket Monthly* in July 1995, was more explicit in its enquiry. Henderson recognised cricket's role as a source of national and 'racial' pride for black and Asian people born in ex-Empire nations. He also understood that cricket provided the basis for a concrete, collective identity for their British-born descendants; and that this was some comfort when set against the uncertainty of a black-British or Asian-British label. As a *sequitur*, the author suggested that representative sportsmen who were not 'unequivocally English' – by which he meant not white and raised in Britain – were likely to have divided loyalties, even when Britain was the country of their birth. This lack of real commitment to the England team and cause may reflect a subconscious desire to overturn centuries of colonial exploitation and oppression. Henderson provocatively stated that these players 'may well be trying at a conscious level', but rhetorically asked: 'is that desire to succeed instinctive, a matter of biology?' (1995, pp. 9–10). The furore resulting from the article partly led to the formation of the independent lobbying group, Hit Racism for Six. As its name suggests, it was motivated by the need to address and challenge racism at all levels of the game.

Chris Eubank and Frank Bruno: England's 'different' sons

During this period, a number of individuals within the sport of boxing also reflected this tension about belonging, and about challenging the limits of British identity. In the 1990s, the behaviour and public persona of black British boxer Chris Eubank clashed uneasily with normative ideas about whiteness and blackness, and created an intense public antipathy that seemed to obscure his successful career in the ring. Frank Bruno, by contrast, slotted more comfortably into a 'safe' black Britishness that seemed to rely on more classic stereotypes.

Eubank committed the 'sin', a cardinal one to sports purists, of besmirching his sport for being base and repulsive (whilst, it should be said, making a comfortable living from it). In itself, this was not the cause of public antipathy towards him. But Eubank combined these utterances with a foppish social attire (jodhpurs, patterned waistcoat and eye monocle); a religious zeal when proselytising about the insights of Plato, Marx and Mao; and an affected vocal gravitas more in keeping with someone who hails from the landed classes. The extent of white public ire seemed to be rooted more in this challenge to the defined contours of British ethnic identity than his sporting pronouncements: contours which, although tightly scripted, were still comforting for some members of both groups. Black reactions to Eubank were arguably more ambivalent.

The jocular persona of former world heavyweight champion Frank Bruno made him easier to situate within an 'ideal type' ethnic identity framework, and could not have provided a stronger contrast to that of Eubank. At a time when tensions over 'race' and identity were at their height, white reactions to him were considerably more favourable, to the point where 'our Frank' became accepted as a true British icon in spite of his colour, and his relative failures in the ring (or maybe because of his failures, as in the case of skier Eddie 'the Eagle'). Bruno's 'easy Britishness', was best captured by his catch phrase, 'you know what I mean' 'Arry?' (a reference to his friend and sports commentator Harry Carpenter). But his frequent appearances on talk shows, and as the 'Dame' in British pantomime; the energetic flag-waving that accompanied his ring performances, and even his support for the Tory Party, also confirmed his role as a true symbol of Britishness (see Gilroy, 1993, for a discussion of Bruno and Salman Rushdie). In this regard, and with reference to the normative codes that reinforce whiteness, Carrington (2000, p. 134) has noted that:

> Bruno . . . works prodigiously to endorse a conservative conceptualisation of the nation, supposedly at ease with itself and free from racial antagonisms, and is thus accepted unquestionably into the nation. Bruno is thus presented as the acceptable face of Black masculinity, supposedly symbolizing what Blacks as a whole could achieve if only they would stop 'whingeing' about racism and commit themselves more fully to being British.

The politics of 'race' have produced a very different reaction among British black people. Bruno's public persona was perhaps interpreted as evidence of political and cultural compromise, and not necessarily as a cause for celebration: contrasting as it did with their own struggles, and the profound impact of racism on their lives (see for example Eboda, 1995). So whilst Bruno's non-radical blackness and non-threatening persona were prime elements of this easy Britishness, they merely exacerbated the black sense of unease about him.

Signs of the future

Whilst these questions of cultural allegiance and British identity surfaced, sport in the 1990s (football particularly) witnessed growing numbers of black men and women who have continued to achieve spectacular success at domestic and international level. They appear to have developed a strong rapport with supporters and, in the process of extending their craft, have forcefully challenged worn-out racial assumptions about their aptitudes and abilities. For instance, through a combination of their determination to make sport a worthwhile career choice, the sheer impact of numbers, and changing societal attitudes, British black people have succeeded in debunking ideas about their lack of aggression, their lack of versatility; and their lack of commitment to the national team, and the group ethic in team sports. Today, an impressionistic look at the English premier football league would appear to provide evidence of how comprehensively these barriers have been breached. Not only can black players comprise between 10 and 80 per cent of first-team selections, they play in all roles from goalkeeper through to attacking forward, as well as captaining the side in some cases.

Black British sporting success has been interpreted in some quarters as a symbol of unity for the nation as a whole. In 1993, ex-Manchester United and Liverpool footballer Paul Ince achieved what would have been considered unthinkable just a decade earlier when he became the first black player to captain the national side. Other symbolic and visible manifestations of black nationhood included Linford Christie's habit of draping himself in a Union Jack after victories at major athletics championships, and the obvious and open patriotism of the boxer Frank Bruno. And although minority ethnic figures in management and other roles such as refereeing are disproportionately low, former players such as John Fashanu, John Barnes and *Viv Anderson* have made inroads in coaching at the élite level. Furthermore *Garth Crooks*, along with other former players Robbie Earle and Ian Wright, regularly feature as television commentators on the game. In combination, these players and former players challenge the (hitherto pervasive) 'stacking' thesis outlined in Chapter 4; as well as the view that black people have no tactical or technical contributions to make to their sport.

This is not to suggest that narrow, clumsy theories concerning aptitude and temperament have been totally consigned to the mantle of history. In 1993 for instance, the former England Chairman of Selectors, Ray Illingworth, claimed that West Indians needed less training than English players, because they were 'bigger' and had 'looser shoulders' (cited in Marqusee, 1995a, p. 2). And *Daily Mail* sports writer Steve Curry reactivated a stereotypical idea concerning British black people and their spurious loyalty to the nation. Curry adopted an inferential tone reminiscent of Henderson (see above) when assessing the international debut of black footballer Michael Ricketts. In Curry's view: 'For all his influence at Bolton [football club] . . . Ricketts was out of his depth. His future may yet be with Jamaica's *Reggae Boys*, where he will have a more suitable platform for restricted talent,' (2002, p. 95). For some commentators, it would seem that black allegiance to the 'nation', and the self-identity that is invariably bound up with this, can be changed as easily as a football shirt.

Asian men and British sport

1889 to 1939

In common with their black counterparts, an Asian presence in football can also be traced back to the genesis of the modern game. Nonetheless, appearances before the Great War were scarce, and records of Asian contributions to this sport have been marginalised. The Anglo-Asian Cother brothers attracted some press attention and spectator curiosity playing for Watford in the 1890s, as did the Calcutta-born Salim Khan in the 1930s. The Cother brothers appear to have had a 'physically uncompromising' style of play (KIO/FURD, 2001*b*), for example Khan, eschewing football boots, preferred to play in bandaged feet for Celtic reserves! In theory, the contributions of such players to overturning stereotypes of Asian men as passive, and lacking the physical strength to play football seriously, could have been significant. In the case of Khan however, it seems as if his unorthodox apparel may have had the effect of further marking him out as an exotic 'Other', and not contributed to challenging these ingrained notions (Dimeo and Finn, 2001).

If not the number, then certainly the profile of Asian men in cricket was higher than in other sports, due to the popularity of outstanding individual players. Before the First World War, a small cadre of non-whites played first-class county cricket. These were mainly overseas-born players who had toured England and decided to stay on, or had returned specifically to play cricket. Reference has already been made to Ollivierre, one of the few black players in the first-class county game, and to the impact of other black players in the professional Lancashire leagues. Before 1939, the presence of Asian cricketers in the first-class county game, and the relative absence of African-Caribbeans at this level, reflected the importance of class and status, and a legacy of different Empire relations. By the end of the nineteenth century, cricket in both the Caribbean and India had provided the means to affirm imperialist ideas essential to the maintenance of British political, cultural and economic hegemony. The exclusive status of the élite and the aspiring Caribbean cricket clubs (organised along social ranking and colour hierarchy, rather than ability) was an important mechanism by which this was achieved. And whilst cricket in the Caribbean effectively mirrored the wider exclusions of the black population from the dynamics of power, the British established the game in India to include the indigenous ruling élite as a means of engendering their loyalty to the Crown. This more even power-balance, based as it was on education and proselytism, helped to establish a tradition of Indians of high social status playing cricket in England from the turn of the century, many of whom attended public schools, and the universities of Oxford and Cambridge (see for example Stoddart, 1988; Holt, 1989).

Undoubtedly the most famous 'product' of this tradition was K. S. Ranjitsinhji. An Oxford cricket blue, Ranjitsinhji played first-class cricket between 1880 and 1914, and was described as 'one of the biggest stars of English sport in the late-Victorian and Edwardian periods' (Williams, 2001, p. 22). As a Prince (possibly self-proclaimed) from a wealthy Indian aristocratic family, Ranjitsinhji was a popular and well-received figure among the literati and higher echelons of British society. His status and popularity also meant that his white team-mates were more inclined than they might otherwise have been to play under him as captain. Evidence of racism directed towards non-whites in county cricket between the wars is scarce. However, at a time when innate white superiority was assumed, there is little doubting the significance of 'race' for social relations. It is probable that despite his playing form at the time, and in spite of his enhanced status as an Indian Prince, the lack of a concerted press campaign for Ranjitsinhji to captain the national side was due to increasing anxieties over 'race': of what having an Indian captain, a colonial subject in spite of his wealth, *says* about the nation. As Williams (2001) has shown, it was not unprecedented for the England captain to be born abroad.

Broadly speaking, social class continued to supersede race to account for why the very small number of non-whites playing first class county cricket between the wars were overwhelmingly of Asian origin. Two overseas-born players followed Ranjitsinhji, and were also products of the élite tradition. Kumar Duleepsinhji, a nephew of Ranjitsinhji, and Iftikhar Ali Khan, hailed from privileged backgrounds in India, were Oxbridge educated, and played for England in this period. Like Ranjitsinhji before him, Duleepsinhji met with covert racial hostility: in this instance, over his selection for a team to face South Africa. White establishment figures were understood to be anxious about the ideological challenge presented by an Indian posting a high score against a racialised regime, and the overtones this might create. Duleepsinhji was dropped after the first test in 1929. In the same period, the Asian presence extended to the professional game: most notably Amar Singh, playing for Colne, 1935–38, and Lala Armanath for Nelson, 1938 and 1939, in the Lancashire leagues (Williams, 2001).

From 1945 to the present day

After the war, football and cricket continued to represent rare avenues for Asian professional sporting aspirations in Britain. It has already been mentioned that many clubs urgently cast their nets outside Britain in the search for less expensive footballers. Despite this overseas focus, a small number of British-born, 'Anglo-Asian' players are particularly well known. In the 1955/56 season, Roy Smith played for West Ham and Portsmouth; whilst in the 1960s, Paul Wilson played for Celtic and was capped for Scotland in 1975 (more later). Ricky Heppolate was arguably the most well known of the cadre of post-war Anglo-Asian footballers. Heppolate joined Preston North End in 1964, and played over 250 games with distinction for this and a number of other clubs. This chapter has already made reference to the impact of legislative measures such as stricter immigration controls, and discrimination in housing and education. Despite these constraints, Williams still felt that '[f]irst-class cricket in England in the 1960s fostered racial harmony in Britain' (2001, p. 53). Certainly, the popularity and success of such cricketers as Farouk Engineer at Lancashire, and Asif Iqbal at Kent lends some credence to this idea, presenting the acceptance of talented individuals as an antidote to the societal racism common in this period.

By contrast, accounts of the careers of notable and talented Asian footballers such as Heppolate instead highlight how their sporting ambitions were partly frustrated by entrenched, negative perceptions about their limited motivation, physical frailty and limited mental capabilities (Bains with Patel, 1996; Bains and Johal, 1998). These stereotypical 'character traits' are the antithesis of normative sporting values such as physical aggression, and courage and competitiveness, which lie at the centre of male supporting cultures.

A purely 'recreational' experience?

Sport for South Asian groups in Britain has consistently performed a specific, traditional function: acting as 'an effective means of maintaining ethno-cultural solidarity in the face of geo-political and social dislocation'. In 1963 for instance, one year before Peter Griffith's racist 'nigger for a neighbour' campaign slogan appeared on the hustings (see above), the first Asian Games tournament also took place in Smethwick. From humble beginnings, it grew to become an annual national sporting event, encompassing an ever-widening range of sports: from the traditional *Kabaddi*, to weightlifting and athletics (Johal, 2001, p. 161).

The limited presence of Asian men in British professional sport has meant that racist reactions have been specifically directed to black sportsmen at this level. But given the social context, it is also likely that racial antipathy surfaced between white and Asian groups at other sporting levels (see also Chapter 1). In the 1970s, a press focus on Asian groups as a threat to British culture and way of life contributed to a 'moral panic' about the social consequences of non-white immigration. 'Fresh extremes of media sensationalism' (Ben-Tovim and Gabriel, 1987) were generated by the arrival to Britain of some 27,000 African-Asian refugees from Uganda, Kenya and Malawi in 1972. In the 1980s, the same themes were adopted by the political right, exploiting fears about a 'flood' of Tamil refugees; prominent reports about the 'bogus' marriages of Asian couples for the purposes of securing a British passport; Indian family members ostensibly visiting their relatives but with the intention of remaining here indefinitely; and stories of state scroungers (Gordon and Rosenberg, 1989).

Against this background, sport continued to represent a site of tension around nationhood and identity. In this way, a narrow, racialised definition of Asianness (Chapter 1) may explain why the playing successes of Paul Wilson have not been greatly publicised as Asian achievements. Wilson, an 'Anglo-Asian', played for Celtic in the 1970s, the period when they were one of Europe's premiere teams, and where he enjoyed a successful career. Wilson was also capped by Scotland in 1975, some three years before *Viv Anderson* made his England debut. At a time when black achievements in professional sport were starting to be more widely recognised, the significance of Wilson's selection for Scotland was ignored. To add insult to injury, the racist abuse he regularly endured from opposing team's fans when playing for Celtic was trivialised by the club's failure to classify it appropriately. And of course, a more easily recognisable Asian heritage was no guarantee of sporting acknowledgement. In the 1980s, Rashid Sarwar was one of the few Asian players ever to play for Kilmarnock. In common with Wilson, he had his playing achievements marginalised, and the extensive racist abuse he encountered was neutralised by a similar wall of denial (see Dimeo and Finn, 2001).

In the summer of 1981, uprisings by Asian youths in Southall, London, were a violent expression of their discontent with the scope of lives limited by racism, and in defiance of anti-immigrant demonstrations in their local communities. Sport was not widely presented as a solution to this outpouring of Asian 'aggression'; in contrast to Britain's African-Caribbean groups resorting to the same means of protest. Long-standing ideas about Asian identity and culture remained fairly unchallenged, and obviated sport's assimilationist function for Asian youth.

For instance, writing in the early 1980s, Cashmore (1982, p. 34) remarked that: 'Asians were products of a culture emphasising the value of education as a means of social advancement and, because of the tight control they were able to exert over their children, could imbue the second generation with similar values'.

In the 1990s, the success that Asian groups have achieved in the 'professions' (law, medicine, commerce) has sustained the view about career interests outside of sport, and the influence of the family (Modood *et al.*, 1998). A recent study found that Asian parents remained disdainful about their children's sporting career interests, although attitudes are changing (Bains and Johal, 1998). There are signs that a significant number of British Asians regularly play recreational cricket: in proportionally greater numbers than their African-Caribbean and white contemporaries (see for example Verma and Derby, 1994; Fleming, 1995*b*). And according to a recent Sports Council study, proportionally as many Asian as white boys regularly play football (47 per cent compared to 46 per cent; figures cited in Moore, 1998). Having spent over a decade living in West Yorkshire, I can personally attest to the interest, high levels of support, and enthusiasm for Asian football tournaments amongst the local communities. For reasons outlined in Chapter 1, this Asian sporting presence is found in predominantly all-Asian leagues and clubs. For instance, the Quaid-e-Azam (father of the nation) league is regarded as one of the premiere Pakistani cricket leagues, with its clubs located in the North of England. Tournaments, which are well-supported by Britain's Asian communities, are prestigious and competitive, with a high standard of play. However, there is also increasing evidence of Asian men joining integrated playing structures, and aspiring to professional sports careers (Carrington and McDonald, 2001*b*). In football, this is being facilitated by schemes such as the Leicester Asian Sports Initiative, which seeks to provide increased opportunities for young Asian players to join a professional club's school of excellence.

Contrary to ideas about their non-association with the professional game, Bains and Johal (1998) provide detailed evidence of the central role that football has continued to play in the lives of British Asian males. In their book *Corner Flags and Corner Shops*, they detail the extent of Asian involvement from playing and supporting, to financial controlling interests. There is also a significant level of support for British football teams and players in India, due partly to post-imperialist ties and the impact and reach of satellite television coverage. In this light, both the appointment of the first Asian referee to take charge of a game in the league's top division (1989); and the signing of India's captain

Bhaichung Butia by Bury FC a decade later, seemed long overdue. However, there are currently no British South Asians playing regular first-team football in England's premier league.

When the LKR campaign was launched in 1993 (see above), the subject of Asians in football did not emerge as a prominent focus for discussion, in spite of evidence suggesting a significant involvement in playing, and in the numbers of 'armchair fans' (Bains with Patel, 1996). At a regional level, there has been an attempt to redress the marginal- isation of Asians in football. A lack of knowledge about the relationship between Asian communities and football has been the focus of such organisations as the Midland Asian Sports Forum. Professional football clubs, and supporters groups have also attempted to redress this mis- match between perception and reality. For instance Bradford City and Sheffield United, located in cities with sizeable Asian populations, have sought to be more responsive to the needs of these groups; whilst 'Foxes Against Racism', a supporters' initiative at Leicester City, have actively campaigned to rid their ground of racism, and to promote greater minority ethnic attendance (Garland and Rowe, 2001).

Although Asian sportsmen have challenged pervading stereotypes about sporting aptitude and ability, these still persist. Spracklen's research (2001) indicated that rugby league coaches and other person- nel continued to view Asian men as not 'built' for sport; and believed that they prioritised religion and other cultural concerns over an inter- est in sport. Typical reflections of rugby league personnel concerned Asian men not liking the intensity of the game: 'I have heard it said that they do not take kindly to being covered in mud – I understand it to be a religious thing' (cited in Long *et al.*, 1995, p. 27). Other 'folk tales' concerned Asian men (presumably of any religion) stopping football matches in mid-flow to unroll prayer mats; and not playing rugby because they couldn't wear turbans in the scrum. And as Bains (1997, p. 169) indicates, these ideas about Asian lack of interest and aptitude have continued in the face of quite contrary evidence:

> Perhaps someone ought to explain this notion to those Asian sports- men playing professional club and international rugby league, or to the many lads who have represented the Great Britain weight-lifting and wrestling teams . . . the Indian game of 'Kabbaddi' – a sport which demands great strength and speed, and is participated in by a great number of Asians . . . let's not forget that squash, tennis and hockey are not only physically very demanding sports but also require high levels of tactical awareness and appreciation – not unlike football.

And so on. The perpetuation of mainstream views about Asian men and sport imposes its own weighty constraints on their legitimate sporting aspirations.

Cricket and 'race'

It has been noted that the history and cultural heritage assigned to cricket make it a potent symbol for anxieties around 'alien' threats to an English identity, and to the 'national character'. The spurious questions asked by Tebbit and Henderson (see above) were accompanied by 'other' anxieties. These ostensibly focused on overseas Asian cricketers, but had consequences for the sporting identity of British Asian men too.

Of all England's test match opponents in the 1980s and 1990s, relations with Pakistan were the most strained; characterised by bitterness, suspicion and recrimination on both sides. To add 'spice' to these encounters, Pakistan had a long-standing grievance against English cricket, and felt 'slighted' by the English game. Hostilities were arguably at their most pronounced during the English tour to Pakistan in 1987, and the Pakistan tour of England in 1992. Racial stereotypes of the 'wily' Indian spin bowler, the 'wristy' Indian or Pakistani batsman and the 'corrupt' Pakistani and Indian umpire were particularly commonplace at this time, and inferred cheating by ball tampering, illegal bowling action and 'dubious' umpiring decisions. The extent of this belief is supported by Williams (2001, p. 140) who states that:

> English cricket saw Pakistan cricket as riddled with cheating. There was a long-held belief that Pakistani umpires, with the encouragement of Pakistan captains and officials favoured Pakistan teams on a scale that constituted cheating. The conviction that Pakistan players and officials colluded with umpires to cheat was found even at the summit of English cricket.

In his country's defence, the former Pakistani cricketer Imran Khan viewed extensive tabloid press allegations as a manifestation of post-colonial hegemony, and evidence of the enduring legacy of colonial relations. In relation to umpiring, Khan had argued that when English and Australian officials made 'controversial' decisions, they were interpreted as mistakes, rather than (as in the case for Pakistani umpires) evidence of cheating. In the 1990s, Khan felt that:

> Pakistanis were still being treated as natives out to cheat their colonial masters. The untrustworthy native was the 'white man's burden', as

Kipling had put it, and had to be taught the higher British values. Imran felt the more sensational English newspapers still seemed to believe that the native was going to cheat whenever the Englishman was off his guard.

(Tennant, 1994, p. 121)

Against this background, it is not surprising that the success of the Pakistani cricket side in 1992 was undermined by a concerted press campaign against them. Inflammatory headlines and press allegations focused on the bowling actions of the Pakistani fast bowlers Waqar Younis and Wasim Akram, and the ways that alleged tampering with the cricket ball led to 'reverse swing' (see for example Marqusee, 1998; also Chapter 4). The atmosphere of recriminations was further heightened in the courts, as a number of high-profile libel cases ensued between English and Pakistani cricketers. The tenor of the (mostly tabloid) press reports also nurtured a climate in which physical and verbal abuse was directed against Asian players and cricket fans (Searle, 1996); and arguably helped to ossify beliefs about different cricketing 'cultures' existing at all levels of the game. According to Carrington and McDonald:

> a large number of Asian players ... especially at the recreational level, have had to face accusations and tolerate suspicions. Thus in a cricket discourse replete with racial stereotypes and competitive bowling, enthusiastic appealing by an Asian bowler can very easily be interpreted by umpires and others as 'intimidation' and cheating, typical of 'Pakistani' players. To protest at such treatment merely confirms their 'volatile [and dishonest] nature[s]'.
>
> <div align="right">(2001<i>b</i>, p. 57)</div>

Rather than being a purely sporting occasion, the 1999 cricket World Cup seemed to crystallise multilayered concerns over non-white *alienness*: be it expressed as a fear over immigration, the mode of fans' celebrations, or the recurrent theme of Pakistani cheating. For example, hundreds of cricket fans from the Asian subcontinent travelling to England for the World Cup were required to take a verbal test on their knowledge of the game and the team they supported before being granted entry visas (Chaudhary, 1999). The suspicion of a racialised agenda was strengthened by the omission of this particular 'cricket test' for fans travelling from South Africa, New Zealand and Australia, who were asked only to show proof of a return ticket.

Similarly, criticism of the traditionally 'colourful' behaviour of West Indian and Asian fans at test matches has led to restrictive responses and rule changes by the English cricket authorities. To some, these changes have been underscored by a cultural agenda emphasising the superior norms and ethics of the English game (Marqusee, 1998). Finally, despite a burgeoning and well-established local structure in Yorkshire, it is significant that an English-born player of Asian origin is yet to play for the county's first team. For this reason, the former Pakistan cricketer Imran Khan accused the club of 'failing its Asian community' during the 1999 World Cup (Abassi, 1999). But in spite of these concerns over nationhood and British identity, a number of 'Anglo-Asian' cricketers are currently leaving an indelible mark on the professional first-class game. Principally, Madras-born Nasser Hussain became the first person of South Asian descent to captain England in 1999. His England colleague Mark Ramprakash, who made his debut at the start of the decade, is also a regular member of the national squad. In addition, a small number of Asian men have achieved success in other professional sports in the 1990s. The boxer 'Prince' Naseem Hamed is arguably the most accomplished of this cadre, whilst tennis player Arvind Parmar currently ranks among the country's top ten professionals.

By the end of the twentieth century, discrimination against Asian groups has been fuelled by religious intolerance, and one-dimensional perceptions about their cultures and lifestyles (Modood *et al.*, 1998). An over-simplified view of Muslims and their religious practices has exacerbated already-existing tensions between white and Asian groups, and contributed to a rising antipathy towards Islam in Britain. Practices associated with more fundamentalist Muslim groups have been extensively reported, and provided a commonsense framework for understanding the entire Islamic faith. In 1988, noted author Salman Rushdie published *The Satanic Verses*, a book which some British Muslims felt was critical of Islam. In response, Iran's Ayatollah Khomeini pronounced a *fatwa* (or 'license to kill') against the UK-based author; which led to strident defences in the British media of the constitution's principle of freedom of speech. As Werbner (1996, p. 105) states:

> The publication of *The Satanic Verses* ... revealed a deep clash between Islam and British nationalism. 'Islam' was now to be defended at all costs, a matter of personal and communal honour. British Pakistanis 'became', officially, in the media and in their own eyes, 'Muslims'.

The declaration of religious wars or *jihads* against the West were further causes of consternation, along with the repressive Taliban regime in Afghanistan; and stories of Asian brides forced into marriage on pain of death. The combination and profile of these stories, along with the terrorist attacks on 11 September 2001, have arguably reinforced an impression of Islam as a regressive, destructive, anti-Western religion, intensely at odds with British culture and mores (see for example Runnymede Trust, 1997). The decline of the old textile and manufacturing industries in the North of England has increased competition for jobs and other scarce resources, and contributed to a breakdown of wider community relations in areas where poor white and Asian families live. Hostile reactions between Pakistani and English supporters during test matches again highlighted the ways in which social antagonisms were reflected in sports. Whilst the high level of support from English-born Pakistanis for the Pakistan team, reflected how implausible a British identity seemed for these Asian groups (Bose, 1996; Buruma, 2001).

Concluding remarks

The historical and more recent experiences of minority ethnic sportsmen in Britain have been profoundly affected by white reactions to 'racial difference'. In the twenty-first century, a non-white British identity still exists as a site of contradiction and tension in sport and outside of it. On the one hand, the sporting successes of African-Caribbean men have gradually been acknowledged; and their presence at the highest levels has challenged assumptions about culture, biology and an exclusive national identity. On the other, the continued existence of racism can perpetuate hegemonic structures. The relatively fewer sporting landmarks of their Asian contemporaries have not had the same recognition, or generated the same level of interest. It is too simplistic to suggest that Asian groups have an insufficient investment in sport as a career, and that this somehow 'explains' a lack of penetration. The circulation of ideas questioning Asian suitability for sports, and the more overt racism that these groups encounter in a sporting setting and wider social life, have combined to limit their potential sporting aspirations.

The following two chapters will address the thoughts and experiences of the male interviewees who have participated in this study. Broadly speaking, Chapters 3 and 4 will discuss the extent to which issues of 'race' have shaped their sports participation.

3
Sporting Beginnings

Introduction

Chapter 3 is the first to address the thoughts and recollections of sportsmen interviewed for this study. The school years are an important place from which to start (Hargreaves, 1986); and all of the male interviewees showed an unwavering commitment to sports at this formative stage. I have attempted to examine the basis for their sporting motivation by breaking it down into distinct, but related, 'moments'. Whiteness is examined through such factors as teacher expectations, the significance of role models, and a self-appraisal of alternative career options. These provide important markers from which their subsequent sports trajectories can be mapped, and interview testimony will be integrated with theory and research findings.

Winning appeal

'... they'd announce it in assembly ... it was my first indication of how people responded to success'

'I'd finally found something I was good at'

'... I was continually in trouble, fighting. I found that by being in trouble it made me popular ...'

The reasons why black men (in particular) choose to embark on a professional sports career in the first place have been highlighted as a consequence of racialised practices, involving a number of different groups and individuals, that often begin at school (see for example Cashmore, 1992). It has been argued that a mix of social and cultural pressures, and beliefs about biology, seduce black children to the promise of a sports career.

All of the male interviewees could be described as 'sporting all-rounders'. Indeed, almost all (bar Zia Haque) conveyed the sense that they didn't *exist* before sport. In their earliest years, the sports participation of a number of the interviewees had been encouraged by visibly

Figure 3.1 Cyrille Regis

enhanced peer status (that is to say, by the popularity and respect that being talked about as a 'winner' brings); and a self-perceived ineptitude for academic school work. These themes certainly run as lead motives through the relevant sections of testimonies by Cyrille Regis, Jason Gardener and Garth Crooks. In explaining their intense interest in sport from an early (5–12 years) age, they made the following claims:

> *[the appeal of sport was] the social side, the camaraderie, the team spirit, the social team spirit that goes along with football . . . the joy of playing in a team that passed the ball well and won, which was very important, and you scoring goals and being a hero or being a villain if you missed the goal; it was great. It was great emotionally, adrenaline was bubbling and that's when I started developing a deep love for the game.*

(CR)

> *We had a race across a school yard . . . I ran across the yard, and I was the best. And suddenly I got respect for being good at something. Right from those early years. I must have been aged five, six, whenever you started junior school. And that was my first taste of success and I loved it. I'd*

Figure 3.2 Jason Gardener

suddenly found something which I was good at, and it's very strange because, from that age, I knew what I wanted to do and where I wanted to go. I just knew that I wanted to be a sprinter, a one-hundred metre sprinter, and run in the Olympics.

(JG)

. . . I was about seven. I say seven because I have this early recollection of me playing with nine, ten and eleven year olds, they were like men to me at the time. But I was quicker and had a better ball awareness than they had; and

Figure 3.3   Garth Crooks

I sort of enjoyed playing with cumbersome lads who were bigger and stronger than me, but who didn't have the same ability. So I enjoyed that, and sort of discovered that while I didn't have an interest or a great enough interest in the classroom, I enjoyed the attention of my peers and I quickly decided to . . . well, I discovered because I play for my school football team and if the team was successful and if I was successful in that team then they'd announce it in assembly that the team had won and that I'd scored a goal. And I could see, it was my first indication of how people responded to success, and that was my first recollection of thinking to myself: 'hang on a second. I can't get attention in the classroom but I can get attention here, if I can perfect what I do here and I enjoy it, then I can get the attention of my peers.' And I distinctly remember that, and that was around as early as seven.

(GC)

Although most sports had a general appeal for Gurbinder Singh, his early dedication to weightlifting was perhaps more pre-ordained and calculated. Singh's father had achieved notable success as a weightlifter himself, becoming Asian Games champion and competing for his native India. Singh reflected that:

. . . because my dad was successful in it he put me into it and now he's coaching me as well, and my other sports were football, basketball, the natural sports that boys are interested in at school, athletic running. I used to like my physical exercise classes. And my weightlifting was after school. After school I used to go weightlifting with my dad, my dad used to take me.

(GS)

Chris Sanigar's excellence at school-supervised sport was not the only thing that got him the kind of attention and respect accorded to the other male interviewees. Two of the most noticeable features of his testimony that are germane to this issue concern the way that his ethnic 'difference' was signified as a source of conflict in his early years; and the framework he has adopted to explain this conflict. He claimed that:

. . . I was good at running, and was very good at high-jumping, I had the school records, apparently they was set, went on for about 25 years. Played rugby. I represented the school in all the various sports. [But] I suppose the best thing I was at was fighting. I was one of the best [playground] fighters in years, in my school . . . I was always in trouble, I was continually in trouble, fighting, I found that by being in trouble, it made me popular, and I think that's why I continually misbehaved . . . made me feel as if I was one

Figure 3.4   Gurbinder Singh

*of the 'chaps' . . . I think I was the only non-English boy in the whole school.
It was very difficult . . . I was different from everyone else . . . people can get
bullied or singled out if you've got no hair or if you're fat, if you're extra tall
or different coloured skin, then naturally you're gonna be singled out.*

(CS)

The bullying and unwanted attention Chris Sanigar received from his
classmates has been rationalised as an inevitable consequence of 'difference', broadly defined. 'Race' is grouped with height, weight and bald-
ness as a generic signifier, all interchangeable as noticeable somatic
features. The 'colour blind' approach to racist abuse is certainly popular
in team sports and, as we have seen, is a view held by important personnel (Chapters 1, 4). But whilst listening to Chris, I got the impression
that this way of categorising the abuse was more than a sporting mantra.
Perhaps it is more accurately described as an important survival mechanism to counter the psychological strain of living in the 'small town' in
which he grew up. Chris was adopted by a white couple and was also one
of the few non-English boys in the town. The reasons why he was often
'singled out' would have been explained to him by countless individuals
in the same terms as he conveyed them to myself. The explanation
would have had to suffice if he were to survive in that environ.

Figure 3.5 Chris Sanigar

Social class and exposure

Chapters 1 and 2 have emphasised that sport is perceived to occupy a minor role in the construction of British Asian identities. A limited presence in professional sport has skewed research priorities toward the constraints and issues of recreational involvement for Asian communities, particularly where they constitute a significant proportion of the local population. By contrast, the large number of black men who opt for a professional career in sport mirrors the interest shown by black children in their early years. Sociological research on black male sports involvement in Britain and the USA focuses on the relationship between the apparent 'freedoms' enjoyed by these individuals once they make a career in sport; and the ways that their ethnicity obscures concerns about their individual and group participation (see for example Cashmore, 1982; Majors, 1990; Greendorfer, 1992; Maguire, 1995).

When research on black children and sport is cross-fertilised with that looking at the socio-economic position of black groups, then it becomes clearer that a link between early interest and eventual career only tells a part of the story. Statistically speaking, and in spite of the more recent emergence of a black middle class (Small, 1994; Gates, 1997), the majority of Britain's black families are still officially represented within the ranks of the working classes; live in one of the country's larger inner-cities; and send their children to one of the many state-funded schools (see for example Bhat *et al.*, 1993; Modood *et al.*, 1998; Nazroo, 2000). These institutions have less resources available for a diversity of sports.

Economic factors can therefore present a major hurdle to participating in certain sports. Black men tend to be over-represented in a fairly limited range of sports. Athletics, basketball, football, boxing and cricket (especially in the Caribbean) are typically the traditional routes through which they have recognised and profiled their sporting talents. Their presence in these sports markedly contrasts with black under-representation in tennis, golf, yachting, skiing and motor-racing. These pursuits are less attractive, partly because they require consistently large financial outlays. But in addition, they lack a tradition of black participation which might inspire future generations, and suggest the possibility that racist barriers can be breached. If we leave aside the question of financial reward, the (skewed) relationship between black people, and the limited range of sports that they ultimately make careers in, appears to have a real basis.

British Asian populations are more socially mobile than their black contemporaries. But significant economic and social differences between Pakistanis and Bangladeshis (on the one hand), and African-Asians and Indians, suggest that the 'Asian' label is a very misleading one. The literature on Asian people and sport indicates that Asians have traditionally excelled, mainly as amateurs and semi-professionals, in hockey, squash, cricket and weight-lifting; but has not generally considered participation differences by social class and religion (but see for example Johal, 2001). As Cashmore (1992) confirms, such issues as restricted access to facilities and equipment, and limited disposable income, are likely to alienate working-class British Asian youth, whilst they tend to be accessible only to the middle classes.

In the sportsman's earliest years, the opportunity to participate in a range of sports is most likely to be a function of the above factors. Although all the male interviewees shared a similar economic background, the formative experiences of Paul Hull and Martin Offiah differed from the group, and from the general influences on black youth in the 1980s. In this sense, they proved to be exceptions to a tightly

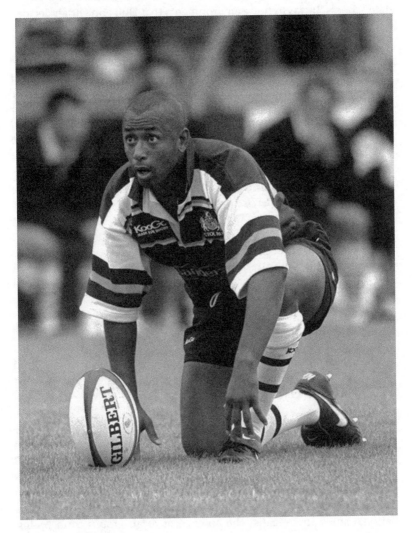

Figure 3.6   Paul Hull

scripted race/social class rule. Unlike the other interviewees who attended their local state comprehensive schools, both Hull and Offiah were able to attend better-resourced and prestigious fee-paying schools. These schools operated means-tested scales to minimise their parents' financial contributions. They were therefore a more realistic option for children from poorer families, and explained their exposure to rugby union: a sport which is not generally part of the curricula for inner-city state schools. It was in these environments that Hull and Offiah decided to commit themselves to the sport, although in Hull's case:

> . . . I only started playing rugby because the school year was split up into three sports. Rugby for the first part, then football, then cricket, and I always played all different sports but football was still my love until really I left school and then had to make a decision what I was gonna do, either play football or rugby. And I already had a trial for Southampton Football Club at the age of fourteen and I didn't make it, I got to the sort of final trials and I didn't actually make it . . . so the decision to go into rugby was sort of made easy for myself and I joined Bletchley, Milton Keynes, rugby club, and went from there. Joined the RAF [Royal Air Force] and started going up the different levels of rugby from there really.

> (PH)

The other notable exception was Zia Haque. Haque attended an (in his words) 'segregated' Asian school in Pakistan. It was here that he was exposed to sports like hockey, squash and badminton, before coming to England at the age of eighteen.

Choice of role model

> 'I don't know why, but when Bruce Lee beat up the bad white guys like Chuck Norris, I felt like he was doing it for me, as a black man.'

How influential are role models for minority ethnic children in their choice of a sports career: someone whose sporting attributes, sartorial style and/or public persona is a source of inspiration and imitation? Research has suggested that the significance of 'race' in society means that young black boys aspiring to a sports career have invariably chosen black sportsmen as role models (Cashmore, 1982). More recently, a national study investigated the absence of Asian groups from professional football (Bains with Patel, 1996). The study found that the very presence of an Asian player would make 90 per cent of respondents identify with the their local professional football team, and thereby seek that player as a role model.

As well as ethnic-group identification (in Gurbinder Singh's case, this literally meant identifying with his father), future career and recreational choices were influenced by the popularity of certain sports; and by the levels of success enjoyed by black sportsmen, whilst the status of more 'global' sportsmen was seen to be enhanced by what Dyson (1993) has termed their 'stylisation': or the unique ways in which they have harnessed their skills to create a much-imitated sporting identity. Equally, a number of the interviewees stressed that their role models discharged a wider, political function for them. This is because uneven power relations have created an additional significance which redefines sporting contests. To repeat the point that Hargreaves made in Chapter 1, sporting contests offer 'new meanings' which are 'constantly being worked out and struggled for'. Hopcraft eloquently illustrates these different meanings when commenting on the relationship between football and social class in 1920s Britain:

> By the 1920s, football was an established employer in a community where jobs were scarce. The clubs had grown out of a pride in athleticism, in local importance, in corporate endeavour. The stadiums were planted where the supporters lived, in among the industrial mazes of factories and hunched workers houses. The Saturday match became more than mere diversion from the daily grind, because there was often no work to be relieved. To go to the match was to escape from the dark of despondency into the light of combat . . . to win was personal success, to lose another clout from life. Football was not so much an opiate of the people as a flag run up against the gaffer bolting his gates and the landlord armed with the bailiffs.
>
> (Cited in Critcher, 1980, p. 161)

It is worth developing this theme, linking the way that sport is *interpreted*, to the social milieu. The all-conquering fighting skills of Bruce Lee, Arthur Ashe's Wimbledon victory over Jimmy Connors in 1975, and even television comedy have provided the interviewees with some relief from feelings of marginalisation.

The majority of the interviewees were teenagers in the 1970s and 1980s: a time when journalist reporting of black and Asian people could not be taken as neutral, and had arguably the gravest social consequences. This reporting was consistently underscored by a 'dysfunctional', socially incompatible view of the black family (see below). The widespread impact of racism in the spheres of education, health, employment and social life, contributed to the acute politicising of blackness, and minority ethnic feelings of alienation from the mainstream of British society (Husband, 1987; Lawrence, 1992*a*; Chapter 2). There was little relief for these groups in the sphere of mediated popular culture. Grosser stereotypes, given an unbridled life in the national press, also informed fictional television characterisations of black and Asian people.

In such circumstances, it is not just sporting deeds which are imaginatively appropriated as symbols of political resistance. The television comedy *Love Thy Neighbour* is one such example. In this regard, I was interested to find it cited as important and empowering by a number of the older interviewees. As a young black boy growing up in South London, I certainly remember how well-received this programme was with *my* black friends and their families. The programme 'relied' (if this is the right word) on the racist jokes and insults directed at a black couple by the husband of their white neighbours. But although the insults were the mainstay of the show, the small ways in which the black couple usurped their white neighbours (the white character's bigotry invariably got him into trouble when he tried to provoke or embarrass his black neighbours) seemed to create a sense of shared victory against the displays of petty chauvinism in our daily existences, and the feelings of hostility that accompanied them.

The sporting context may have provided a different type of 'victory', but the meaning was the same. Bruce Lee (martial arts), Pele (football), Jim Brown (American football), Arthur Ashe (tennis), Hakeem Olajuwon (basketball) and Muhammad Ali (boxing) seemed to bestride the sporting world like colossi. It is certainly true that a number of these men were appealing because they were articulate and intelligent, in strong contrast to a stereotype of black athletes being 'all brawn and no brain'. And in Ali's case, supreme boxing ability was allied with quick, witty, and incisive oratory highlighting issues of racial justice. But their appeal to young black people relied equally on the fact that they took white opponents on and beat them in their sports. So, whilst their sporting deeds were among the most lauded, the social context equated Ashe's Wimbledon victory over Jimmy Connors; or the skills of the Brazilian players who cut a swathe through European defenders during football World Cups, with a blow against 'the system'. A political resonance out of all proportion to the sporting occasion.

For David Lawrence, read Muhammad Ali the boxer, rather than Freddie Trueman the cricketer; for Garth Crooks, Viv Anderson, Cyrille

Regis and Martin Offiah, read Pele rather than English World Cup-winning hero Geoff Hurst (both footballers); and for Jason Gardener, read Daley Thompson the decathlete, rather than Alan Wells the 100 metre sprinter. Gardener states that:

> *I just knew that I wanted to be Daley Thompson. Now I didn't know what event Daley Thompson participated in, but I knew that athletics was associated with Daley Thompson and that he was black, outspoken, arrogant and a winner. I knew he'd won gold medals and the Olympics, and it just grew from there onwards.*
>
> (JG)

By contrast, 'fandom' for Zia Haque, Gurbinder Singh and Chris Sanigar was deracialised, and bestowed on individuals who happened to be foremost in their favourite sports. So a Russian weightlifting champion was as prominent for Singh as Geoff Hurst and the rest of the 1966 World Cup winning football team were for Chris Sanigar. Whether this division between the Asian and African-Caribbean responses reflects the greater significance that sport has for the latter group, is open to conjecture.

In the absence of alternatives . . .

We have read that sporting victories possessed a wider meaning for a number of the interviewees. Politicising the sporting victories of others was a way that their own negative feelings of disadvantage could be (temporarily) relieved. Gramsci's ideas on *hegemony* can yield useful theoretical insights about this question of power relations; and help us to understand why these same negative feelings could lead to such an *empressement* for sports.

Hegemony theory makes reference to subordinate groups struggling to gain worthwhile concessions within a framework of dominant ideas and values. Partly for this reason, it has been appropriated by social researchers looking at the relationship between 'race' and sport. In adapting hegemony theory, research has indicated that black school-children's real and imagined career interests are driven by a strong faith in legitimate social and economic progression, in spite of the obstacles of racism. Within these parameters, and particularly for working-class black children, a specific focus on sport represents a 'concession': the search for a mainstream solution to problems of educational marginality (Carrington, 1986; Carby, 1992a; see below also).

Research published in the 1980s, and looking at the socialisation into sport of white and black children, also revealed the latter's pessimistic view of a lack of other opportunities available to their parents. More recently, evidence suggests that African-Caribbean peoples still fare significantly worse than their white counterparts, across such relevant indicators as employment, household income, health and education. The fourth national survey of minority ethnic groups found that black people (men in particular) are still likely to be unemployed, and for considerably longer, than white people; to be described as living in poverty; to suffer from poorer physical health; and to achieve fewer academic qualifications at lower grades (see for example Modood *et al.*, 1998). The survey also confirmed that, given the same indicators, the 'Asian' descriptor encompasses a much greater diversity of fortunes. Pakistani and Bangladeshi groups continue to fare worse that their African-Asian and Indian contemporaries. In fact, Pakistani and Bangladeshi groups are described by the survey as experiencing a position of 'serious disadvantage'.

For African-Caribbean, Pakistani and Bangladeshi boys, these trends create their own pressures and perceptions about sports as a career. Jason Gardener recalls his father's advice about a sports career:

> *My dad, I remember what he said: 'you've got a talent, you could become famous, successful, earn money'. My upbringing was from a working class, my dad's first generation from the Caribbean. As soon as he was old enough, he didn't have no choice to continue studying and go to university. He had to get a job, as was the case with his brothers and sisters, and other first-generation people from the Caribbean. He saw it for me is I have a talent, I gotta maximise it and become famous, or it was doing jobs like what he does, which are not secure, in and out of one job into another, just making ends meet. I remember him saying that to me. I was very upset, I don't want to be like that.*

(JG)

So it is easy to see why, given the success of black sportsmen, and when faced with the prospect of careers seemingly more blighted by racism, sport would appear an attractive and even 'natural' option. Partly due to a perception about limited career options, black children were seen to 'over-emphasise' their sports participation (Oliver, 1980; Cashmore, 1982; Carrington, 1986). The testimonies of Viv Anderson, Cyrille Regis, Garth Crooks and David Lawrence indicate the extent to which this was true. None felt sufficiently encouraged at school to *'think beyond their race'*, as Crooks put it: a pointed reference to the negative association linking black people as a group, with low expectations and abilities. All felt that they were steered by school teachers into sport (see below); or into vocations which required little formal training, and afforded little career autonomy and prestige.

White working-class children have also viewed a career in sports as a viable means for social and economic advancement, and there is a strong historical tradition of this. A popular saying in Yorkshire, 'whistle down a mine shaft and up comes a fast bowler', is strongly evocative of how sport has been used to escape restrictions of social class. But whereas black children were seen to be more influenced by a perception of limited opportunities elsewhere, whites were equally hopeful about career prospects in other spheres. Although failing to adequately control for related demographic factors, a number of other, small-scale studies still indicated a more enthusiastic response to certain aspects of physical education from African-Caribbean boys, than from their white and Asian contemporaries (Ikulayo, 1982; Carrington and Wood, 1983).

Research also suggested that black enthusiasm for sport is nurtured by sports coaches and administrators, school teachers, peer groups, the media and 'public opinion'. To appropriate Gramsci, this 'ensemble of relations' promote a particular worldview of the black person's aptitude for sports (and, as indicated elsewhere, ideas about Asian people's unsuitability for aggressive contact sports); one which meets with the acceptance of a wide spectrum within society. Research has highlighted the existence of stubbornly held, broadly congruent viewpoints expressed by these groups, concerning physical sports performance and mental aptitude, which are actively created and re-created in specific social contexts (Small, 1994; Jarvie, 1995). And as Small (1994, p. 105) notes:

> It takes little effort to formulate it [racialised stereotyping] as a doctrine of 'natural ability'. Nor is it done in any deliberately demeaning or disparaging fashion. We are not talking about racialised abuse, diatribes or invectives; but simple, plain, praiseworthy 'common sense'. It is as if the holders of such views are praising Black 'natural' superiority in much the same way that white slave masters espoused the 'natural' superiority of Blacks in the plantation fields.

The biological basis to these views may be endorsed by black people themselves. In this sense, Foucault's ubiquitous notion of *power* is relevant, and can be appropriated for a sporting analogy. Foucault argued that power circulates widely through a network of individuals and institutions, and has positive effects (to varying degrees) for everyone. It is possible to see how the degree of social power that black people gain from sport is linked to other ideas about blackness. That is to say, high self-esteem about black sporting ability and tangible success may constitute the adoption of a positive belief about physiological advantage, at a cost of intellectual underachievement (Collins, 1991). Chapter 4 will look more closely at the interviewee's self-perception of whether 'race' determines sporting prowess. In any event, the comments of Viv Anderson, David Lawrence and Garth Crooks conveyed a sense that the pitfalls of sport compared favourably with other, seemingly more precarious, careers; and that sport was *the* way that they, as black men, could make a 'mark' in life.

Teacher expectations

> ' . . . no matter what we're gonna do, they're gonna under-achieve anyway, so let's throw them into sport'

So far, a number of interviewees have confirmed previous research findings on the attractiveness of peer kudos, the significance of role models, and a pessimism about alternative careers as key factors driving their interest in sports. Equally, research has suggested that due to ideas about black physical rather than intellectual prowess, school teachers encourage their sporting aspirations to the detriment of a focus on their education, and attainment of formal academic qualifications (see for example Gillborn, 1990). Writing in 1986, Hargreaves' study of popular sports in Britain found that:

> PE [physical education] teachers widely assume that blacks are naturally better at sports, and promote black participation as an *alternative success system* for these pupils, as a way of integrating them into the school culture and of gaining prestige for themselves and the school.
>
> (cited in Small, 1994, pp. 102–3, emphasis added)

More recently, evidence suggests that teachers still adhere to these views (Sewell, 1997; Hayes and Sugden, 1999). Therefore, the failure of black children, particularly black *boys*, in the British education system is still an enduring and sensitive issue. This group are over-represented within the ranks of those subject to exclusion orders from school. In fact, they are between four and six times more likely to be excluded from school than their white counterparts (Sewell, 1997; see also Klein, 1996). Racism is seen by black parents to be at the root of this educational failure, and is being tackled by community schools run by black parents for black children (Gillborn and Gipps, 1996; Reay and Mirza, 1997). It is not surprising therefore that black boys may feel that they have no stake in the formal education process; and that sport compensates for their problems of educational marginality. The contrasting success and visibility of black people in sports reinforces both sports' value to promoting 'cultural assimilation', and the 'myth' of genetic aptitude.

The interviewees in Cashmore's study of black sportsmen confirmed teacher 'over-enthusiasm' for their sporting progress. Furthermore, they claimed that the marked interest shown by teachers for their sporting prospects was commonplace for black children in British schools (1982. See also Hargreaves, 1986; Harris, 1995). The creation of 'athletic scholarships', which black students in the US have applied for in large numbers, is evidence of how sport has been 'over-emphasised' there too. These scholarships are a fairly unsatisfactory and piecemeal effort to address learning problems in further education. In theory, they are designed for talented sportspersons who want to study for formal academic qualifications and enhance their prospects in the jobs market. In practice, they do not seem to help black students. Majors (1990, pp. 114–15) claims that:

> Despite the large number of black males who participate in sports, less than 6% of all the athletic scholarships given in the United States go to blacks. Just as damaging is the fact that an estimated 25 to 35% of high school black athletes do not even qualify for scholarships because of academic deficiencies. Of those black athletes who ultimately do receive athletic scholarships, as many as 65 to 75% may not ever graduate from college . . . Among the approximately 25 to 35% of the black athletes who do graduate from college, about 75% of them graduate with either physical education degrees or with degrees in majors that are especially created for athletes. As one might suspect, such 'jock degrees' are not acceptable in the jobmarket . . .

All of the sportsmen in this study showed an early interest in sport, which was encouraged by equally enthusiastic teachers. Interview accounts were replete with descriptions of them being 'pushed' and 'steered' in a sporting direction. Whilst this is not indicative of coercion, it does convey the strength of teacher priorities for them. It is also significant that a number of the interviewees felt a less-than-committed attempt by teachers to uncover their 'hidden' academic talents. Of course, the issue is complicated because British schools have a long tradition of orienting 'non-academic' and/or 'boisterous' (read 'disruptive') children of *all* backgrounds into sport, as a way for them to 'let off steam' in a controlled way (Parry and Parry, 1995); and because black enthusiasm for sport is fed by a self-belief about aptitude. Nonetheless, it is difficult to escape the impression that teacher enthusiasm was infused with racial 'myths' about black people and sport.

For instance, in spite of an initial interest in his schoolwork, David Lawrence's commitment to sport appeared to be fuelled by his teachers' belief in racial stereotypes. Lawrence referred to the 1970s and 1980s when personally reflecting on this:

> *I think, especially in the seventies, statistics always come out every year, and it seemed in the seventies it was always that black, Afro-Caribbean children was always underachieving. So I think the attitude of the teachers was that: 'ok, no matter what we're gonna do, they're gonna underachieve*

Figure 3.7 David Lawrence

anyway, so let's throw them into sport.' The first thing they do is say, you know: 'can you run? can you bowl? can you kick a football?' you know: 'you can play rugby 'cos you're fast. Naturally, because you're black.' That was the attitude in the seventies. So I suppose I was an all-round sportsman. I took up all sports.

(DL)

Lawrence neglected his academic studies and sought to 'find himself' through sport. Considering the large numbers of young black males who looked to sport as a way of constructing a more valued sense of self, this private decision resounds with the certainty of a definitive public statement on black male identity in Britain at the time (see for example Maguire, 1995). He further reflected that:

Growing up in the seventies, there was very little academic support from teachers . . . It was all negativity more than anything else . . . I mean the teachers, I could [only] pick out one or two. One was a sports teacher and the other was, I think, was an English teacher and they were the only two. [One or two of my teachers] were keen cricketers and sportsmen, and they helped me a lot. But the rest of the teachers did not encourage me academically. They probably look back and say that they did this and did that, but they did nothing. They were poor.

(DL)

Garth Crooks provided a similar reflection, repeating his points as if to emphasise them:

I fell out with a lot of teachers, a lot of teachers, largely due to the fact that they had a jaundiced view of black children. They had a limited view, a limited view and a jaundiced view would be too fair an assessment of some of the teachers I had. Some of it . . . lots of it I don't think it was their fault, but I think they had a limited view of black kids and black people particularly in that area, in Stoke-on-Trent, the mining town. Yes they'd been to university, but they'd probably come from certainly white, certainly middle-class backgrounds, and they probably hadn't any idea of what black people were like culturally, historically, traditionally. None of those things. I'd say they had a very limited view of black people and black children. So I often fell into conflict with many teachers, but the one that had reached me to try and understand me a little bit I still have a great deal of time for, and still keep in contact with today.

(GC)

We have read that when Jason Gardener won his 'race across the school yard', victory was the spark that lit his sporting ambitions. In the short term however, this enthusiasm was not encouraged. One particular teacher's low assessment of his academic ability, which Jason is convinced was fuelled by racism, actually worked to block his initial progress in sport. This seems strange, given the emphasis placed on sport as a coping strategy for teachers to deal with 'difficult' young black people. According to Gardener:

> *I went to a Catholic [primary] School, and I had a very unhappy childhood there . . . I was experiencing difficulties with a particular teacher. The teacher was purely a racist, and I'm not one to use words like that to describe anybody unless I really feel that way inclined. Not only to me, of different coloured skin, unlike the majority of children in class, but more so to an Italian boy who was quite plump. It appeared that he was not that bright in class. She was very nasty to him. She made my childhood not very nice at all, and we were not allowed to join in sports . . . When my sister and myself joined our new school we changed. We were welcomed. I was allowed to participate in sports and felt very welcome there, and loved doing it. I didn't want to leave the school. It transformed our childhood.*

(JG)

Jason's reflections on the role of sport in his secondary school are a closer match to the template of experiences of other working-class black boys. And his assertions about his school's failure to discharge its academic function are also tempered by honest self-appraisal. He states that:

> *I knew I was good at sport, especially in the senior school. [But] I felt . . . that I was pushed more so in representing the school in sport than actually in my education . . . by teachers. To be honest with you, the reason why I attend school should be to be pushed in my education, but I did feel that I was more so pushed the other way. Obviously, I play a part in applying myself but I found something I was very good at, naturally I was very good, and I eventually found myself in a certain group who were inclined to do other things and not be committed to schoolwork.*

(JG)

Leaving aside questions of social class, and academic differences *within* this group (see earlier), South Asian pupils generally continue to perform as well as, if not better than, their white counterparts (see for example Skellington, 1996; Modood *et al.*, 1998). Again, the contrasting success of Asian children in school, and the lack of a 'presence' in professional sports, helps to confirm ideas about their higher intellect, and their less intense relationship to sport. In stark contrast to the tenor of findings on black people, research conducted by the Midland Asian Sports Forum found that Asian children were being overlooked by PE teachers for team sports, due to ideas about prohibitive Asian cultures and physical disadvantages. Research also pointed to teachers encouraging Asian pupils in their scholarly activity instead (Fleming, 1995a).

The experiences of Chris Sanigar and Gurbinder Singh did not correlate with these findings. Both showed strong early promise and commitment to sport, and these factors undoubtedly played a part. Chris Sanigar's testimony reveals the extent of his optimism about sport, but also regret about the lost potential of other career opportunities. Indeed, a theme of 'wasted opportunity' runs consistently throughout his early recollections. He claimed that:

> *I always thought I would be a footballer, and then just at about 13, I sort of just lost my way. I got into bad habits, getting into trouble, just too many distractions. And also, as a 13 year old, I was one of the best, suddenly started playing with adults, but I just didn't transform. And when I came to Bristol at 17, I just played in the Suburban League, but I didn't work hard. It was hard.*
>
> (CS)

In his view, the attempts by his teachers to educate him foundered because:

> *. . . I think I abused my education and likewise I sure I must be guilty of abusing other people's, my class mates, I was continually misbehaving, but when you're young you're just so irresponsible, and you just can't realise it . . . I don't think they [teachers] thought that I would be a top sporting person, I don't think they thought anyone would be. I don't think they thought I would be anything.*
>
> (CS)

Zia Haque was born in Kenya, went to school in Pakistan and came to England at the age of 18. For these reasons, he did not feel qualified to comment on the significance for British minority ethnic groups of teacher expectations, and the role of sport. However, he felt that his son could. At the time of interview, Robeel Haque was 22 years old. Born and raised in Britain, he attended a local school where the ethnic background of the children was described as 'mixed'. Robeel had this to say (this question only) on the relationship between sport and minority ethnic groups:

> *I wouldn't say that we were actively encouraged. I'd say generally that black children tended to be more boisterous and more dominant. So, they would tend to take charge. They weren't very academic in class so when it came to sports they were generally better than most other students.*
>
> (RH)

Five of the eleven men interviewed for this study (Zia Haque, Paul Hull, Martin Offiah, Gurbinder Singh and Sean Viera) felt encouraged to concentrate on their academic schoolwork, *and* supported in their sporting ambitions. Of this group, Hull and Offiah were educated outside of the state school system (whilst Haque was educated abroad). I believe that the distinction between the private and state school sectors accounts for the different interviewee responses.

Britain's larger inner-city state schools are expected to operate effectively whilst under increasing constraints. Larger class sizes, longer teacher working hours, fewer resources and facilities, chronic teacher shortages in key subjects like mathematics and physics, and more reported incidents of serious disruption and physical intimidation of staff, are factors which have a cumulative effect on learning provision. Staff are perhaps less predisposed to search for individual solutions to what is perceived as a collective black educational disinterest. Smaller class sizes in themselves facilitate a closer attention to individual development rates and needs. But these are a scarce and valuable resource, and increasingly the overwhelming preserve of the private school sector. In addition, a less pressurised working environment, and students with a background of fewer social problems, make it easier to discharge a school's ethos of academic excellence for all.

Viera and Singh were the only interviewees who attended a state school and who felt *holistically* encouraged by their teachers. For Viera, this encouragement sometimes took the form of novel ways to combine his love of sport, and academic study:

> *Yeah, [my school teachers] did encourage me in my education, and also they did encourage the martial arts as well. Because when I was at school . . . you had to do a talk for examination, and they encouraged me. Certain teachers encouraged me to do one on martial arts and the Chinese history behind martial arts, and it really helped me. It really*

Figure 3.8   Sean Viera

helped me a lot, and these teachers did actually help, and made me think:
well, you know, I can have both, I can sort of pursue education and sport
and go ahead with it.

(SV)

The family

'it was always drummed into me from my parents point of
view to get a trade. Education, education, get a trade . . . But
they were always quite supportive in me playing football . . .
so long as your work was done academically.'

What role does the family play in the formative process of its children's careers, or the seriousness with which recreational sports are

taken up? The family is perceived as a primary site of cultural reproduction, and an area of autonomy for minority ethnic groups
(Lawrence, 1992*b*). The ways in which black families are structured,
and pervasive ideas about their lived practices, continue to underpin
discourses about the patterns of behaviour exhibited by some black
youth (see for example Cashmore, 1979; Pryce, 1979; Carby, 1992*b*;
Mirza, 2000). By contrast, ideas about the strength of traditional Asian
family structures and cultures have resulted in a less damaging assessment for their British-born children. Not surprisingly therefore, it is
the black family that has functioned as a site of ideological tension
between those seeking to reclaim its worth, and those who see it as the
basis for black children's social exclusion. This is therefore a sensitive
and controversial area.

The 1991 census indicated that the black 'community' has a disproportionate representation of (teenage or older) single mothers (see also
Modood *et al.*, 1998). This is seen to have important cultural and social
ramifications in a society that privileges the traditional *nuclear* family as
the basis for stability, and as a site for nourishment and psychological
well-being. As Heidi Mirza (2000, pp. 304–5) explains:

> This phenomenon [of single parent households] has caused an outcry
> concerning the crisis of the Black family. The failing Black family we are
> told, is classically dysfunctional. The weak and marginal male is absent,
> feckless, lazy and emasculated. He is left to dwindle on the fringes of
> family life while the domineering matriarch, that insatiable workhorse,
> that larger than life 'superwoman', heads the household, pushing all
> aside in her singleminded, determined quest for self-satisfaction.

Politicians, the police and the media (key members of Gramsci's
'ensemble') have grafted a well-defined pattern of consequences onto
the assumption that a pathology, a sickness, lies at the heart of black
family life. The activities of 'lawless black youth', and the much-
publicised failure of black children in the British education system,
have been rooted in paternal absence, and the pressures exerted by an
emasculating mother. In the aftermath of the thirty-plus inner city
disturbances that seemed to define the 1980s, the black family was
heavily implicated in explaining the behaviour of the rioters
(Lawrence, 1992*b*).

It is significant that this model of black family life has also formed the
basis for sociologically credible accounts from the sub-discipline of 'race
relations' (Gilroy, 1987. See for example Pryce, 1979; Cashmore and

Troyna, 1982). These studies have essentially charged black families with saddling their children with unrealistic academic expectations, and for not being sufficiently interested in their chosen sports careers. The following quote (1982, p. 82) is taken from Cashmore's study of black sportsmen:

> The black parents are often apathetic and perform no positive function in their children's progression in sport and stir from their inertness only when some measure of tangible success has been achieved . . . The passive role of the black family in the children's sport jars with the discordance of a cracked bell when compared to the part played by the white family, usually a source of encouragement from which affirmative, strengthening and, when necessary, consoling influences come.

Cashmore's remarks create a strong impression of black parents as opportunistic and disingenuous; and of the black family's failure to nourish its children. Sport, then, is the means by which young black people can construct a more 'positive' identity. Carrington (1986) has highlighted that Cashmore's findings were based on an atypical study of black male athletes competing in a narrow range of sports, and failed to fully account for class-related factors in explaining the different attitudes to sport between the African-Caribbean, Asian and white populations. But I believe that his study is still regarded as influential because of the continued message of authoritative discourses about the black family (Mirza, 2000). Furthermore, the *external* conditions and circumstances understood to orient black children to sport still, to a critical degree, exist.

The vista of career opportunities has widened for black people. Young black Britons (women particularly) are now more likely than their white counterparts to continue their post-16 education, and the gap in the levels of formal qualifications between black and white groups has narrowed. However, key structural conditions (greater incidences of poverty, higher levels of unemployment, higher incidences of one-parent families and educational failure in British schools) still affect disproportionate numbers of black people in Britain (Modood *et al.*, 1998). Furthermore, young black boys have consistently been identified by the police as largely responsible for rising youth crime, in cities like London, Manchester and Liverpool (see for example Wright, 2002; also Chapter 2). When the psychological strain associated with poverty and disadvantage is contrasted with seductive ideas about biological determinism and sporting success, then sport has an obvious appeal.

Have the 'absence' of a father-figure and the presence of an 'authoritarian' mother combined to create a crisis of black male identity: one that the interviewees ultimately resolved through sport? Their responses range from accounts of parental trepidation and lack of knowledge about the viability of sport as a career, to full support and encouragement. Furthermore, testimonies reveal a strong concern by *both* parents about their children's education and career opportunities that does not appear to be unrealistic and over-bearing. Garth Crook's reflections perhaps typify this. If anything, they illustrate the ways that inter-generational differences can be 'played out' over such an important issue (in this case, a worthwhile career). The bolder aspirations of youth are counterbalanced by older sights trained on a more modest vista of opportunities: a 'lesser vision' that owes its apprehension to relations of social class. Crooks states that:

> *I think [my parents were] both [a hindrance and a help]. I think in some cases they were definitely a hindrance and some cases they were a help. They were a hindrance in as much that they didn't appreciate how seriously I was taking this sport [football] at the ages of eight, nine, ten and eleven. It was only until I got to fourteen, fifteen and they started to see in the papers that the sort of attention I was getting and they thought: 'Oh Christ! This kid, we're going to have to take him seriously.' They were scared for me, I've absolutely no doubt . . . they had no conception of what future professional football held for their son, it was alien to them . . . my father was a labourer, my mother was a nurse. These were sound professions, or sound jobs. My father worked for Michelin tyre factory for twenty-five years. That was a job, you know. My mother was a nurse, that was a job, [but not] professional football. 'What happens if you get injured? What happens if you're not chosen? What happens if, what happens if [they would ask]?' . . . My attitude was markedly different. It was 'what happens where? What happens when?' That was the difference in approaches. I had been brought up here, I'd been to football matches, I'd seen . . . I understood the industry a little bit, they didn't understand the industry at all. It was only when my school report came around that my parents looked and said . . . 'well, is this good enough for him to devote so much time to sport?' And the answer being a conditional yes. I doubt very much whether my parents could do any better. They did what they thought was their best. It was their best, they gave it their best shot.*

> (GC)

We have read that Martin Offiah had strong encouragement from his teachers to consider his education alongside his sporting aspirations. His parents prioritised the education route too, seeing in this the means to a more worthwhile career. In common with Garth Crooks' parents, their decision was based on a failure to appreciate that élite sportsmen can claim substantial financial reward, *and* a measure of job security. Rugby union is a strong case in point. Before 1995, it was officially regarded as an amateur sport. But in fact, the sport has been accused of 'sham amateurism' (or shamateurism) because it traditionally operated a kind of sinecure system for its international-calibre players. Offiah explains that:

> ... *my parents have been similar to a lot of Nigerian, I suppose West African, parents. Obviously they feel that education is the be-all and end-all, and I wouldn't say they were particularly sporting. My dad, God rest his soul, my late father, was certainly more supportive than a lot of people. If we were a success at anything, he was quite keen on that. My mother wasn't too keen when I was playing rugby, you know what mothers are like. They think you're gonna get hurt, and they also think it takes time away from your studies, and she didn't really see a future. But obviously when she went to Buckingham Palace with me to pick up my MBE, she probably, by that time, she'd changed her mind. But she didn't really see no future in me playing rugby. I suppose, to a certain degree she tried to dissuade me [from making] a career out of it, but she ... didn't really understand the nuances and how if you were good at rugby, you could get a decent qualification, then that would lead onto a better job. Jeremy Guscott's a classic case [the former Bath and England player]. I think when he started off he was just a labourer or something, and then he became a British Gas Executive all from playing rugby. So you know, it does help. But she didn't really understand that, so it was hard for her to encourage me.*
>
> (MO)

Sean Viera also met with some initial parental resistance in his pursuit of a sporting career. In his words:

> ... *they had a slight interest in what I do but as they see it, it was just like not something you were going to get an income from, or it's nothing you're gonna progress out of it. So it was not like yeah, yeah, yeah, you're gonna be this and that. It was more like, well yeah okay, you're doing your martial arts. But you've got to do your study, and you've got to get a job ... you should find more time to do your study and work, rather than just doing the martial arts.*
>
> (SV)

Figure 3.9   Martin Offiah

Viera pursued a vocational qualification, becoming an apprentice mechanic. But as a product of Britain's increasingly aspirant culture, he felt that this was an unexciting and routine job that held little long-term appeal for him.

Before his highly publicised move in the 1970s to West Bromwich Albion, one of Britain's top football clubs at the time, Cyrille Regis had progressed through the ranks of various semi-professional football clubs. He had been 'spotted' as a promising youngster plying his trade in Sunday league football. I have noticed a smile form on Regis' face as he ponders this phase in his career. We both agree that his survival in this environment, and subsequent progression, were no mean feats. Anyone who is even vaguely familiar with Sunday football will confirm that the 'beer and bellies' leagues are not for the faint-hearted. My personal recollections are of full-blooded and potentially injurious tackles on sodden pitches (affectionately known as 'puddings'); or on bone-jarring, solid-hard ground. Sunday League football attracts a combustible mix of younger players with dreams of being spotted, and asked to play professionally; and older 'diehards', resentful that their chances to do so had passed. But I digress.

Whilst trying to fulfil their ambitions to play professional football, both Cyrille Regis and Viv Anderson had a realistic sense about the prospects of failure. Although a professional career has been and continues to be the dream of countless thousands of young boys, very few, less than 10 per cent, actually make the grade. Viv Anderson's parents proved particularly supportive and helpful about his football career, given that he had a number of setbacks. The most notable of these was being 'released' as a registered player from Manchester United's books. It was at this point that Anderson's parents helped him decide about an alternative career option as a silk-screen printer, which he could combine with playing football on a part-time basis. Cyrille Regis' testimony also indicates how an alternative career path was encouraged by his parents, who emphasised the value of education as a way of maximising his opportunities:

I was working as an apprentice electrician on a building site installation, and going to college. So at the time of me moving on to West Brom[wich Albion], I was a fully qualified electrician, so therefore it wasn't a big gamble for me if I didn't make it as a professional footballer. The firm I worked for, they said to me if you didn't make it [as a full-time professional] within a year, then you could have your old job back. So I had a foundation there, being a qualified electrician . . . that if things didn't work out for me as a professional footballer, I could go back and carry on as usual. But as it was, as things turned out, it worked out quite well. Laurie Cunningham was there, and Brendan Batson came four or five months later. We were affectionately known as 'the three degrees'

[Chapter 1] and went on to win 'under 21' caps, 'B' caps and full caps over the years . . . but it was always drummed into me from my parents' point of view to get a trade. Education, education, get a trade. And that's the road you went down. But they were always quite supportive in me playing football. Sunday mornings, Friday night, whatever, going out to football clubs, playing for whatever club you were playing for. So long as your work was done academically. My parents were quite pleased that I had a job as an electrician – doing quite well, and playing football, and holding your own, and growing up as a person, as a man. It was hard work working on the building sites two or three days a week and playing semi-professional football. But once again you love the game, you love the camaraderie, you love the social side, you love the buzz of winning, and the whole atmosphere of football – the game itself was wonderful to me. I had two aspirations – one was to finish my apprenticeship and become a qualified electrician which I attained, and two was to see how far I could go as a professional footballer. When West Brom came in for me my parents gave me all their blessing, knowing that I had a foundation if nothing came of it. It might have been a different story if I never had a foundation, I might have lost a year out or whatever . . .

(CR)

The West Bromwich Albion fans, and the manager at the time (Ron Atkinson) regarded Regis as a player who was never afraid to 'try new things' in a game, and to 'express himself'. Perhaps the option of a genuinely viable fall-back career gave him the confidence to re-assess the significance of not 'making the grade', even whilst striving to establish himself as a footballer of note. There is some evidence to suggest that fears about a career being truncated through serious injury, or the setback of rejection, can result in acute feelings of distress for footballers. Houlston's now dated (1982) study of post-football occupational careers (among all ethnic groups) not only found that the experience of downward social and economic mobility was fairly common, but also that ex-footballers were unprepared to make the necessary psychological, social and financial adjustments to accommodate quite dramatic status changes. Football is beset by uncertainty, and only the élite are likely to be financially secure. It is feasible that the continuing burden of racial discrimination would accentuate the psychological and social consequences of change.

Considering the occupations and income levels of their parents, the majority of the interviewees were representative of the working class. Perhaps it is not surprising that parental help to foster a sporting career was 'in kind' rather than being financial. The tone, rather than the details, of Regis' reflections was typical. He argued that:

> ... *we came from a fairly poor background ... My father was a labourer, my mother she was a seamstress, and so you're really just got your bus-fare, and it was down to you to travel across London at whatever age or get back home at whatever time necessary ... Your parents didn't have that money. It's no reflection on them, it's just that they didn't have it. You just have to do what anybody else does in that situation.*

(CR)

The family circumstances of Paul Hull highlight him as the exception to the majority. Not only does he convey possibly the strongest sense of parental influence and support in all respects, financial and otherwise; but his father also provided the resources to pursue a range of sports as 'comprehensively' as possible:

> ... *my dad took me to the clubs [and] made sure, you know, I had the proper coach and everything else, for whatever sport it was gonna be. And when I decided I didn't want to play that sport he wasn't sort of annoyed or anything like that because [he thought that] it was good, the fact that I sampled all different sports. And I think that's helped me out in the long term. Especially, you know, for the skill for part of the rugby game.*

(PH)

Hull's job as a Physical Training Instructor in the RAF enabled him to combine his love of sports, specifically rugby union, with a career. By the mid-1980s, he was playing for Bristol Rugby Club in the West of England, and the RAF proved an accommodating employer. Approximate postings near the club were complemented by time off from work for rugby training. There is a tradition of this 'understand-ing' in the British armed forces, as press interviews with Tim Rodber, Will Carling (both Rugby Union), Kris Akabussi and Kelly Holmes (both athletics) have indicated. Zia Haque joined the army at 19, trained as a motor vehicle technician, and was also able to indulge his love of sports in this way.

In 1991, David Lawrence was forced to take a prolonged break from cricket, after an horrific accident shattered his kneecap during a test match against New Zealand. He reflected that it was this career-ending injury, rather than his parents advice, that caused him to consider the need for alternative career plans. We have already read that he considered his teachers neglected their pedagogic responsibilities. But in relation to his parents, he felt that:

> *... at the end of the day, I had 100 per cent support from them ... Obviously they would have liked me to go on to get qualifications whatever, but I decided that I wanted to become a professional cricketer ... I didn't go on to get any qualifications. I did a lot of right courses, but I did it really just to improve on all my English and everything else. But I didn't go on to go back to college and try and get any qualifications ... which, you know, if I look back, probably, it would have been the best thing to do. If this injury came ten years or 15 years earlier as I was starting my career, I wouldn't have had anything to fall back on.*

(DL)

Jason Gardener's approach to his sport and his education appear to have been profoundly influenced by his mother, and by the practical guidance of a coach related by marriage, and regarded as a family friend. Gardener's mother already had an extensive knowledge about the 'culture' of athletics (the importance of rest and diet, maximising the benefits of seasonal training), whilst his coach David Lease promised the family that Gardener would maintain an equal commitment to his studies. Under these influences, Gardener developed a realistic perspective about the pitfalls of exclusively pursuing an athletics career; instead attempting to balance short-term ambition with long-term investment. Reflecting on the roles of his parents, and that of Lease, Gardener claimed that:

> *... my dad had to work all the time, in a working-class job. He didn't have the time to really spend with me ... he didn't have time to do what some of the other fathers were doing, taking their children to places. But my mum, she was very good. When it came to club nights, when I was too young to catch a bus into town to Percy Boys Club, she would take me down and watch me train or go off for an hour or two and come back and pick me up. She would take me to some of the school competitions. Especially my mother, she done all she could to help me out ... My dad was the one who provided the money for me to go to competitions, to have the right equipment and stuff. But it was my mum who took on the role of actually being there ... Dave Lease said that only a handful of British athletes make a lot of money from the sport, make any money from the sport. I could become an international sprinter and not make a penny.*

I didn't know that. I thought that if you compete for Great Britain then that is it: you open the door to a pot of gold! . . . so many people think that. But Dave made a contract with me . . . redo my GCSEs and I had to succeed for him to keep coaching me . . . it's a great motivation . . . and I got there. And the most important thing I learnt from sport, from athletics, was that if I worked for something and I worked smartly, correctly, the right way, and I wanted it, I could become successful, and that's what's happening. And once I realised those two things, work hard and work correctly, you get results.

(JG)

Jason was able to maximise the benefits of a supportive environment, in spite of financial restrictions. Having successfully completed his GCSEs, he decided to combine competing at the highest level with study for a university degree.

The traditional view of Asian family/kinship systems does not wholly contrast with the African-Caribbean model advanced earlier, since it is seen as a source of strength *and* weakness. On the one hand, Asian households are seen to provide the structure and cohesion vital to stability and psychological well being. On the other, the potential for conflict exists. More assertive and confrontational Western attitudes are seen to clash with Asian hierarchical family structures, and parental authority (see for example Khan, 1979; Lawrence, 1992a). The racial disturbances that took place throughout May and June 2001 were partly explained in terms of Asian youth having a greater intolerance of racism than their migrant forebears (see for example Wainwright, 2001). Chapter 1 has shown that a whole genetic and cultural 'apparatus' exists to link black groups with sport. For British Asians, sport was not promoted as a social 'release valve'.

Do these ideas have any significance for the Asian interviewees? We have already learned that Gurbinder Singh's father was a former national weightlifting champion in his native India. Not only did his parents travel with him to competitions, but his father's technical coaching was complemented by his mother's dietary knowledge. Singh claimed that:

My mum was encouraging as well, 'cos she's been through it with my dad. When my dad used to lift she was there and she used to support him, and now she's supporting me in the same way . . . particularly food-wise: she makes all the proper food for me, whilst my dad coaches me, tells me what's wrong and what's right.

(GS)

A career in sport was not considered to be a viable option for Zia Haque in his formative years. Indeed, his parents seemed indifferent to the fact of his sports participation. Their lack of enthusiasm was, he believes, due to the casual way that sport was regarded by his and other Asian families. Instead, it was emphasised that sport should be sidelined whilst he obtained his academic qualifications. Haque claimed to have no knowledge about British teacher expectations relating to minority ethnic groups and sport (see above). He nonetheless had this to say on the subject of why sport is more popular amongst black than Asian children in Britain:

> These are just personal views. A fair few section of the African-Caribbean community do not pay enough attention to the academic side. Whether that's lack of encouragement from parents I don't know . . . it's purely my personal view. And they seem to excel in sports because you still need to do something to burn your energy . . . and they seem to naturally excel in that. From the Asian side the parents place a very, very strong emphasis on the academic side and the children are not encouraged, or encouraged very little towards the sport side. The Asian parents look at it that . . . the Asian parents do not consider sports to be a paying career. Hence, they encourage their children on the academic side to do home study . . . and that's borne by the fact that you see very few Asian kids in the higher level . . . in county sports or national sports. Having said that, that's changing. Parents have started to realise, certainly parents of younger age are starting to realise that sports is important. It's not only important for physical exercise, it's also important for health as well. The younger generation of parents are starting to encourage their children to play sports, partly because maybe they play sports. But if you look at the older generation of Asians . . . the generation of my age or older, very, very, very few play sports.
>
> (ZH)

Haque's answer points to a generational shift in the attitude of Asian parents towards sport. However, it is most striking for what it reveals about the perpetuation of commonsense thinking on race and sport. When considered alongside his son's remarks on non-academic and 'boisterous' black youth (see above), it presents a cross-generational picture that is remarkable in its consistency. Haque was equally forthright on the question of inter-generational conflict over cultural values. His ideas on the traditional 'Asian temperament' also resonate with commonsense ideas about their unsuitability for 'aggressive' sports:

Figure 3.10 Zia Haque

Generally, it is recognised that the Asians do not retaliate. And that quite often is seen as weakness, and that's true of adults. Certainly people of my age, they don't want to retaliate . . . they know whatever happens . . . they are more interested in preserving the security of their family life. To give you an example, I would think very, very hard in either getting into a fight or getting into a situation where I might end up in prison . . . I think much more so, I'm not saying other people don't . . . but for the Asians, it's a stigma if you end up in a prison, it's also considered very bad for the family and for the children: more so for the black or the white and I must emphasise that I'm not saying that the white people don't think for their families but Asians think about it very, very strongly . . . they would rather walk away from something that's humiliating. So, if somebody's hit me, quite often people of my generation will walk away rather than create a scene where you end up hitting somebody else and it goes to court. So the option, two options, is to walk away. Quite often, that's considered as a weakness. But the current generation, the youngsters who were born in this country, who have gone to schools here, are not tolerating abuse. They will stand up.

(ZH)

Concluding remarks

This chapter has looked at some of the ways that 'race' has shaped the early sporting experiences of the interviewees. Dominant ideas about black and Asian groups, and their relationship to sport, are central to establishing 'races' as indelible categories, and for normalising *whiteness* (Chapter 1). The idea that black children have a genetic predisposition for sport, whilst their Asian peers lack the aptitude and temperament for it, is reinforced by a network of institutions and personnel. Patterns of social mobility are affecting all groups in British society. However, important structural impediments, arising out of racial disadvantage, have continued to disproportionately affect black people, and Pakistani and Bangladeshi groups. This has had a number of consequences for black people and their relationship to sport. The search for sport as a social solution for the 'problem' of black youth has been intensified; discourses which implicate the black family as dysfunctional have been strengthened; and ideas of biological determinism are being confirmed at a 'commonsense' level. In the 1970s and 1980s, the term 'black' was disaggregated to become a less inclusive category. The ethnic separateness that this encouraged (see for example Modood, 1994) further emphasised how professional sport had less significance for Asian groups.

4
Sport in the Later Years

The names of certain individuals and organisations connected with the interviewees have been changed to protect confidentiality.

Introduction

Like the previous chapter, Chapter 4 addresses the interviewee's personal experiences of, and general awareness about, racism. Unlike Chapter 3 however, it proceeds from the point at which hard decisions have been made about sport as a recreational pursuit, or as a way of making a living. For reasons of coherence, Chapter 4 begins with an account of popular racialised ideas; and follows this with an examination of racial manifestations (practice and consequence). At the level of policy measures and targeted action, anti-racist initiatives tend to focus on the need to tackle *overt* (Chapter 2) abuse directed towards minority ethnic sportsmen and supporters. This focus has obscured the need to confront more subtle, difficult-to-detect forms of racism, which are still pressing concerns in some popular sports. Chapter 4 will address the interviewee's experiences of overt and covert reactions, and will finish with a look at how racist ideas and practices are perpetuated in media representations. Ideas about 'natural ability' are, as will be shown, linked to such practices as 'stacking'. Media portrayals of black sportspeople have also supported these ideas, through journalism that emphasises instinct, skill and 'natural' ability, before such qualities as intelligence, nerve and effort.

Racialised ideas and practices are given life through stereotypes. A *racial stereotype* can be defined as an over-generalisation about the physical and intellectual attributes, and behavioural patterns, of a category of people (in our case 'blacks' and 'Asians'). This is an important area of enquiry. Such over-generalisations form the bedrock of thinking on why black men and women have achieved so much in certain sports; why they are absent from coaching and management; and why Asians are generally absent from both.

Sport and racialised ideas: 'natural' ability?

'Why have we got to look for some other reason to take away the magnitude of victory?'

'I was a boy from Stoke of Jamaican parents, not a Brazilian from Rio!'

'Asian kids . . . they're very good at yoga, brilliant at stretching, aren't they?'

Football has enduringly served as a site for stereotyped ideas about 'natural' abilities and weaknesses. In the 1970s and 1980s, two oft-quoted weaknesses about black players were that their 'instinctive' play was spoiled by an undisciplined and lazy approach to the game; and that they were keen to avoid the hard physical challenge necessary to win the ball from an opponent (see for example Mason, 1988). We can add the view that black players cannot play in the centre of midfield, as this position requires leadership skills; and that even though they prefer to play in the centre-forward position, they are not 'natural' goal scorers. Jim Smith, ex-manager of Birmingham City Football Club, claimed that black players 'seem to use very little intelligence; they get by on sheer natural talent most of the time' (quoted in Cashmore, 1982, p. 45). In 1987 Graham Taylor, then manager of Aston Villa, made the following remarks about one of his black players:

Like a lot of lads with a West Indian background, he's a free spirit. You don't want to lose that, because now and again he'll take your breath away. But I'm trying to stop him running all over the place to get the ball . . . I want him to come off tired from mental application, rather than just plain knackered.

(cited in Hill, 2001, p. 94)

How can we make sense of these and other similar comments (Chapter 1), using the ideas of Roland Barthes? To Barthes, the power of a *myth* such as 'race' lies in its self-evident, 'natural' qualities. In his view, the fact that a myth 'hides nothing' means that its revelatory power is the very means of its distortion. Black people's sporting success, and contrasting failure to make an impression in coaching and management, 'self-evidently' indicates that they are more gifted physically, have more of a '[care]free spirit', and are less endowed intellectually. In addition, one of the underlying strengths of Barthes' myth is its dynamic, protean qualities. This means that quite diverse and sometimes oppositional facets of a myth can coexist without apparent contradiction, thereby defying attempts to reduce it to a single uniform principle. For example, a predominant stereotype of black athletes as 'naturally' large, strong and quick, can coexist beside the image of the 'natural' African long distance runner, who is small and lithe to suit the discipline.

Sport is an area of contested and shifting ideologies, rather than a consistent and functional ideology working in the interests of a dominant group. Therefore, the possibility exists that racialised perceptions about playing and managing can be overturned through time, broader access to a greater array of sports, and individual performances that challenge traditional beliefs. Football again provides a powerful illustration of how this works in practice. As noted elsewhere, the emergence in the last ten years of midfield and defensive players like Paul Ince and Sol Campbell, whose muscular and aggressive style of play is 'typically English', have challenged the myth of the talented, but soft and erratic, black player.

However, commonsense understandings about the physical and mental capabilities of different 'races' may not be abandoned altogether. The 'transformative' qualities, or 'plasticity', of Barthes' myth (Chapter 1) mean that these particular football stereotypes are being replaced by equally significant others. The Wolverhampton Wanderers and ex-England player Paul Ince would appear to be instrumental in debunking both the myth of the black player who lacks 'bottle' in the tackle, and who cannot captain a football team. As any devotee of English football will confirm, Ince is noted, in fact castigated, for his aggressive style of play. He has also captained England from the centre of midfield on a number of occasions, being the first black player to do so. When considering the other, high-profile, black players who adopt a similarly 'aggressive' role in midfield (such as Arsenal's Patrick Viera and Juventus' Edgar Davids), it is further tempting to believe that stereotypes about temperament and ability have been consigned to history. Nonetheless, each of these players is contributing to a new and in some ways ambiguous image for black players. In my view, the 'reticent' black footballer has been replaced by an 'over-committed' one in media commentary: whose actions verge on, or extend beyond, the legally permissible. This particular view of black players is much closer in keeping with the overtly physical and aggressive stereotype attributed to black sportsmen in general. At any rate, it illustrates how ideas are not consistent over time, but are modified to take account of new developments.

David Lawrence, Jason Gardener and Garth Crooks reflected on how the stereotyped thinking their school teachers had subjected them to was a feature of their professional careers. Although his own club was progressive in this regard, Lawrence was adamant:

> . . . *there's no doubt about it. I mean, if you're a black cricketer, people automatically straight away think 'oh, he's a bowler, he's a fast bowler', that's what they think straight away. The problem we're all gonna have . . . there's a lot of English-born African-Caribbean players playing county cricket, and Gloucestershire is probably one of the better examples where black cricketers have been given responsibility here . . . we've had Courtney Walsh as our county Captain for four years, and now Mark Alleyne has taken over as our county captain, both black cricketers. So, really they've been able to ease their way through and they're not just bowlers, they're not just batters . . . they have the ability to have leadership skills . . . But if we retire today, could we get a job in management, could we get a job coaching? . . . it's still early days . . . you've only got to look at football . . . it's early days despite Viv Anderson. We're still climbing up the ladder. And it will happen, but it will have to take time.*

> (DL)

For Gardener:

> *Stereotyping is part of most sports which I have been involved in from a youngster. In rugby, I was 'fast on the wing Jase'. Picking a team, if there were a few black guys in the school they would usually be thrown out to the wing, or they wouldn't really play the acute [central, influential] positions, and that was really frustrating for me . . . rugby is a good sport . . . I enjoy rugby, but I didn't enjoy playing it because I never got the damn ball! And every time I got the ball I'd score a try, but scoring one or two tries in 80 minutes, 90 minutes of play in the freezing cold wasn't appealing to me . . . I could never understand why they didn't put me in the centre, where I could break free and nobody could touch me. In athletics, if you come along to a club firstly they think: 'you're black'; secondly they think: 'let's check him out, he's probably a good sprinter' . . . I think it's because of what people see and the 'knowledge' they have available to them. They see certain*

groups do certain events on television. They don't mean to stereotype but that's just the impression they have and then they say: 'let's see how good they are at playing that role'.

(JG)

Crooks remarked that:

. . . some white people in particular are ready to write black people off, they're all too ready to write them off at school and push them into particular areas that they think they fit. That was prevalent in my day, and I'm absolutely convinced that it's prevalent today, probably more so today . . . I think that teachers, along with members of the public, find it all too easy to put people into a convenient little compartment. 'This is what you're supposed to be good at.' I remember Gordon Banks [ex-England goalkeeper], and again, it was born out of his experience, and I'm not being critical of Gordon. I have an enormous amount of respect for Gordon, as a goalkeeper and a man. I remember I was doing some practises with him one afternoon, probably just the two of us. He was in goal, he was a tremendous man for perfection and practice, and I was bending shots around him, and one or two would beat him, and it was a tremendous thrill for me to be beating one of the greatest goalkeepers in the world. I was seventeen at the time, and after the session he said 'you should try that more often, you should do that more often'. And I went yeah, you're right, I should try that more often. And then he said: 'you people are good at that'. And I thought even then without even dissecting it or intellectualising it and I doubt whether he'll even remember this, but it stuck in my mind because I couldn't understand why black people should be any better at this than white people, it was the technique and the practice that was important and crucial here, not what colour your skin was. I was a boy from Stoke of Jamaican parents, not a Brazilian from Rio! Anybody could do this if they set their mind to it and apply themselves.

(GC)

Both are British, but to Banks, Crooks' colour attained more significance than his nationality. In this sense, Crooks recognises the ways in which blackness and Britishness operate as mutually exclusive categories. Today, Crooks feels that 'attitudes have changed', with the arrival of numbers of foreign players to English football. Certainly, being able to 'Bend it like [David] Beckham', as the popular film title suggests, is testimony to how the skills previously associated with an exotic 'Other' are being co-opted as part of British style. However, the idea that racial characteristics are expressed through national sporting styles and attitudes is still embedded in the British psyche; and reflected in media commentary opining about African 'naivety and indiscipline', Brazilian 'flair' and Argentinean 'cunning' (see for example O'Donnell, 1994; Ladyman, 2002). Crook's culinary metaphor is brilliantly apropos:

> *I think that . . . the images of Brazil and their World Cup successes left football people thinking that we [black people] all had a greater propensity to do these things than white people, and it's utter nonsense. There's no evidence to support that whatsoever and . . . again I think that a lot of English people have put themselves in a category as well, not just us, but put themselves in a particular category . . . I think that traditionally English people have wanted their staple diet of football to be rather like their food, to be a bit bland. 'This is what we like, this is what we're used to, and this is what we want. We're not into any exotic, flashy, culinary delights'; and I think that football is not dissimilar. I think that when black players born in Britain burst onto the scene, there was room for a little bit of spice flashing down the wing and it had it's place, but there was no other room for it: 'this is not the way we play football'. And there wasn't any room for development, there wasn't any room for creativity, 'this is what we knew, this is what we understood, this is what worked'. It was born out of stiff-upper-lip get on with it, roll your sleeves up, this is who we are.*

(GC)

Racialised preconceptions had a less profound effect on the mind of Sean Viera. In his view:

> *I was fortunate really because in my class . . . the majority of the group was black . . . they sort of spurred me on, my instructor was black as well so he spurred me on as well . . . it was important because . . . it felt like you was in a community, not saying that I don't know how it would work if it was a white person doing it, but we sort of could relate to each other . . . we had that goal within us to go ahead and obviously win as much as we can and then . . . quite a few of us out of that team got to the national team. Again, the thing for us was like, again, the head coach [of the national team] was black, and half the team, 80%, was black. So we didn't have to worry about: 'how do we act in front of these people, and what do you say to these people?' It was just like you go in there and everybody could relate to each other because they were from the Caribbean or origins were from the Caribbean, so whether you're from Jamaica, Barbados, whatever, you could still relate.*

(SV)

Viera's testimony supports an important research finding concerning the social and cultural function of these predominantly black/Asian settings (Williams, 1992). The ethnic origins of his classmates and instructor was seen as key to developing his confidence, in an environment where aptitude and ability would be fostered with minimal recourse to stereotypes.

Chris Sanigar's thoughts on genetic attributes illustrate that stereotyped groups can themselves co-opt and assimilate dominant ideas into coherent philosophies, even in the face of contradictory evidence. Having finished a successful professional boxing career in 1984, Sanigar eventually turned his hand to managing and promotion. He reflected on the different levels of commitment to boxing between young black and Asian men:

> *I just think it's something naturally that black kids are good at . . . Jack Johnson was the first heavyweight champion, and I think that he was some focal-point naturally for black kids. Naturally, black kids are just naturally strong, they're not great swimmers, but they're good runners and that. [A lack of Asian interest in boxing is] I think, just heritage . . . likewise they're very good at yoga, brilliant, aren't they, at stretching? But just recently, in the new era, they are beginning to play football, and there are quite a few Asian boxers as well in this country, such as the British Welterweight Champion . . . the IBO Champion both at same weight [67kg].*
> (CS)

Sanigar's testimony is replete with references to 'nature'. It conflates biology with culture to create a popular discourse on race and sports aptitude, even whilst recognising that important changes invalidate the arguments. Nonetheless, Zia Haque also endorsed this philosophy, suggesting that: 'generally, the Asians are not big in size, and I would imagine they might feel intimidated [in contact sports]'.

Irrespective of much-stated cultural barriers, ideas about Asian groups and sport can be seen to have impeded their real desires for access and participation (Chapters 1, 2; see also Bains with Patel, 1996). This point was agreed upon by all of the interviewees. The comments of Garth Crooks are in particular worth noting, given that his work involves widening sports access:

> *I think there's gonna be another surge, and I think that it will probably come from the Asian community. But I think they are experiencing the same things that we did in the sixties and the seventies, that's with the*

exception of people like Charlie Williams who played in the fifties and people before him – Henry Wharton at the turn of the century. There have been exceptional black people who have played but I'm talking really from 1970 and post-'70. Asians are, I think probably, where the next surge will come from. But they're telling me they're experiencing prejudice where football is concerned, and they're experiencing the same stereotypical arguments about their unsuitability for sports.

(GC)

In contrast to (predominantly Western) ideas about the frailty of South Asian people, Punjabi Sikh culture actually places a premium on the physical strength of males. Such sports as weightlifting are popular in this part of India, and account for the successes and popularity of Asian lifters at the all-Asian games, and wider stages such as the Olympics, and the Commonwealth Games. Gurbinder Singh's testimony confirmed this when he stated that:

Weightlifting is popular amongst Asian people. If you are strong and you can lift a lot of weight, you are really respected a lot. According to other religions it's not that important. I think in the English [religions] they'd rather be more intellectual . . . but in ours if you're strong you're more respected than anybody else . . . We have Asian tournaments, and in those Asian tournaments we use our weightlifting to give shows, performances for Asian people, in England and abroad. And whoever wins, the audience give money to them, in respect like, for entertaining them.

(GS)

But the idea that South Asian groups possess strong business acumen has an equally popular currency in Britain, and again serves to locate their interests outside of sport. The disproportionate number of Asian-owned 'corner shops' – newsagents, confectioners and tobacconists in the main – partly inspired the title of a book on these groups, and their relationship to sport in Britain. *Corner Flags and Corner Shops* (Bains and Johal, 1998) was so named because of a 'joke' popular in football circles, and one which I clearly remember from childhood. According to the joke, Asian footballers can't take corner kicks in the game because, rather than kicking the ball, they would open a shop instead! The point is that the 'joke's' central meaning is reinforced, even whilst its message is not taken literally. Just as 'white men can't jump' (a reference to basketball), Asian men are business entrepreneurs who have concerns other than sport. Chris Sanigar, Zia Haque and Gurbinder Singh all endorsed ideas about Asian groups and business acumen, with Sanigar attributing his success (as boxing promoter and manager) to a mix of ethnic 'heritage', and experience.

'Race' practices: 'stacking'

> '... if you are black you are fast. You know you were intended to go on the wing, in the same way in America that a lot of wide receivers are black as well because they tend to be the fastest.'

> '... not only are you faced with being black, you're faced with doing the wrong martial art as well.'

One of the most significant outcomes of racial stereotyping in sports is the assumption that black sportsmen and women lack stamina, courage and intellectual abilities. This has led to coaches and managers pushing black players into wide, peripheral positions on the sports field. Here, their 'natural' abilities and good 'instincts' would be best used, primarily against black opponents with similar attributes; whilst opportunities in central, decision-making roles would be denied. By contrast, white competitors are preferred in positions 'likely to influence the pattern of the game', and ostensibly requiring leadership, thought, precision and the ability to make rational decisions under pressure (Brower, 1972; Calhoun, 1987). In the USA, this practice is most commonly referred to as 'stacking', or 'centrality', and has generated a substantial body of academic enquiry there (see for example Chu and Seagrave, 1983; Medoff, 1986; Hoose, 1989; Omi, 1989; Greendorfer, 1992).

According to this research, stacking conditions teachers and coaches to look for and encourage certain skills in some players, at the expense of other skills. How *applicable* this process is differs between sports, so that it has less significance for soccer and cricket, than for basketball and US football. Nonetheless, it is still a useful concept. Malcolm's research (1997) indicated how racial groups in British cricket are stacked in different positions, with black men as low-status bowlers and Asian men as high-status batters. We have seen that the experiences of Lawrence confirm research findings on how black British cricketers are 'stacked' in certain positions. And in line with Gardener's observations about his rugby playing days (see above), evidence suggests that a close variant of stacking also occurs in this sport.

Both codes of the game (union and league) appear to have the majority of black players in 'non-central' positions that rely primarily on speed: such as the wings. Rugby union is traditionally associated with more prosperous social groups in both the North and South of England. The stacking of the sport's black players, the majority of whom belong to these groups, shows therefore that power and oppression in sports can transcend the traditional black, working-class profile (Maguire, 1995). As a (related) aside, research suggests that the limits imposed on black physical and mental ability are even reflected by economic discrimination in sports. Szymanski (1997) found that the financial market works less effectively for black football players in Britain, as there is evidence of lower wages paid for a given level of team performance.

Breaking the mould

The process of stacking arguably makes it more difficult for some athletes to realise their true sporting potential. Despite this, black sportsmen have developed creative and imaginative styles akin to those of minority ethnic groups in other cultural spheres. These responses show how individuals are both determining and determined, and can exploit as well as being exploited (Hargreaves, 1994). Dyson's interesting essay, on the black basketball superstar Michael Jordan, provides a potent illustration of cultural and personal agency achieved through athletic competition. Characteristics in his play, variously described as the 'will to spontaneity' and the 'stylization of the performed self' are seen to reflect the influence of African-American culture (1993). The need for expression within the confines of structure is also recognised by Majors (1990); although he conveys a stronger sense that black males contrive to worsen their own oppression. Majors adopts the term 'cool pose' to describe the way that black men have co-opted sport as a site for masculine self-expression. He acknowledges that black Americans use legitimate cultural responses to their restricted spheres of opportunity, and that an 'expressive lifestyle' is adaptation of the limits of structure, rather than submission to them. But by defining black expression as a cultural resistance to racism, and as almost 'post-modern' in its preoccupation with style over substance, Majors seems to diminish the ways in which cultural practices can *in themselves* be political; and how sport has been used to challenge the actions of governments. To recognise these meanings is to acknowledge that powerful, subversive ideas can motivate sporting actions, and challenge the *status quo*. Hence, the dominant groups' hegemonic hold over subordinate groups can never be totally guaranteed. Sport has famously served as a site for political empowerment for disadvantaged groups, through drawing attention to their cause: for instance, in the case of the former heavyweight boxer Muhammad Ali (Marqusee, 1995*b*; Hartmann, 1996).

Rugby union player Paul Hull's amateur and professional careers do not seem to have been affected by stacking. Indeed, Hull was moved around the various key positions understood to influence the flow and pattern of a rugby match, and associated with intellect and decision-making (such as fly-half and centre), before eventually playing at full-back for both Bristol and England. Ironically, given the direction of research findings, Hull's England career seems to have suffered because of his positional versatility. Perhaps not surprisingly then, the issue of 'stacking' for Hull can best be explained not in terms of positional centrality; but through an analysis of sport which focuses on the consequences of uneven class relations:

> . . . *I went to boarding school. I'd never played rugby [before] . . . if I didn't have that opportunity, I wouldn't have gone into it . . . In certain schools football is their sport, and they don't play rugby, and that is the barrier: the fact that people aren't going to get the opportunity to play sport. With a lot of private schools, boarding schools, schools like that, rugby probably is a number one sport, and it goes on to university and college and stuff like that . . . if you haven't got the opportunity to play in one of these places then you know you're just not going to get it. And I think a lot of the black people in the sport at the moment over the past sort of x amount of years have been people that have gone through university. You know, Victor Ubogu went to Oxford University and Andy Harriman [former internationals, both black] went to university and people like this . . . when a black person or their kids have started playing sport it is natural to say 'right, who's the fastest in the team? Okay, if you're the fastest in the team, you'll play on the wing'. And that happens all round. I mean in football it does as well . . . [but] you don't actually find many black people in other sports, especially in England anyway, playing key positions like fly-half or scrum-half . . . the one good thing about rugby is the fact that there's no barriers, I mean generally speaking.*

(PH)

It seems essential to consider whether class supersedes race in the view of Martin Offiah, the other interviewee to be educated at a fee-paying school. Like Hull, he spent some time after his school years playing rugby in a variety of influential positions, before settling on the wing. He explained that:

> ... *I always played centre, I always played fly-half and centre at school and even at Rosslyn Park I only played on the wing when I got into the first team* ... *[but] there's always the stereotypes about young black people being fast playing on the wing and all that, but at the end of the day, you know it did suit the attributes I had especially in [rugby] league. So that's why I went to it, but there were lots of other players who had been successful in lots of other positions* ... *I do agree with the fact that in certain sort of rugby environments they assume that if you are black you are fast. You know you were intended to go on the wing, in the same way in America that a lot of wide receivers are black as well because they tend to be the fastest. And you only need to look at the 100 metre final in the world championship Olympic Games. How many white people are there? There's none, the same way there's no black guys in swimming. These things are nothing to do with culture, it's more a physiological thing. I think that's more probably the case.*

(MO)

Offiah concurs with Hull's point about the 'colour blind democracy' of rugby union (but not rugby league; see below), but also recognises the ways in which sports coaches and managers in general link black people with certain roles. And not unlike Chris Sanigar, he endorses a view that black people (himself included) are genetically endowed with attributes like strength and speed.

Jason Gardener has been dubbed the 'Bath bullet' in that area's local press, and so has similar physical attributes to Martin Offiah. His approach to this question of centrality is more politically engaged, since it attempts to consider the nature and form of social organisation:

> ... *from studying and reading how difficult it has been for black people to progress in Western society, there's been lots of barriers, and this is a way where black people are able to express themselves – if I cross the line first, I am the winner, no one's taking that away from me. It's not like team sports, where you could be the better player and you find that you're on the bench or you're out of favour with your coach, and that could be subjective reasoning* ... *There's lots of discussions and writing about black people being genetically different, but I agree with what I've read from black writers when they say: 'why can't you just accept we're all equal,*

that black people through social circumstances try harder in certain sports?' Why have we got to look for some other reason to take away the magnitude of victory?

(JG)

Gardener's testimony revealed a heightened awareness of stacking in his own sport, and about the assumptions that coaches make concerning black athletes. He also reasoned that the singular discipline of sprinting would still be less prone to the racial stereotyping that leads to stacking in team sports like rugby and football. His greatest frustration was a failure to appreciate why, even when black athletes were stronger and quicker than their white contemporaries, these attributes could not be used to enhance their decision-making in a central area. Finally, Viera suggested that black martial artists are 'stacked' in Chinese rather than Japanese-based disciplines; and that the latter styles are regarded as 'superior' by the 'experts'. He confirmed that: 'It's a double negative really. The judges don't look kindly on us because we're black, and we do a Chinese art that is seen as a weaker form.'

'Race' consequences

(i) Coaching and management

'. . . if we retire today, could we get a job in management, could we get a job in coaching? . . . it's still early days.'

Ideas about 'natural' ability have obvious implications for black and Asian sportsmen aspiring to a post-playing career in sport. As noted earlier, stereotypes about Asian groups possessing a high degree of intelligence and business acumen are qualitatively different from the more sports appropriate ideas associated with their black contemporaries. But despite their high representation in such popular sports as football and baseball, few positions in management or coaching have been taken by former black professionals (see for example Majors, 1990; Carrington and McDonald, 2001*a*). The ex-England and Liverpool forward John Barnes had a short and fairly unsuccessful tenure as assistant manager at Celtic. Barnes was not only the most notable exception in managerial terms, but also with respect to his social background, as he comes from an upper-middle-class Jamaican family (Hill, 2001). The high-profile appointments of black managers in the English premier league (previously Ruud Gullit at Chelsea, then

Newcastle; currently Jean Tigana at Fulham) ostensibly points to progress in this area. But as Back *et al.* (2001) point out, their 'foreign-ness' (Gullit is Dutch, Tigana French) makes them less threatening to the white, British male identities that are central to football culture.

The prospects for aspiring black and Asian managers appear more bleak at the lower levels of football. A recent study into racism in the semi-professional leagues found that: 'There is a continued adherence to the stereotype of the less intelligent black athlete, unsuitable for the organisational demands of managership and coaching' (cited in Dobson, 2002, p. 11). The news is equally stark in other non-playing areas of football, with no more than a handful of black referees refereeing professional football in England, and an Asian referee pursuing a claim of unfair dismissal from the same organisation.

At the time of writing, Viv Anderson was the only non-white English assistant-manager in the premier league. How did he negoti-ate 'racialised barriers' (cf. Small, 1994), predicated on black ability and temperament? Interestingly, Anderson claimed to have not per-sonally experienced the negative stereotyping that these barriers are premised on (see below also). Indeed, due to personal contacts, he had previously accepted the offer of manager at Barnsley Football Club before his current post. By contrast, Cyrille Regis has found it harder to break into football management, and eventually became the reserve team coach at (previously) second division West Bromwich Albion. Regis was reluctant to talk about this role, and his silence on this question was out of keeping with his reflections else-where. Perhaps it revealed an anxiety about how criticism of the club would affect his career, as well as the efficacy of normative 'codes' in certain sports (Chapter 1).

(ii) A role model?

> 'Are they gonna react violently, kicking out or having a verbal reaction? How do they behave outside of football, are they determined, are they disciplined?'

> 'I'm representing my religion, other Asian religions and my culture in that sport.'

Continued debates about the significance of 'race' mean that the actions of sportsmen, and other visible members of minority ethnic groups, are still susceptible to framing in stereotypic terms. Chapter 3 highlighted the importance of role models to the interviewees in their formative years. As adults, were they aware of a wider 'burden of responsibility' to represent black and Asian people in Britain? There was total agreement from all of the interviewees on this point. Cyrille Regis reflected on the 1970s when he claimed that:

> ... *you were aware that there's not many of you around, and so therefore the media, the public so to speak, are saying: 'well, we've got this image of black players or black people, is it true? Are they gonna react violently, kicking out or having a verbal reaction? How do they behave outside of football, are they determined, are they disciplined?' And so yeah, it was very paramount to me in the 1970s ... even more later on in life. I think when you're 19/20/21, you're just getting on in the game, but if you talk to second-generation black footballers, they will say it's important. Seeing Cyrille Regis and Laurie Cunningham and Justin Fashanu and Garth Crooks playing football and being interviewed inspired me to go and play football and say, yeah, if those boys can do it, I can do it. But it's only then that you feel well, yeah, you're a role model in bits and pieces too – when black players start telling you that you were an inspiration to them ... When you are much more mature you know the system, you know how the media works. And you are very conscious that your behaviour has an affect on your community, and black men and young boys in general.*

> (CR)

By the 1990s, a more established minority ethnic presence in Britain still prompted a similarly self-conscious response from Jason Gardener:

> *I'm conscious of the way I behave for my own self, me as Jason Gardener ... how I've been brought up by my parents, you know ... good family, manners, discipline. I want to be able to do well in society, and my actions hopefully display good behaviour. But I'm also very aware that a lot of people don't have much involvement with black people or people with different backgrounds, and that the information they have available, that may be TV coverage and newspaper coverage, to make decisions about certain groups ... is often bad. So I'm very fortunate when I can at least provide a positive portrayal of people from different backgrounds. And hopefully I can do it in a good way, that I'm not seen as just another arrogant guy with chips on his shoulders. I want people to think what a nice guy ... he's doing a great job for our country Britain, which is my country.*

> (JG)

Gardener places an emphasis on belonging ('Britain, my country') which is characteristic of a second generation of black people more assertive in their attempts to reconcile blackness with Britishness (see for example Hall, 1998). But by not wanting to be 'just another arrogant guy with chips on his shoulders', he unwittingly reveals that being black *and* British is still likely to create a defensiveness in public, and an uncertainty about belonging (Chapter 2).

The minor presence of British Asians in professional and semi-professional sport presents a more fundamental 'burden' for Gurbinder Singh: representing the diversity of Asianness in its religious and cultural forms. Singh was selected for the British weightlifting team and claimed that:

> *I'm the only Asian in there, and I'm very aware of that, and of what people might think, and also what they say, particularly when they haven't met Asian people before. I'm proud because I'm the only Asian in there [British weightlifting team], and then I can say at least there's one Asian in there. There's other black Afro-Caribbean people there as well, but I'm the only Asian in there so it makes me proud. So I think that towards me, I'm representing my religion, other Asian religions and my culture in that sport.*

> (GS)

This task of cultural bridging is arguably made more difficult because of the ways that the mainstream media misrepresent different Asian religions and cultures. For instance, Malik has referred to a lack of: 'cultural authenticity when it comes to detail – thus mosques are confused with Hindu temples . . . Muslim characters are given Sikh names, and so on' (1998, p. 320). But what emerges from Singh's testimony, nonetheless, is the degree of pride that he takes in possessing a *distinctive* cultural identity within the British context. In this sense, his reflection conveys less ambiguity about identity and belonging than all the other interviewees.

A burden of wider responsibility has particular resonance for Garth Crooks. During his playing career, Crooks served as a member of the PFA committee. In 1988, he sought election as chairman, explaining that:

> *I'd been on the management committee since 1982, the longest-serving committee member, perfectly equipped to take the job, I seemed the obvious choice. And in the election, I suddenly had two people opposing me, which I thought was very strange because there had been no sign of this in the first place . . . and then there was an atmosphere change in the meeting room, and there seemed to be what I can only describe as a coup d'état, where*

one or two people had been canvassed to stand against me. It only later transpired, and I hadn't known anything about this, that a member of the committee didn't feel it appropriate that a black man should be leading the Association. It wasn't until the Chief Executive, Gordon Taylor, made it absolutely clear and reminded one or two individuals of their obligations to pick the right man and the best man, no not the right man, the best man for the job. Now he didn't have any voting rights. But he felt it his duty to remind those who did have a vote of their obligation to the union. And when I got the nod I was very proud, but I was quite prepared to walk away from it if they didn't think I was suitable. But when I did get the nod I did feel the enormous pressure of this . . . I had to be successful because a lot of people are looking, a lot of people were prepared to knock, I was very aware that people in certain quarters, particularly the media, thought that – well, they hadn't said it publicly, but they thought: 'what's happened to the union? the deputy chief executive's black and now the chairman's black'.

(GC)

Crooks held the post for two years and during that time was overly conscious about the prospect of failure. There is a marked absence of senior black and Asian personnel in football's hierarchy, and failure to discharge his role competently would simply reinforce ideas about limited black capabilities. Perhaps the less intense relationship that Asian groups have with British sport explains why Singh appears content just to be included. By the same token, it is likely that the central place that sport occupies for black male identities underpins Garth Crooks' desire to prove a point about black people, and wider sporting roles.

(iii)   Overt and covert reactions

We have seen how general ideas about 'race', reflected in specific practices and consequences, have influenced the sporting experiences of the interviewees. This section will detail their experiences of overt racist abuse, along with the more subtle and difficult-to-detect forms of racism. Both are still a pressing concern in popular sports like football and cricket.

iii(a)   The 'have nots'?

'. . . there's no racism whatsoever in rugby, I'd say.'

Four of the interviewees (Gardener, Haque, Sanigar, Hull) claimed not to have experienced racist abuse directed at them from spectators, team mates, or opponents during sporting occasions. In Gardener's view, the conspicuous presence of black athletes in the British and other national squads mitigates against this. Nonetheless, his comments about the differential media coverage of black and white athletes (see later), do convey a sense that racial antagonism is *contained* rather than absent. A recent, highly publicised 'spat' between former British athletes Linford Christie and Sebastian Coe also hinted at an underlying racial tension when the two were competing as part of the same team. Reflecting on this period (the 1980s), and to Christie's captaincy, Coe racially slurred Christie, accusing him of conducting team talks which were 'unintelligible . . . to all but those who had a passing knowledge of jive' (cited in Toolis, 2001, p. 9).

Like Gardener, Hull was unequivocal about the absence of racism in his sport:

> . . . there's no racism whatsoever in rugby, I'd say. I mean, you hear of many classics. A player . . . who played rugby for Wales, and was a legend in his time . . . when he first started out, it was really unusual seeing a black player playing for Wales, and he's Welsh and everything else . . . and I remember a story . . . someone from a crowd chucked a banana at him and he just peeled it, ate the banana, chucked the skin back at them and that was it, you know, he was loved by the Welsh from that moment on. Not that he wasn't loved anyway, but they knew he was a character. No, I'd honestly say there was no sort of racism whatsoever. I'd be very surprised if anyone black in the sport would tell a story where they felt, you know, uncomfortable on the pitch. I think obviously the crowd would get on your back if you played poorly. But apart from that you know you would get nothing at all, and you don't get any trouble in the crowds . . . it's a sport where both sides' supporters can mingle, have a beer, have a laugh . . .
>
> (PH)

The 'classic' example that Hull cites is 'interpreted' using a conformist sporting vocabulary. By treating the appearance of a banana as a joke, and not an incident with racial overtones, the player showed 'character', and also gained the affection of the crowd. Equally, he adhered to the normative codes referenced in Chapter 1.

For Haque, Viera and Singh, racial prejudice was most operative at the level of *feeling*, rather than articulation. By their very nature, feelings about the existence of racist practices are nebulous, and difficult to substantiate. But for Haque, there was a strong feeling that he was tackled a little more ferociously than his white colleagues in inter-divisional

Army hockey matches. Whilst for Viera, white judges in competition seemed keener to obey the letter (rather than the spirit) of the law, when his predominantly black team were competing. In similar vein, Gurbinder Singh expressed a palpable sense of frustration with what he felt was a 'hidden' racist agenda behind national team selections:

> *I've noticed one thing . . . if you're equal with a white person, they'll take the white person to championships. I've noticed that, yeah. So if you're equal, like say that there's a white person and me doing the same weight, they'll probably take the white one . . . when I was a schoolboy, I didn't notice it at the time, because I was younger, and didn't realise why I seemed to have to work so much harder [than the white competitors]. I was under-15, and this under-16 lifter was lifting no more than me. And if I had gone on the competition he had gone on, I would have gained experience, and next year, the following year, cos I was in the same age-group, I would have probably got a medal or something. But I wasn't taken either year, because he was white – I didn't know this at the time – but like, he was white and probably, because I was black.*

> (GS)

When Regis and Lawrence won their first England caps, and Crooks stood for the PFA Chair (see above, and Chapter 2), the antipathy greeting them supported the notion that, for some, to be non-white and the 'face' of England was implausible and contradictory.

For Viera and Lawrence, the iniquities of a repressive apartheid regime in South Africa provided an extra moral and political dimension to their sporting contests: again, with nothing more concrete than 'feelings' of personal offence. Viera referred to an international competition in 1987:

> *There was this 'supposedly' anti-racist, 'multiracial' South African team . . . all these South Africans were in track suits and stuff . . . and this one black [South African] . . . they didn't give him a track suit, he wasn't allowed to sit by them, and he was the only one that came first, that had a medal. And he was going around talking to anyone else. And the funny thing is no one would chat to the [white] South Africans, and he's the only one everyone was chatting to . . . and I tell you the team went out there and one of us had to fight a massive white South African guy. And we just all said like if we have a South African, we're gonna try so hard because their mentality, their attitude was like . . . everyone was inferior, you could tell the hatred they had for you . . . you knew it was because you were black, and you were standing in front of them. They thought it was an insult for*

you just even coming on the mat here to face them. I can remember being in the changing room and saying 'boys, we're gonna have the South African guy, they're gonna have to be scraped off the mat because there's no way we're gonna hold back on these guys, no way he's gonna win' . . . because that just gives them more fuel for the fire.

(SV)

These feelings and experience were similarly replicated by Lawrence in the 1980s, when facing South African-born white players in English county cricket. In his view:

. . . the South African players I played against, I would say, took it on a personal level: that they didn't want a black man to get them out. I always sensed that: that they would try harder not to get out, to give their wicket away . . . and saying that, I used to try harder as well . . . I used to feel it subconsciously, whether it was true or not I don't know. But I always tried harder, and I always felt they tried harder as well.

(DL)

The white sportsmen's levels of competitiveness towards Lawrence, and vice versa, may have acted as a proxy for their different attitudes to South Africa's political system. Lawrence's colour attained the most significance in perceptions of his identity, defining him in opposition to a specific definition of whiteness. For this reason, Lawrence made it clear that his very presence, and his most significant sporting acts (taking wickets, fielding catches, hitting runs), were invested with a political symbolism over-riding any sporting meaning.

iii(b)   The 'haves'?

'There was a lad called Terry Hennessy, who had a bald head, and everywhere we went he used to get abuse, just because he had a bald head, and it was somebody to focus on that afternoon.'

Unfortunately, a larger number of interviewees *have* experienced abuse at the level of articulation. For Lawrence, this reached its nadir when playing at Headingley in the 1980s. On one occasion, he was subjected to a tirade lasting over two hours, and including the 'classic': banana-throwing. The football contingent are all ex-professionals who believe that the 'problem' in their sport is being alleviated. Their accounts of the abuse they faced in their playing days (the 1980s) are consistent with the profile painted of the sport at that time, and relayed in Chapter 2.

The research of Les Back and associates has highlighted the 'uneven' nature of racism amongst football supporters. They call for a more textured, multilayered approach to understanding the apparently inconsistent 'psychology' behind racist abuse. In their view: 'differences with regard to the level and intensity of racism need to be understood in terms of the way racist practices are nested within the ritual and collective symbolism of each fan culture' (2001, p. 37). During his time as a player in the 1980s, Crooks commented on these same inconsistencies. The *home* support were:

> ... *very supportive, if only superficially. And I say that because it was only when the opposing team had a black player, who was getting racist abuse, that you said to yourself: hang on a second, why are they [the home fans] ... abusing that black player on the other side? I'm playing for you, how can you cheer me one second, and be slagging him off the next? And that happens today ... I could detect in my early days that there was a little bit more affection and a little bit more protection from the fans. They were conscious of the fact that I was black, and very aware of what the other fans were saying about one of their players. It was rather a mixed loyalty. It was only when other fans gave their black players stick that they didn't like it ... but they were quite at liberty to give other [opposing] black players stick.*
>
> (GC)

Recognising that there is a structure and a logic to apparent blind hate, it becomes easier to understand why the adoration of some black players can exist beside the crude racist baiting of others. An awareness about the uneven nature of racist reaction may also explain why some black players are less willing to accept it as having a genuinely racist motive; and instead see it as an attempt to distract them. This is not the same as naively assuming that all verbal abuse is a diversionary tactic, rather than an authentic statement of belief. But Regis, Offiah and Anderson have endorsed a more 'neutral' assessment of the verbal racist abuse they received. These three have successfully plied their trades for large, well-supported clubs, and claimed to have received the extremes of abuse and adoration from both sets of fans. Anderson reflected on his playing days in the 1970s:

> *I remember ... I made my debut [for Nottingham Forest] on the Saturday and we played Newcastle ... they had a fantastic team then ... and the*

atmosphere was incredible. I wouldn't go out on the pitch prior to the game because I was so nervous, 'cause you always go out and look at the pitch to see what studs you need and things like that ... but when I came out ... the reaction was unbelievable ... the atmosphere and everything else ... I got lots of cheers and boos. But the longer the game went on, and the more they saw I could play, the more the boos diminished, funnily enough. [In] ... Newcastle, they didn't see many black faces anyway, and you couldn't have gone to a worse place at that time for that sort of [racist] abuse, so it was a learning process. And at certain times in certain situations it does happen but now there's only isolated incidents and ... they're more personal than generalised, just like they were when I started because they'd never seen many black faces ... I always hark back to the times when I was at Nottingham Forest. There was lad called Terry Hennessy, who had a bald

Figure 4.1   Viv Anderson

head, and everywhere we went he used to get abuse, just because he had a
bald head and it was somebody to focus on that afternoon. [Colour wasn't
important]... but I was the reason at Newcastle that night... if you go for
a throw and somebody says something, I just used to smile and that used
to infuriate them even more, so that was my way of just saying you're an
idiot... I'd say something quick that they couldn't reply to, 'cause I just got
on with the throw-in, but it never ever affected me, I made sure it never
affected me... I wanted to be in the team next week.

(VA)

Regis, too, can be said to have turned a 'negative into a positive'.
Reflecting on the 1970s, he claims that they were 'difficult times', when
a cacophony of abuse from supporters was often accompanied by abuse
from fellow professionals. Like Offiah (see below) and Anderson, his
riposte was to do his job well. Regis's view on the 'tactical' nature of this
abuse was reinforced because, once outside the sports stadium, he
claimed to command the 'respect' of the self-same people who hours
earlier had been baiting him.

And according to Offiah:

... Some people may not be intentionally racist but you know don't get me
wrong, there are people who are, and I have received that. If you're gonna
go into sport, any kind of sport, you're gonna have to be pretty strong to
battle against a lot of negativity, and I think I can be quite sort of philo-
sophical about it because I've been successful... stuff like that [racist
abuse] spurred me on... for some reason... I kind of flourished in that
environment... I just felt that I was the centre of attention. I was this
black guy that just came from nowhere. I scored lots of tries. The people
that I was playing for [Widnes] adored me, and loved singing songs that
praised me... it was a bit comical really, a bit like watching wrestling...
the ones who hate you hissed you and the ones who loved you cheered you,
and you was the centre of attention... but if my career was not success-
ful, then I might be sitting here telling you a different story, which some
people do. Some people say I don't believe that people should have to go
through that... [but] people abusing me and throwing bananas at me or
whatever, it just made me want to score a hat-trick even more... just
'cause a few people are throwing bananas at me, I wasn't going to let that
make me go back and live in my mum's small back room again... some-
one calling you a black bastard, that doesn't really hurt me to be that hon-
est, at the end of the day.

(MO)

By ignoring the terrace abuse, and letting their skills 'do the talking', Anderson, Regis and Offiah believe they showed 'character', not to mention a professional attitude. And not unlike Hull, they reproduce a popular sporting vocabulary and rationale on the issue. Anderson claimed to be aware of the (past and present) negative experiences of his fellow black professionals. But remarkably, he could not recall personally being affected or impeded in football because of his colour; let alone being abused by his fellow professionals (by contrast, see Parkinson *et al.*, 2001).

The significance of 'race' in the construction of British identity has been emphasised, to varying degrees, by both Henderson and Tebbit (Chapter 2). On first reading, Lawrence's own experience of playing for England, against the West Indies, seemed to endorse Tebbit's scepticism:

> *I would honestly say that I got more negativity when I played for England in ninety-one, against the West Indies, from the West Indian supporters, than I did with the English supporters, which just disappointed me more than anything else. The fact is that I'm born here. A lot of black kids, second generation, third generation, are born here. It's no good us saying 'I don't wanna play for England, I wanna play for the West Indies' and this, and that . . . that is no good. It's up to us, to lead the way . . . It was a question of 'why you playing for them'? Well, because I'm English. I was born and bred here, that should never be an issue . . . I remember when Tebbit said that there was more West Indian supporters supporting the West Indies. But where are they when the West Indies are not playing? Why aren't they shouting for England, and a lot of them are from here?*
>
> (DL)

A decade later (June 2001), and one week after racial disturbances in the North of England (Chapter 2), England captain Nasser Hussain queried why the large number of English-born Asian fans present at a test match were not supporting England against Pakistan (Buruma, 2001). Echoing Henderson, black and Asian people would simply appear to be expressing a 'natural, instinctive' aversion to supporting their country of birth. However, what really emerges is the need for an analysis taking account of how and why sport is used by non-white groups in Britain to re-establish diasporic identity connections; and a recognition of how global processes have made it more difficult for some migrant groups to conform to a singular national identity.

'Race' and media representations

> There are teams where you have got players who, from a distance, look almost identical. And, of course, with more black players coming into the game, they would not mind me saying that that can be very confusing.
>
> **John Motson, sports commentator**

Research on the media representation of minority ethnic groups in sport has focused overwhelmingly on *black males*. The general tone of these findings is that the mainstream media plays a key role in perpetuating the types of racial stereotypes about black and Asian people in sport that have been encountered elsewhere in this book; and which mirror stereotypes about these groups in other areas of social and cultural life (Davis and Harris, 1998). A more polite language of 'cultural difference' is less blatantly racist today than in the 1970s (Gilroy, 1993). The resultant media discourses, which no longer emphasise 'race', are more elusive and abstract when referring to the effects of genetics and biology.

Media representations of black sportsmen have helped to reinforce the idea that their success is due to 'natural' athletic gifts; and is reflected in commentary about 'silky' skills and 'natural' rhythm. By contrast, white success in sport is due to hard work and application (see for example Jackson, 1989; Coakley, 1994; Staples and Jones, 1995; Andrews, 1996; Carrington, 2000). Whilst looking through my small archive of newspaper material, I encountered a more subtle manifestation of this racialised polarity. The front page of the *Guardian* sports supplement headlines the fortunes of two British athletes competing at the 2000 Olympic Games. Whilst white athlete Dean Macey 'pushes himself into decathlon contention', black boxer Audley Harrison 'dances his way to a boxing semi-final' (28 September).

As a 'natural' sequitur to this thinking, white sportsmen rely on their intelligence and powers of mental acuity; whereas black sportsmen rarely do. Descriptions of the playing talents of black and white footballers have been viewed through this particular lens. For example, in a 1993 television documentary, Ron Noades, then chairman of Crystal Palace football club, commented on the level of physical fortitude offered by his (predominantly black) team:

> The problem with black players is they've got great pace, great athletes, love to play with the ball in front of them . . . when it's

behind them it's chaos. I don't think too many of them can read the game. When you are getting into midwinter in England, you need a few of the maybe hard white men to carry the artistic black players through.

(cited in Bose, 1996, p. 84)

And Rosenbaum (1995) found that while black sportsmen were portrayed as self-centred, selfish, arrogant and money-oriented, white sportsmen were portrayed as unselfish team players.

Sport is a key site of white male ambivalence about the black male body (Mercer, 1994). Whereas black males are highly visible in the tabloid press particularly as threats to civil society, in sport they are also revered for their athleticism and prowess. Given classic stereotypes about black sexuality, it is not surprising that this ambivalence can spill over into the sexual objectification of the black sportsman. Nowhere in Britain was this perhaps better illustrated than with the Olympics of 1992 and press coverage of Linford Christie. Having distinguished himself by winning the prestigious 100 metre final, the tabloid press chose to run a series of features about Christie's 'lunch box': a crude reference to his anatomy, based on sexual stereotypes about the black body (see for example Kitching, 1992).

For Mercer, any white antagonism about the black body has been resolved through the media's 'paternalistic infantilisation' of such sportsmen as Frank Bruno: a strategy that elevates them 'to the status of national mascots and adopted pets' (1994, pp. 178–9). The essence of this characterisation, that black people are childlike, irresponsible, and playful, has an historical linearity in media portrayal. For instance, Cashmore remarked that the popularity of the Harlem Globetrotters basketball team in the 1970s was 'accountable in terms of its members conformity to the image of a black man as physically adept but lacking in the intellectual equipment to harness his skill to firm objectives' (1982, p. 20). More recently, it is clear from media commentary on the 2002 football World Cup that African players perform 'tricks', whilst European players show flashes of 'skill'.

Even views on racial aptitudes which appear laudatory can be loaded with subtly negative inferences. Arsene Wenger, a (French) manager of English football club Arsenal, was interviewed in a British newspaper on the subject of French football. In the course of explaining the recent spectacular success of the French national side (in 1998, France won the football World Cup; in 2000, the European Championship), he asserted that:

The make-up of the national team benefits from the variety of ethnic origins of the players ... For example, our black players have special qualities. I think black sportsmen have a certain advantage, and in football it shows itself in an explosive speed ... And that bit is genetic. The rest is culture and education. But the genetic bit can't be added.

(cited in Williams, 2000, p. 5)

Intentionally or not, Wenger infers that black sporting attributes do not 'naturally' extend to constructive thought on the field of play: this must be taught. And as he doesn't mention what their white team mates bring to the game, we can only assume that these are the 'traditional' virtues of intelligence, and control of the direction of play. Wenger's prognosis brooked no dissent with the author of the article. Williams failed to challenge the basis of the link made between sport and biology, concentrating instead on how best to maximise it. In this vein, the article went on to suggest that once Britain's 'explosive' sportsmen are 'nurtured within a culture of trust and encouragement', then their genetic attributes could be exploited in the same way. Both the standing of Wenger in the British game, and the aforementioned success of the French 'formula', give his views a strong credence and legitimacy. Once again, we can see how whiteness is reinforced through a sports culture that prioritises attributes such as 'explosive speed' in black athletes, over others. And as we have seen (Chapter 3), these views are endorsed by minority groups themselves, further extending their influence.

A binary division between 'instinct' and 'intelligence' is specifically constructed with reference to the attributes of black and white centre-forwards in English football. Writing anecdotally, and as an avid fan of the English game, I have very rarely heard a black forward described as 'intelligent'. The accolade is regularly extended to such white players as Eidur Gudjohnsen, Teddy Sheringham, Alan Shearer and Ruud Van Nistelrooy, even though black strikers Jimmy Floyd Hasselbaink and Thierry Henry face the same opponents on a weekly basis and score as many, if not more, goals. The strike partnership of Gudjohnsen and Hasselbaink is a prime illustration of the different ways that black and white players are racially ascribed. Hasselbaink is regularly described in televised commentary as having pace, power, strength, and possessing a ferocious shot; whilst Gudjohnsen provides the intelligent runs and crosses, and scores intelligent goals. When Dwight Yorke and Andy Cole formed such a devastating strike partnership in Manchester United's treble trophy winning season (1998/99), their understanding was described as 'telepathic': again, an inference to its 'instinctual' nature.

Chapter 3 made reference to a link created between 'pathological' black family structures, and black children's enthusiasm for sport. According to media research findings, the black family is also responsible for the *adult* sportsman's 'excesses'. Cole and Denny (1994) found that the almost exclusively black American Basketball Association was depicted by the media as an uncontrolled and addictive 'ghetto' in the 1970s and 1980s: principally with regards to sexual appetite, substance abuse and an unrestrained style of play (see also McDonald, 1996). The deviant behaviour of black athletes was simply a consequence of the moral turpitude to be found in black communities, and reflected in disproportionate levels of welfare dependency, single-parent families and drug-taking. McDonald (1996) argued that the re-marketing of a cash-strapped, 'ghettoised' NBA, and of Michael Jordan, its most remarkable star, involved distancing both from the eroticism, atavism and drug excesses that were seen to characterise it. In other words if not the athletes themselves, then certainly the 'spectacle', would be less stereotypically 'black'.

Research has suggested that media reporting over-emphasises the degree to which white 'father-figures' have aided some black men in their professional and private lives. Again, this inflection is consistent with a narrative of black family dysfunction. By the same token, a white patriarch is essential to control excessive black masculinity, so that the black sportsman can be refocused towards more socially beneficial aims (Carrington, 2000, p. 135). In recent times, the most powerful confirmation of the need for a guiding mentor was seen with the careers of two high-profile US sports figures: baseball star Darryl Strawberry, and boxer Mike Tyson. Media coverage of both athletes has highlighted the ways in which their self-destructive, errant behaviour resulted in them wasting their 'natural' talents. In the case of Strawberry, a number of white mentors and coaches have publicly bemoaned that they should have done more to save his career; whilst Tyson's much-reported slide into trouble outside the ring has been traced to the loss of his white mentor, Cus D'Amato (see for example Steen, 1999). The true significance of influential figures in both of their lives is really a matter for conjecture. However, the emphases in each account, and therefore wider public understandings of them, correspond with an historical stereotype of black people as child-like, undisciplined, and unable to look after themselves.

In the absence of a representative proportion of professional Asian sportsmen, the worst excesses of British sports journalism have been focused on overseas cricketers such as the Pakistan national team. It has already been noted that relations between the two cricketing sides were characterised by rancour and accusations of cheating (Chapter 2). Headlines were at their most inflammatory during the tours of 1987 and 1992, and had social consequences for Asian groups outside of the professional game (Williams, 2001). The following headlines provide a flavour of this representation:

PAK YER BAGS (*Sun*, 10th December 1987)

HOW PAKISTAN CHEAT AT CRICKET (*Daily Mirror*, 26th August 1992)

PAK OFF THE CHEATS FOR FIVE YEARS (*Sun*, 28th August 1992)

To some, headlines and articles in the British press were the thin end of a malignant wedge, stereotyping Pakistanis in general as untrustworthy and treacherous. A historical stereotype of the cunning native, out to dupe his colonial master, provided a strong subtext to this narrative (see for example Tennant, 1994; Marqusee, 1998).

What were the interviewee's experiences of, and broader awareness about, the sorts of trends noted above? A number (Anderson, Singh, Hull, Sanigar, Haque) claimed not to have been aware of the ways that language, headlines and photographs combine to produce racialised media coverage in sports (or, indeed, in other spheres). In my view, Hull, Anderson and Sanigar have most easily endorsed a construction of the nation as relatively free from limitations imposed by racism; and in which skin colour is less of an impediment than relations of social class. Hull's thoughts about 'stacking' and Anderson's reflections on the abuse he encountered as a player (see above) are consistent with this ideological framework.

The remainder of the interviewees expressed the view that sports coverage of black and Asian people was prone to stereotyping; even though Regis was emphatic that black football players were now exploding myths about temperament and limited tactical awareness. The majority described their *own* media coverage as ranging from 'good' (particularly in the local media) to 'satisfactory'. At one end of this spectrum, Hull claims that both the local and national press conveyed their shock and sympathy that he wasn't selected for the England World Cup squad in 1995.

Even when media coverage was interpreted more 'ambivalently', this was rationalised strategically. The more high-profile names (such as

Offiah, Lawrence, Regis) referred to an inter-dependent relationship existing between the media and popular culture. It was recognised that the
(mostly entertainment-oriented) media lays increasing claim to people's
private lives as a consequence of burgeoning 'celebrity culture'. This is
accompanied by journalism which seeks to extend the margins of exposé,
stereotyping, chastisement and praise, in its efforts to 'sell' media product. Offiah in particular has experienced negative and positive extremes
of reporting, and now recognises this as 'part of the media game'.

But Gardener and Viera found journalist codes about the *quantity* of
coverage less easy to accept. Referring to Linford Christie, Gardener
noted:

> *The lunch box story [above] ... is a classic from the* Sun. *I mean ... he's*
> *become a national joke ... That's not nice to see when he's won an*
> *Olympic gold medal ... It's so strange that if you win an Olympic gold*
> *medal, and achieve the highest possible award there is in the sport, it might*
> *only make a small paragraph on the back page ... but as soon as Michael*
> *Owen scores a goal, for instance England versus Germany which is only a*
> *world cup qualifying game ... front pages, every newspaper ... Certainly*
> *the media just go crazy, and that's not the same for other sports, especially*
> *when the athletes like [Mr X] are not white ... and all the athletes are*
> *aware of that, and it is a problem.*

> (JG)

Gardener's use of 'all' (last sentence) is a reference to the high number
of non-white athletes in the British team. Gardener hinted at the feelings of resentment that sometimes manifest themselves against white
sprinters. To him, and apparently to his black colleagues in the Great
Britain squad, these athletes are portrayed as 'Great White Hopes' in a
predominantly black discipline like sprinting. As such, they are seen to
command a level of media attention inappropriate to their relatively
modest achievements (see also 'Joice Maduaka', Chapter 6).

Viera took umbrage with a martial arts publication that had promised
him a full front-page picture and lead story. Instead, his picture was rele-
gated to the top corner, and the lead story was given to an up-and-
coming (white) martial artist. Viera felt that this 'mistreatment' of black
martial artists, new or established, was 'typical', and commented:

> *This guy, nobody really knows him ... I've been around a lot longer, more*
> *people are going to know me ... the interviewer told me that he [white*
> *fighter] couldn't string a sentence along, because he hasn't done nothing. In*

his interview . . . all you see is loads of pictures . . . they're trying to promote him but he hasn't got a lot to say so they can't write a lot about him . . . but if you look at my interview . . . look how much more writing there is . . . I'm not trying to make myself out as a big head, but I'm looking and thinking . . . is that a racial thing or what? . . . do they think, 'well, we can't have him central?' . . . for years there's been a big influence of black people within the martial arts . . . with a black face winning the competitions . . . and it's like they've <u>got</u> to put them in the magazine <u>because</u> they're winning . . . but once some white guy comes in and starts winning, they'll spread it everywhere. Boom boom boom boom, new white guy on the block, boom!

(SV)

For Viera, there is less of a political (read commercial?) will to promote black sportsmen. He referred to a nebulous, difficult to measure *feeling*, even when coverage was forthcoming. The sense of a disparity between actions and personal beliefs is supported by Back *et al.*'s reference to a 'dual vocabulary' on race; this time in football. Their findings pointed to less 'palatable' views conveyed in the private sphere of the boardroom, bar and training ground; and more inclusive noises, aimed at fostering good relations with minority ethnic groups, for press releases and the like (2001).

Crooks considered the 'ambivalent' nature of ideas about black prowess. He recalled that:

. . . some of the people who were covering me while I was playing for the Spurs [in the 1980s] . . . I've got to know personally and I've been in the company of many of them . . . nevertheless, the coverage [was] . . . typical of people of their generation. So what I'm saying is that they would respond to me and what I did with clichéd comment. It would be the 'Black Pearl' or the 'Black Panther'. I remember one particular opening paragraph from a journalist which talked about chickens and signs that were attributable more to voodoo than the copy on the sports page. But because he was talking about a black player, and obviously been reading some novel, he thought he'd be very clever by making some correlation between the black player, and the occasion, and the moment . . . but he couldn't understand why it bothered me . . . why I was so sensitive.

(GC)

Leaving aside the hilarious reference to Haitian practices, Crooks earned the same sobriquet assigned to rugby league player Ellery Hanley at the time ('Black Pearl'). Both names define their 'Otherness', as *black* men, and their unique status in the white, male culture of their sports (see Spracklen, 2001).

Small has commented on a racialised typology used for black sportsmen during international competition. In his view: 'when a black runner came first in a race against foreigners, he was "English". If he came second, he was "British". If he lost, he was "coloured". If he cheated he was "West Indian"' (1994, p. 62). A number of the interviewees supported the theme of this observation, concerning the media's 'de-nationalising' of black athletes. In Gardener's words:

> *The press only want the sportsperson to be British, part of 'us', when the athletes are winning, not when there is a dispute or problems. Look at Linford Christie. Whenever he's done well, he's British. As soon as there were problems he would be Jamaican, back to where he's come from.*

(JG)

In Gardener's view, 'race' is conflated problematically with nation because, for black and Asian athletes, national belonging is contingent on the degree of sporting success. Not unlike Henderson's biological assertion (Chapter 2), these comments point to a spurious way of measuring national loyalty and allegiance, and imply that black and Asian people who don't win aren't trying hard enough.

Gardener also made reference to what can be termed a 'normative code of comparison' in media sports commentary. He stated:

> *... it's funny, because I was talking to Carl [Saunders] who played for Bristol Rovers, and he said that they used to call him Billy Ocean [after the singer] and that it's about his perm. And it's funny because now he's got dreadlocks he says: 'I can't get away from that nickname you know, now that Billy Ocean's got dreadlocks!' ... Why is it that we always get nicknames, and the white players don't? Emile Heskey [football] is Bruno, and so is Devon Malcolm [cricket]. Just more black players being stereotyped.*

(JG)

In his view, the media's sport's 'primary definers' (the coterie of sports writers and commentators whose opinions are well-respected and frequently referred to) invariably compare the physical attributes of one black sportsman with another black sportsman. By this criteria, sports identification is reduced to the primary basis of 'race'. This tendency was strikingly illustrated by veteran sports commentator John Motson (whose quote appears at the start of this section (cited in Bowcott, 1998,

p. 2)). In a radio interview, Motson suggested that it was difficult to tell black players apart.

Given the prevailing feeling that some of the interviewees have about racialised media coverage, do they aspire to contribute themselves? All, with the exception of Haque, have written media articles and/or been studio guests commentating on live sport. Most notably, Crooks works as a high-profile BBC sports journalist and interviewer. From his comments, it is possible to discern the kernel of a wider political philosophy, as well as career motivation:

> *In 1998, if you're a professional footballer coming to the end of your career or effectively finished your career, you'd better be in a position to articulate your views and understand the arguments otherwise much of what you will have achieved will be wasted. Because it's my view that if you don't have those views itemised and analysed, it's lost. So I would encourage black players to understand what has happened to them, and what is happening to them. Understand the argument, sharpen your argument, and enter the debate. Otherwise, the abuses will continue to abound . . . I'm particularly concerned at this moment in time that there are no black players on the PFA management committee, so how will the management committee understand what black players are thinking, what they're feeling, what the fears are for the new generation, for Sol Campbell and Rio Ferdinand, and players like that coming in? There's no use limiting your arguments and your discussions [about racism] to the pubs, the clubs, the shabeens and the raves . . . and that's what I've learned over the years. If you can articulate your arguments then people have to listen! And by asking them questions, they've got to go away, and come back with damn good answers.*
>
> (GC)

Concluding remarks

This chapter has looked at the impact of racialised ideas and practices on the interviewees' 'career' years. In making sense of racist abuse and racialised media coverage, a number of the more successful black sportsmen have endorsed a conformist sporting vocabulary. As indicated in Chapter 1, 'conformity' is a feature of the *whiteness* of sports cultures, and seems essential to progress and longevity at the highest levels in sport. But the diametral interpretations of two successful sportsmen, Garth Crooks and Paul Hull, are worth commenting on. Both convey a sense that their sport's traditions, and the social class base of their supporters, are fundamental to how they are received as black sports-men. Isolated incidents of overt racism obscured institutionalised forms for Hull; and could be interpreted neutrally precisely *because* they were isolated incidents. Whereas the predominantly working-class game of football, less influenced than other sports by the 'civilising processes' moderating aggressive behaviour (see for example Murphy *et al.*, 1990), have a long and intense tradition of racist abuse. For Crooks, the char-acter of this abuse provided a quite different interpretation as to its meaning, and heightened his awareness about more subtle racist processes.

The Asian sportsmen, with a lower presence in professional sport, and qualitatively different stereotypes around their participation, have been less affected by the racism directed at black sportsmen. Furthermore, and in common with a number of their black compatriots, they have endorsed views and attitudes which are central to reinforcing whiteness in sports.

Part II will look at the ways in which sport, race and gender interact to shape the experiences of minority ethnic women in sport.

Part II
'Race', Gender and Sport

5
Women and Sport

Sportswomen interviewed for this study will have their names printed in italics.

Introduction

Chapter 5 will highlight the ways in which patriarchy (or structures of male domination), has constrained women in sport, and show how the struggle for gender equality has obscured concerns of 'race', social class and sexuality. Certain sports have featured prominently as sites of struggle over women's rights to participate on their own terms. And whilst changing social ideas have led to greater sports access and freedom, women's sport illustrates that certain expectations, assumptions and patterns of behaving still serve as 'norms' for female behaviour.

Women's sport, men's control

Chapter 1 has outlined the value of Gramsci's hegemony to understanding whiteness in male sports. Sports *feminists* (see below) have also adapted the concept, as a tool to analyse gender relations in this sphere. Victorian Britain has been identified by feminists as a critical time when the dominant power role of 'élite' (white, middle and upper class) males was being threatened. Sport was seen as a key site on which social struggle for control of the physical body took place. Conflicts centred on the differences and similarities between male and female bodies: in terms of what each was physically capable of; and how they should be allowed to exercise from an early age (Connell, 1987; Crossett, 1990; Majors, 1990). Control over the leisure patterns of women was partly achieved by limiting their participation to 'feminine-appropriate' sports which emphasised aesthetics and grace over strength and speed (Polley, 1998). Not surprisingly, women have historically enjoyed most autonomy in supposedly 'gendered' sports like tennis and croquet, and faced most discrimination in traditionally 'masculine' ones like cricket and football. The latter were classic examples of sports deemed unsuitable for women because they were seen to transgress established norms about masculinity and femininity. A brief account of their past histories can only provide a *flavour* of the ideological struggles over women's right to participate.

Women's cricket and football have been shaped by uneven relations of power, and sex stereotyping. Women's cricket has a history of having to fight the men's hierarchy for legitimacy, partly because cricket was one sport that seemed particularly threatening to conventional images of femininity, and to traditional ideas concerning women's inability to play sports (Flint and Rheinberg, 1976). Due to the intransigent attitudes in the men's game, women's cricket was forced to develop its own bureaucracy and administration and, as a result, the Women's Cricket Association was formed in 1926. Not surprisingly, the Association struggled for sufficient resources to develop and encourage women's cricket. And despite organising and winning the sport's first-ever World Cup less than fifty years later (1973), it spent the intervening years hampered by the failure of the men's game to recognise women's cricket, and to take it seriously. Hargreaves has shown how, at various times, the professional men's game sought to sideline women's cricket, and endorse a masculine ideology and culture which have proved to be exclusionary, and denigrating of women (1994). Women's football has also been characterised by struggles for recognition and legitimacy, even whilst growing as a spectator and participator sport. The popularity of the women's game was evident in 1920, when the first international held between two women's teams drew a crowd of over 25,000. This success was followed by the largest crowd ever recorded for a women's game. Around 53,000 people saw Dick, Kerr's Ladies team beat St Helens Ladies 4–0.

Football, like women's cricket, has been reliant on the largesse of the men's game for playing resources and sponsorship, and has also been subject to men's control. An FA ban in 1921, which prevented women from playing football on league grounds, illustrates the magnitude of struggle for the women's game to acquire credibility. The ban was ostensibly due to concerns about the correct use for money raised for war. But in truth, it was a move to stifle the women's game, as evident from the following statement released by the FA. As a result of 'complaints' being made about 'football being played by women', wrote the FA, 'the

Council feel impelled to express their strong opinion that the game of football is quite unsuitable for females and ought not to be encouraged' (FA, n.d). Motivated by this belief, the FA failed to develop and encourage women's football. Not surprisingly, attendance at women's football games declined, as did the numbers of women's football teams. The ban, which effectively ended the inter-war interest in the women's game, was not lifted until 1972.

Strategies for change: feminism(s)

Feminism, both as an intellectual activity and a political strategy, has a long history (Spender, 1983), having developed in response to gender inequalities and oppressions in society. More directly, feminist literature has paid little attention to women's involvement in sport before 1970, because wider gender struggles assumed priority. But by the late 1970s, feminist sports sociology emerged as a reaction to male dominance in this area; and sport (along with the family, and work and pay) came to be viewed as an important site for the reproduction of gender oppression. Feminist analyses of sport developed mainly in the US and, according to Messner and Sabo (1990, p. 2):

> uncovered a hidden history of female athleticism, examined sex differences in patterns of athletic socialization, and demonstrated how the dominant institutional forms of sport have naturalized men's power and privilege over women. The marginalization and trivialization of female athletes, it was demonstrated, serve to reproduce the structural and ideological domination of women by men.

Three main feminist perspectives have provided theoretical frameworks to analyse the problematic of sport and gender. Broadly speaking, these *radical*, *liberal* and *socialist* approaches have had an uneasy coexistence: although their ideological differences have been overstated (Donovan, 1985; Tong, 1989; hooks, 1994).

To facilitate a movement for greater equality, liberal feminists call for unconditional increases in participation, access at all levels, and resources. However, a number of feminist writers have perceived serious limitations in the liberal feminist agenda for change. It has been argued that the changes advocated by liberal feminists cannot exist in a vacuum, and would need to be accompanied by a fundamental transformation of capitalist and patriarchal structures (Birrell and Cole, 1994; Costa and Guthrie, 1994). Without these transformations, increased opportunities for women to compete in male-dominated sports (and to wield power at administrative levels) would simply result in their co-option by a 'dominant patriarchal value system'. In other words whiteness, existing as normative *male* privilege, is reinforced through the adoption of sexist values which limit how women access and engage with sport. Equally important for this study, liberal feminism has been criticised for assuming that women are an homogenous group who experience gender oppression in the same ways and that, therefore, an increase in participation rates would benefit them all as a whole.

In many ways, the process towards a more inclusive feminism was helped by a closer examination of patriarchy. Radical feminism views patriarchy as the fundamental source of women's oppression, universalising male domination and female subordination (see for example Strinati, 1995). However, an emphasis on patriarchy has given rise to a focus in feminist scholarship on the cultural politics of sexism; obscured the varying forms that male domination takes; ignored women's power to resist and subvert these; and used a white, middle-class template for understanding the experiences of *all* women. 'Liberating' feminist strategies (both in the US and the UK) therefore compromised women who felt that the real weight of their own disadvantage would be better understood with reference to social class, 'race', religion, sexuality or permutations of these factors (see also hooks, 1981; Baca Zinn *et al.*, 1986).

In the 1960s, a vibrant black liberation movement defined the politics of civil equality and cultural liberation in terms of a 'racial' struggle. In so doing, the movement obscured issues of gender oppression and sexuality affecting women in black communities. For this reason, black American women argued that they had been positioned as black first, and black *women* second. A distinct, self-conscious black feminism developed in the US in the early 1970s, to challenge black male politics, and to address perceived limitations in white feminist agendas. With white and black feminisms seemingly moving in parallel, bell hooks conveys a sense of the frustration felt during crosscultural exchanges aimed at finding common ground for 'progress'. In her view:

> Visions of solidarity between women necessarily became more complex. Suddenly, neither the experiences of materially privileged groups of white females nor the category 'woman' (often used when the specific experiences of white women were referred to) could be evoked without contestation, without white supremacy looming as the political ground of such assertions. These changes strengthened

the power of feminist thought and feminist movement politically. They compelled feminist thinkers to problematize and theorize issues of solidarity, to recognize the interconnectedness of structures of domination, and to build a more inclusive movement.

(1994, p. 102)

Academic literature on both sides of the Atlantic prioritised the interests of certain women's groups. In the 1980s, British black and Asian feminists challenged the epistemology of this white feminism (Scraton, 2001). In common with their African-American counterparts, they argued that issues of ethnicity and racism were marginalised in this area, with stereotypes of sporting femininity only recognisable as those of middle-class, privileged, white (heterosexual) Western women.

The specific struggles of black and 'coloured' women in South African sport, and of women in Muslim countries, can illustrate the dangers of standardising a female experience of gender oppression. The unremitting significance of 'race' in apartheid South Africa had created an effective smokescreen hiding the perpetuation of gender inequality. And, in the struggle for racial liberation, gender issues were seen to be of secondary importance. This meant that non-white women, in contrast to their white Western counterparts, had to contend with virtually no consideration for their particular needs; whilst men claimed the lion's share of sports access, resources and facilities (Hargreaves, 1997). And when Hassiba Boulmerka won the 1500 metres final at the 1992 Olympic Games, she returned to Algiers to be booed and jeered by Islamic fundamentalists, objecting to her competing in shorts and a vest (Mackay, 1998). These reactions confirmed her unwitting status as a symbol of the struggle between liberal modernisers, and traditionalists fearful of the spread of Western ideas and influence.

By ignoring the significance of such factors as 'race' and religion, British black and Asian feminists argued that they too were part of a wider feminist movement that limited the full expression of their identities: in other words, that they were women first, and *black* women second. Furthermore, the usefulness of feminist academic literature was seen to be diminished by the practice of *theorising* itself. In Birrell's view:

Women of color fear that under the auspices of White feminists, feminism and feminist theory are losing their critical and radical edge. And these women strongly resist the tendencies in theory to abstract, generalize, and to reword experience, fearing that their concerns and experiences will be overlooked, devalued, or actively subverted. They do not trust White middle-class academics, both women and men, who act as custodians and guardians of theory. It has not escaped the attention of women of color that those of us who have the most to say about theorizing difference say it in the most inaccessible way, to privileged audiences who need specialized schooling to render the discourse comprehensible.

(1990, pp. 188–9)

As indicated above, British women's *access* to sport and leisure has partly been defined in social class terms (Wimbush, 1986; Talbot, 1988; Hargreaves, 1989; Pahl, 1990). Women's sports are seen to have a 'middle-class' character, because of the disproportionately high rates of access and control exercised by members of this group, relative to working-class women. Partly as a consequence, British socialist feminism is concerned with understanding complexities in the relationship between class, gender and power.

Due to the influence of black and Asian feminists, socialist feminism also links gender inequality to other forms such as 'race', and perhaps offers a more sophisticated and relevant critique than its radical and liberal counterparts. In theory, even a minor recognition that not all women experience gender oppression to the same degree, or in the same ways, represented an advance in feminist scholarship on freedoms and limitations. In practice however, the importance of 'race' as a source of women's oppression has become marginalised by an overall focus on patriarchal capitalism. Within this intellectual paradigm, a *new critical sport studies* fails to account for the full variation in systems of domination, disproportionately focusing on class dynamics (Messner and Sabo, 1990). By assuming that class structures women and black people's oppression in sport, complexities in the relationship between class, 'race', gender and sexuality are still 'glossed over' at best, and ignored at worst (Birrell, 1989; Jarvie, 1995; Mirza, 1997).

The development of a more sophisticated epistemology has to battle against certain 'traditions' that have preoccupied sports sociology generally, being chiefly an almost exclusive focus on black male athletes (Jarvie, 1995; see also Part I). The presence and accomplishments of black British sportsmen have generated considerable academic enquiry, focusing overwhelmingly on working-class males of African origin. Critical sports analysis has paid little attention to experiences of black and Asian women, and to the ways that sports are engendered and racialised (Zaman, 1997). Sports sociology has also been slow to recognise the significance of masculine identity constructions.

The critique of whiteness is important to de-centre men as a dominant, hegemonic group wielding power (Hearn, 1984; Frankenberg, 1993).

'Race' and gender in sport

Given the priorities of sports sociology, it is not surprising that the involvement of South Asian and black women is an under-researched area of social enquiry. A small but growing body of research presents a sporting 'profile' of British Asian women that is more complex and less involved than for other women's groups: a fact increasingly recognised by community leisure providers (Parmar, 1995). The issues surrounding Asian women and sport further illustrate the danger of using a standard template to interpret the sporting experiences of all women.

South Asian women

If a positive commitment to sport is forthcoming in an individual's early years, it is likely to be maintained throughout their lifetime (Choi, 2000). School is perceived as the arena where Asian girls can achieve the most freedom and autonomy in sports. But research points to Asian girls being more likely than other groups to conform to traditional ideas about femininity and womanhood: ideas which are not easily reconciled with sporting activity. In the 'space' between traditional ideas, and failed strategies for reconciliation, common stereotypes about Asian girls have become widespread. Accordingly, the Asian girl is frail, has a meek temperament, and needs to be excused from school PE classes for religious reasons. Research findings suggest that these stereotypes condition teachers to assume that Asian girls will lack sporting ability and commitment, and to therefore not encourage them to take sport seriously (Verma and Darby, 1994; Lovell, 1995; Parmar, 1995; Bains and Johal, 1998). And in a context of low participation, widespread common beliefs and no representational role models at any level of professional sport, Asian girls are likely to endorse this general perception of themselves. In spite of these factors, research has challenged myths concerning Asian girls' lack of interest and enthusiasm for sports. For instance, studies found that an increase in Islamophobia (Chapter 2) has limited but not stopped Asian girl's enthusiasm for extra-curricular school sport (Parmar, 1995; Bains and Johal, 1998).

It is not surprising that stereotypes regarding women's unsuitability for physical sports become magnified for Asian women; since they are affected more acutely by ideas about 'passivity' and 'frailty' (Lewis, 1979;

Lyons, 1988; Raval, 1989). In fact, the extent to which sport is an almost exclusive male preserve amongst Britain's Asian groups has led Bains and Johal to ask some rhetorical questions:

> Have you ever seen an Asian woman running to catch a departing bus? Have you ever seen an Asian woman kicking a football, going for a jog, riding a bike or taking a swim in the local baths? . . . One of the rarest sights that is scarcely beheld in this country is that of an Asian female in the throes of physical or sporting activity.
>
> (1998, p. 194)

There is an almost total absence of Asian women in British professional and semi-professional sport. Instead, 'leisure' for South Asian women centres around religious events, weddings and community gatherings (Lovell, 1995). And since South Asian groups are generally likely to have more children, and extended family responsibilities which fall to the women (Modood *et al.*, 1998), this further limits their time for sports involvement. Whilst it is true that Asian groups in Britain generally experience greater social mobility than their black contemporaries (see Part I), economic factors affect certain communities disproportionately. Pakistanis and Bangladeshis are more likely to suffer deprivation broadly characteristic of non-white groups in Britain. The poorer, inner-urban areas where these women are concentrated limit the types of sports available. They are also areas where fears about racial and sexual harassment undermine the confidence to pursue a sporting interest after dark.

But the above is just a part of the story. Asian women *do* have an interest in sport, and research has advanced the need for a less orthodox model of sports development. A more inclusive model would consider different religions and cultures, and recognise the very real fears that some Asian groups have about becoming alienated from traditions. As such, Asian women's support for single-sex community sport is bound up with religious ideas about women not being scantily dressed in public, and not participating in 'mixed' sports activities (Hargreaves, 1994; Lovell, 1995). The model of sporting development is complicated because of the different attitudes that religious affiliations have to mixed sport, and to what constitutes 'appropriate' attire. So, as we will see in Chapter 6 below, these issues present *Myra Barretto* with fewer problems than *Azmina Mitha*.

African-Caribbean women

Historical debates on women's sport have endeavoured to uncover a 'hidden history' of their participation. But it perhaps indicates the magnitude of the gender struggle that, in general, there is silence on *black* women's historical contributions to, and experiences in, British sport. British football, for example, has no history of reference to players of African-Caribbean (or Asian) origin. The first comprehensive account charting women's (historical and current) involvement in professional football (Lopez, 1997) makes no specific reference to non-white players, or how they may have negotiated the additional hurdles of colour prejudice. This silence exists even in feminist accounts (Vertinsky and Captain, 1998).

In the last thirty years, there has undoubtedly been a greater presence of black than Asian women at all standards and levels of sport. Black British women looked to the US for sporting role models, following African-American women by making most progress in track-and-field athletics. In the 1970s and 1980s, the accomplishments of black British male athletes (Chapter 2) were accompanied by (for example) those of Mollie Samuel, Sonia Lannaman, and Tessa Sanderson. More recently, Denise Lewis, Ashia Hansen and *Joice Maduaka* have achieved a high degree of success in their respective disciplines. The greater presence of black than Asian women in sport is partly due to the different impact of cultural factors, and stereotypes about biology. And whilst these ideas have made sports participation more accessible for black women, they again signal the dangers of assuming that all women relate to sport in the same way. Racist stereotypes about African-Caribbean women challenge the boundaries between 'femininity', and the showing of physical aggression. As a result, the mainstream feminist focus on patriarchy obscures the cultural differences that give black women greater economic independence, and equality within the family (Phoenix, 1987; Mirza, 1992). According to research, black women's relative freedom to determine their own leisure patterns combines with a less constrained (although still racialised) culture of black femininity. This culture of femininity encourages 'sports appropriate' qualities such as physical assertiveness, aggression and competitiveness (Lovell, 1995). But the relationship between black women and sports participation creates a paradox. Enhanced potential for self-actualisation through sport is contained within an overall system of patriarchal values, and sustained by racist stereotypes around the 'over-sexed', 'aggressive' and 'naturally gifted' black woman. At any rate, given these cultural ideas and sporting stereotypes, it is feasible to suggest that black women's historical contributions to British sport have been under-stated.

In common with men's sport (Chapter 4), issues of 'race' can supersede gender in representations of black females. For instance, when black women have achieved in sport, their success has been credited to 'natural' ability; whereas white women's success is due to hard work and dedication (Hargreaves, 1994). English media coverage of the tennis playing Williams sisters (Venus and Serena), similarly illustrates the primacy of race in representations. The Williams sisters are arguably two of the most high-profile sportswomen in the world, plying their trade in a predominantly white sport. The classic story of their rise from the 'ghetto' to the pinnacle of the women's game fits comfortably into a narrative of racial prowess negating the effects of formidable obstacles, and sport as a realm of opportunity and meritocracy. Constant references in television commentary to their 'overtly physical' style of play, obscure the few references to their technique, skill and intelligence. The dominant narrative therefore fits into a race reductionist framework of black athletes with brawn and no brain.

Although black British women now have a strong presence in women's sports, close scrutiny of their participation highlights their continued concentration in a fairly narrow range of them (athletics, volleyball and basketball); and the low numbers who actually participate. Black women's sporting involvement is concentrated in the aforementioned sports, even though swimming, hockey and tennis are three of the most popular female sports. The latter two certainly require more in the way of resources to participate. It would appear, then, that issues of 'race', sport and social class are as inter-linked for black women as they are for black men. But since black women have fewer problems in formal education, they are less likely than (working-class) black men to see the urgency of sport as a career option (Chapter 3). Research suggests that black women perform as well as, if not proportionally better than, white women in education; and are also more likely to gain employment commensurate with their academic achievements (Modood *et al.*, 1998). And although there is no significant black female presence in sports management, coaching or administration, the appointment of Hope Powell (see below) is a sign of change.

Recent trends

A number of new paradigms have been discernible in women's sports participation. These changes, which are affecting women of all ethnic groups and social classes to some degree, are symptomatic of diminishing gender stereotypes about women's capabilities and temperaments, the impact of feminist research, and changing societal attitudes. Although, generally speaking, women still participate in sports less than men (Choi, 2000), it is significant that an increased interest in recent years encompasses traditionally 'male' sports. Women's rugby and football are growing in popularity. Both sports now have their own world cups, with England's footballers claiming the championship in 1988. Boxing, a sport deemed even less 'appropriate' for women than cricket, football or rugby, has a British champion in Jane Couch, and the daughters of two former male heavyweights (Muhammad Ali and George Frazier) also providing the inspiration for hopefuls. The achievements of élite women athletes bear close comparison with all but the finest men, particularly in running events like the (26 mile) marathon. Black women have a growing presence at the élite levels of rugby and football. Most notably, Paula George and Maxine Edwards are established rugby union internationals, whilst Hope Powell was appointed coach of the England women's football team in 1998.

Where their religion and culture are more adaptable to the Western pattern, the evidence also suggests that Asian women are joining football and netball leagues *en masse*. This is particularly the case in British cities like Leicester and Nottingham, where significant numbers of Asian groups have settled. Some local football clubs are responding to this interest by becoming more sensitive to the specific needs and constraints of Asian women, and are fairly successful at implementing schemes to promote the game of football among them (Arnot, 1998). Partly as a result, a growing number of young Asian women are playing top-class football at present. At the time of writing, Amy Sudan, Aman Dosanj and Permi Jhooti are plying their trade for Chelsea Ladies.

On the non-playing side, women increasingly 'anchor' sports programmes, offering commentary on men's events and competitions. A presence in this previously all-male preserve is matched by a (small but growing) cadre of female sports writers in print and radio journalism. Women's roles have also widened from the supporting or servicing functions in sports like cricket and football, where they have been incorporated as match officials and administrators (Polley, 1998). The growing importance of sport in women's lives has been recognised in other ways. Attempts by the FA to increase women's attendance at men's matches are part of a strategy aimed at broadening football's appeal, diluting the 'masculine' nature of live spectating, and allaying general anxieties about safety (Chapter 2). Equally, Powell's appointment (see above) was preceded by the launch of a women's national league, and a football school of excellence for girls. It is worth noting that women's football in Britain is attempting to be more globally competitive. By contrast, the women's game is already fairly well established in a number of other Western nations. On the continent of Europe, and in the US, women's football is growing far more rapidly, receives an enviable amount of media exposure, and is followed by large crowds at live games.

But in spite of more progressive attitudes towards women and sport, feminists of all persuasions argue that uneven relations of power continue to sustain men's overall power and privilege in this sphere. Gender is a constant, exacerbating the multilayered effects of discrimination also based on 'race', social class and sexual orientation. The vestiges of classic sexism that remain in women's sport indicate how, to paraphrase Hargreaves (1994), a hard-won acceptance needs to be defended; even whilst new meanings and definitions are being fought for.

As one symptom of this ambivalence, attempts to develop more inclusive sports cultures can instead highlight women's limited agency. In March 1991, the English FA rescinded its Rule 37, which had effectively banned mixed football in schools for under-11s. However, mixed football continues to face informal barriers to acceptance, with many schools failing to incorporate girls' football into their curricula. Scraton's research (1992) has also indicated that prevailing conceptions of 'femininity', and a limited definition of 'real' sports, still contribute to discouraging girls' participation, and to the labelling of sport as a masculine pursuit. This 'genderising' process starts in earnest in the childhood years. As well as ideas about femininity, powerful images of gender-appropriate behaviour, women's physical capacities, motherhood and sexuality are reinforced by the structure, content and teaching of girls' PE in British schools (Scraton, 1992). British ex-swimming champion Sharron Davis commented on the relationship between sport and these ideas for young girls. In so doing, she highlighted the ways that society and culture impose powerful conditions on the terms of participation. 'Sport', she stated, 'is part of the real world and it's normal to want to look nice. If we can stop talented girls leaving through making sport look sexy, it can only be good in the long run' (cited in Lindsey, 2000, p. 12).

Whereas males learn to be 'masculine' through sport, Young has written that females 'often experience our bodies as fragile encumbrances, rather than the media for the enactment of our aims' (1980, p. 147). This has obvious implications for how girls, when they become women, will have learned to approach and engage with sport, since confidence and aggression are valued in sporting relations. But it is unlikely that women will feel confident to participate if, as Choi (2000) argues, they do not conform to a 'sporty type' in the first place. Her research found that women who do not correspond to a thin, beautiful and sexy stereotype feel discouraged or unwelcome to participate in sport. Whilst Guthrie and Castelnuovo (1992) have made reference to patriarchal movement cultures that oppress women when they do engage in sport.

The predominantly masculine culture of sport determines that women's sexuality is expected to be heterosexual (Griffin, 1998). For sportswomen of whatever sexual preference, this can mean acting in ways which celebrate dominant definitions of heterosexuality, and which confirm rather than threaten norms about masculinity and femininity. There is an obvious analogy to be drawn with the ways that sporting codes constrain black and Asian men, preventing them from expressing more complex sporting identities (see Part I).

Gendered divisions are represented in numerous ways at the higher and more formalised levels of sport. In 1993, the Women's Football Association was incorporated into the FA. Whilst this has led to associated benefits for the women's game (greater financial backing, increased exposure and sponsorship; better coaches and facilities); it still indicates how development of the women's game is reliant on the men's. In spite of the recent success of the national side (winning the 1993 World Cup), women's football has received scant media coverage. And when this *has* been forthcoming, such as at the 2002 women's FA Cup final, half-empty stadia reinforced the impression that women's football is patronised, not taken seriously, and subject to indifference. And despite the aforementioned incentives for female supporters, a more 'family oriented' atmosphere at live sporting events can still be exclusionary of women. The 'lived realities' of football and rugby cultures are often celebrations of an exclusive, heterosexual masculinity (Polley, 1998).

The survival of these attitudes is graphically reflected in other sports regarded as traditionally masculine. Former British women's golf champion Vivien Saunders has written about the *informally* dissuasive attitudes of some golf clubs towards women players (2002; see also Horne *et al.*, 2000). And in a highly-publicised move in 1999, the Marylebone Cricket Club (MCC) finally opened its doors to admit women as members. However, the MCC has an 18-year waiting list, and operates strict criteria for membership. In short, these examples indicate that patterns of institutionalised discrimination are as difficult to tackle when women engage in sport, as they are in the context of minority ethnic participation.

Women and media representations

The under-representation of sportswomen in the media is accompanied by portrayals which emphasise their sexual attractiveness, and their roles as wives and mothers. Tuchman's claim that media representations of women 'symbolically annihilate' them (1978) therefore has a continuing relevance. Socialist feminists argue that the cultural industries produce representations of women that reflect society's dominant social values, rather than the diverse reality of women's lives. These 'symbolic representations' enable men to maintain their control of women through their bodies and sexuality (see Kane and Greendorfer, 1994).

Although overt media stereotyping of women in sport has decreased since 1990 (Duncan and Messner, 1998), feminist research has uncovered the ways in which journalistic norms contribute to the construction of racial and gender hierarchies (Messner *et al.*, 1993; Birrell and Cole, 1994; Creedon, 1994). 'Gender marking' of women's sports events is an important linguistic device that serves to diminish the significance of women's sport. For instance, references to *women's* world cups establish the men's event as the more significant norm. Evidence of the 'infantilising' of adult sportswomen, where they are referred to as 'girls' rather 'women', further contributes to sustaining a view that the 'serious' sporting world is a male one (MacDonald, 1995). And since an increasing number of former female professionals are making careers in media commentary, and are being trained within the same system of meanings and values, women can actually strengthen this culture of reporting. Ergo, socialist and radical feminists argue that a *transformation of patriarchal structures* (see above) is essential for genuine change.

When considering women's tennis, gender-marking and infantilising have been accompanied by other features of uneven relations. Evidence suggests that the circuit's more 'photogenic' players are sexualised and trivialised; whilst the achievements of its physically stronger ones are not given the recognition they deserve. In the first regard, the Director of Communications for the Women's Tennis Association claimed in 1997 that: 'Part of the beauty of women's tennis is what the players look like.' In this regard, tennis player Anna Kournikova epitomises the return of 'glamour' to the women's game. Described in tabloid newspapers as 'the Lolita of SW19 [area postcode for Wimbledon tennis championships]', she is noted for her 'good looks', and has a large number of internet websites set up by adoring fans (all cited in Viner, 1997, pp. 4–5). Although she has never won a major tennis tournament, a recent television programme (May 2002) estimated that she earns more from endorsements and sponsorship than the top five female players in the world combined. For this reason, the extensive publicity and quality of coverage given to Kournikova is not just a recognition that sex 'sells';

but is illustrative of how a cultural politics of sexism markets women by appearance rather than outstanding ability.

On the second point, there are noticeable differences in the media coverage of players who confirm dominant ideas about gender, and those who threaten these same ideas. Martina Hingis, the former world number one, has often been celebrated in media commentary for combining 'femininity' with 'intellect'. As such, her playing style is described using terms which are consistent with a feminine vocabulary, such as 'grace', 'finesse', and 'lightness of touch'. When Hingis is opposing more 'physical' players, commentary almost conveys the impression that she is outwitting clumsy and intellectually-regressed giants, whose only weapon in their tennis armoury is to smash the ball over the net. The comments of one journalist are typical. In his article, Hingis is described as: 'the queen of finesse in a women's game dominated by power . . . She is almost a throwback at 5ft 7in and just over nine stone – a woman who uses guile and intuition to repel her Amazon rivals' (Speck, 2002). It is significant also that Hingis is regularly credited as having a 'tennis brain', as a way of distinguishing her from her more 'atavistic' rivals. In this sense, her coverage, and the ways that it contrasts to that of Amelie Mauresmo and the Williams sisters (see also 'Joice Maduaka', Chapter 6), further illustrate how 'progress' in sport can be ambivalent. Similarly, lesbian athletes have been stigmatised through negative media portrayals, little interest from sponsors, and sustained challenges to their identity in media commentary. Evidence also suggests that women in aggressive contact sports have had stereotypically masculine traits over-emphasised (see for example Cauldwell, 1999; Wright and Clarke, 1999).

Although 'sex appropriate' sports like tennis, swimming, gymnastics and ice-skating receive the bulk of sponsorship and coverage, it generally runs a poor second to men's. At best, sponsorship for some women's sports can be patchy and uncertain, with sponsors concerned that women's sport lacks sufficient television exposure, and a suitable image for their products. This situation has prompted the Sports Sponsorship Advisory Service to advise women to 'play the sex appeal card to attract more media coverage and therefore more sponsorship' (cited in Gillan, 1999). Increasing numbers of high-achieving sportswomen have certainly recognised that sexuality appears to be the most effective way by which they can attract publicity. The 400-metre runner Marie Jose Perec, and the Australian women's football team, have posed semi-nude in an attempt to boost interest in their events, and to attract sponsorship. And as Carrington has confirmed, gender and 'race' collided with soft-porn photos of athlete Denise Lewis playing on stereotypes of the physically animalistic black female (2000). Men's sport seems just as affected by society's visual culture – the English rugby union team recently (2001) posed nude for a calendar. But this tends to be for charitable causes, and is not regarded as a serious way to raise essential funds at the highest levels of sport. The need to reconcile femininity with the sporting woman can be further illustrated by the popularity of 'new' sports like aerobics, that emphasise grace and aesthetics over strength and power (Hargreaves, 1994; Choi, 2000); and by developments in women's beach volleyball. In a move designed to promote the sexualised body, its world governing authority ruled that a compulsory crop-top be accompanied by bikini bottoms with a reduced waistband (Millar, 2000).

Finally, when women display these physical characteristics in more 'strength-based' sports, attempts have been made to 'feminise' them. The development of women's body-building is a case in point. New, aerobics-based categories like 'Miss Fitness', and 'Miss Figure', which have been introduced to appease the sponsors, show how these competitions have become increasingly preoccupied with femininity (Lane, 2000).

Concluding remarks

In spite of more progressive trends, women's agency in sport continues to be stymied by patriarchal ideas and practices. Definitions of femininity have been actively re-created in sport, and have served to perpetuate 'myths' (in Barthes' sense of the word) about the limitations of the female body. These ideas not only mitigate against women's participation, but also perpetuate the trivialising and sexualising of women athletes. The specific needs, concerns and contributions of black and Asian women in British sport have been sidelined by the enormity of a gender struggle which focuses on the effects of patriarchy, and in which white, heterosexual, middle-class women represent the 'norm'. Sport, therefore, still functions as a site of dynamic struggle over meanings, uses and resources (Theberge, 1993; Birrell and Cole, 1994; Costa and Guthrie, 1994).

Chapter 6 will look at the extent to which issues of gender intertwine with 'race', religion, social class and sexuality, and affect the sportswomen interviewed for this study.

6
Interviews with Black and Asian Sportswomen

The names of certain individuals and organisations connected with the interviewees have been changed to protect confidentiality.

Joice Maduaka

Starting out

> **'I spent near enough a year lying on the steeplechase barrier looking up at the sky.'**

Maduaka was introduced to more serious sport at the age of thirteen by default, having shown little interest in it before then. In her words:

> *...I used to have an excuse every lesson as to why I couldn't take part: headache, or time of the month, or whatever...I went to a school that didn't have a playground [but] across the road in the Imperial War Museum was like a gravel football pitch. I just remember one day being over there sitting on the wall and reading a book while the rest of the class was running around on the gravel, and the teacher said to me: 'get up and run, race against the girls'. I beat the lot of them in my school uniform and shoes, and everyone else was like kitted-out and she's like: 'I think we've got something here.' She took me back to the office and said: 'okay, let's cut a deal. If you go to the track and do athletics, you don't have to do canoeing or swimming, but only if you go down and train.' I was like, 'okay fine', because it's like I don't do water, it's the original black girl thing with the hair. I'm not getting into Surrey Docks for anybody! Canoe or no canoe, I'm not going swimming, I'm not going canoeing. So I went down to the track and spent near enough a year lying on the steeplechase barrier looking up*

Figure 6.1   Joice Maduaka, front

at the sky. And I'd go into competitions and wonder why I hadn't won, you know, or wonder why these other girls were so much quicker than me. I remember we were at the first English Schools Championship, and got knocked out in the first round. And that's when I woke up.

Maduaka claimed to have much more of an interest in her education than her sporting prospects (in her words she 'was at school to learn, not to run up and down'). Given her determined sporting inertia, it struck Maduaka as 'odd' that her teacher would surmise that she had any sporting talent in the first place. At any rate, the teacher's bargaining power was strengthened by an awareness about the 'original black girl thing with the hair': or cultural practices which invest black hair with meanings and values (see for example Mercer, 1994).

Over the next few years, the same teacher invested a considerable amount of her spare time to ensure that a still somewhat 'ambivalent' Maduaka remained committed to sport. Maduaka was now achieving some local success, but:

... because my teacher was like taking her Saturdays off and driving me to these competitions I felt like, you know, I owed her one and I should go and actually try and win ... she [recently] said to me, because I still talk to her now ... 'you are every PE teacher's dream, every PE teacher dreams of finding such a talented athlete, and in some people's lifetimes they will never find anybody' and she goes 'and I found you.' And I was like: 'well, cheers.'

Maduaka's mother ensured that her daughter was not over-committed to sport, pushing her to remain focused on her school work. And whilst other family members exerted the same pressure on her, they also contributed financially to her sporting endeavours. Maduaka claimed that:

My education had to go fine ... otherwise my mum would have just said ... you're not gonna run anymore. It was a case of even though I was going training after school, I was still doing homework, I was still studying ... my family have got a lot of common sense in that, at the end of the day, they realise that if you don't have a qualification, you're not gonna get yourself very far. It doesn't matter how fast you can run from a to b, at the end of the day on your CV everyone can see what qualifications you've got. Sometimes, I mean my brother's like the Midland Bank as far as I'm concerned. We're all very close in that if somebody needs something we'll get together. I mean my brother bought me my first spikes, my sister bought me my first track-suit. It's just how it is.

Establishing a presence
'I didn't realise that I was as good as I was'

Maduaka decided to specialise in the shorter-distance sprint disciplines, progressing through the minor representative ranks. She claimed the under-20 indoor 60 metre title in 1992, before first representing England, aged 21. By this time, a second major shift in the way she approached her sport had occurred. Maduaka claimed that:

... in '93, I had the feeling where I went two steps forward and about eight steps back, it was the year when I realised that I was actually interested in what I was doing ... when you're naturally talented, you can get away with doing not a lot and still succeed. But in '93 I wasn't running well at all, and the whole training group went away to South Africa without me, left me at home for six weeks on my own. And that was like the make or break

of me . . . do I still go training while they're away, or do I just sit at home and hang out with my friends?

Maduaka's coach was Mike McFarlane, the 1982 British Commonwealth 200 metre champion. McFarlane is credited with developing Maduaka's physical potential. In addition, her brother had begun to take a more active interest in her sport, employing 'strategies' to hone her instincts and determination. Maduaka explains:

> *My brother's very win, win, win. With everything he does he has to win . . . when I was a junior, I'd run this race against a girl who was a senior, and we both ran the same time, it was 11.9 [seconds], and they gave it to her, and they gave me second place. I remember walking back up the 100 metre start to collect my stuff, and my brother was standing there and he said 'you were rubbish' . . . 'that trophy would have looked good at home, you were rubbish.' And he had me in tears, I couldn't believe he was so horrible. I found myself saying 'I'll show him!' more than I wanted to do it for myself . . . in a bad way yeah he put me down, but in a good way he picked me up . . . and he still does it now. That's my brother . . . you just take it for what it is . . . I realise he's just trying to do it for me. I just don't get upset and cry about it, because crying gets you nowhere . . .*

Maduaka had given up on the idea of becoming an accountant (she had gained an 'E' in GCE maths 'and thought, maybe not'), instead embarking on a career in insurance. It was becoming increasingly apparent to Maduaka herself that she had the talent and drive for her athletics. But to progress even further, she needed to dedicate herself more exclusively to her sport. The decision was made easier by events at work:

> *. . . it got to the point where it was just like a complete clash of personalities between myself and my boss. I had a blatant lack of respect for him, we had a big argument and I left . . . I got a new job through an agency and the week I started, I did the AAAs indoors, the trials for the European Indoors. I came back and said to my new boss: 'I didn't realise that I was as good as I was, I won the trials [convincingly], and they've asked me to go to Valencia to go run in the European Indoors and I'm the only person that's qualified from this country.' And they said: 'oh well, off you go.' So I left and went to the competition and came back and it was like: 'oh, I'm going to America now for six weeks to go training' and they were like 'you're having a laugh now, you can't be this guy's PA [personal assistant] if you're not*

even in the country to answer the phone.' I didn't know that I'd actually spoken to the Chief Executive and I'd been pointed out as: 'that's our athlete over there'. And I chatted away to this guy thinking he was like the photocopying guy for like half an hour! He then got all the executives together and said: 'find her something to do, we don't want her to leave the company so find her something to do'. So what they did was they created a role for me and sent me over to the city office. My boss at the city office wasn't too happy, because it was a case where I was blatantly like put in above his head, and like he had no choice whether he wanted me or not. He then had to plan a budget around me and everything . . . But they were really good to me . . . I got my three months holiday, extra holiday on top of that, and they would literally close down the office when I was on, put up a screen and get all the brokers in the city to come and watch me running . . .

By the time of interview (August 2000) Maduaka had risen 72 places on the UK women's all-time 100 metre rankings to seventh place. Being established as Britain's number one female sprinter had given her the confidence to become a full-time athlete. But belonging to a vital, close-knit athletics culture has not only assisted Maduaka's professional development: it has also helped to shape her ideas about genetics and aptitude. It is to these that we now turn.

'Race' and genetics
'. . . when they picked the slaves, they picked the best . . .'

How, if at all, do 'race' and gender affect sports performance in Maduaka's view? Part I made reference to an ensemble of 'actors' (sports coaches, the media, and so on) who promote a popular view about the strengths and limitations of black and Asian people in sport. To begin with, Maduaka highlighted the limited basis on which black *British* athletes participate in track and field athletics. This participation is:

. . . just in the sprints. You're talking 100, 200, 400 possibly up in the 800 [metres], but then with the longer distances you're getting white athletes out there, but like there's no Asian athletes running . . . most of us are sprinters . . . I don't think any black athlete goes any further than 800 metres other than like people with ethnic origins, Ethiopians. But I wouldn't say we were pushed into it. I mean it's a case of nobody can make you run if you don't want to, but we've found something we can actually excel in.

Maduaka supports a part of the stacking thesis outlined earlier (Chapter 4), relating to black over-representation in certain sports and disciplines. But she rejected the notion of a 'steering' culture: in other words, that sports personnel may *look for* and *encourage* certain skills in black people at the expense of others, and therefore 'stack' them. The explanation Maduaka offers as to why so few Asian peoples are involved in British sport at a serious level is succinct and popular – 'it might be the family background, they're not pushed into sport'. But her view of *black* participation is considerably more engaged. The sports that black people in the West are involved in are:

> . . . *not popular [with black people]. But we're good at them. I mean I don't know, does it go back to slavery? I don't know. But you know we can run, we can sprint, maybe that's what it's all about. Maybe it's our genetic makeup that means we're able to do all of that.*

And although recognising that the miniscule genetic variations between black population groups fudge the boundaries of her philosophy ('I don't think any black athlete goes any further than 800 metres other than like people with ethnic origins, Ethiopians'), she continues:

> . . . *I've heard stuff about the United States, that when they picked the slaves, they picked the best and took them to like where they are now which is the Caribbean and the next place after there is America, so it's like you've got the cream of the crop with the genes, and that's why the Americans run so well. I believe it in a way . . . but then we always laugh. I mean guys in the group will say there's probably a guy back in some rainforest in Africa who's got no shoes and can still run quicker than the world record. But because he hasn't been tapped and hasn't been taken to a track, you know we're never gonna know about it . . . but also there's one Sri Lankan athlete and I can't remember what competition it was, I think it was the world championships. And she came third in the 200 metres. And nobody had heard of her before and so no, I mean there's Asian athletes out there.*

Maduaka has interpreted black genetic 'blueprints' in ways that strongly support Entine's account on the transmission of selected physical attributes from slavery (Chapter 1). As we have seen elsewhere (Part I), the 'nature' versus 'nurture' debate is at the heart of 'scientific' and cultural explanations about race and sports performance. But it is obvious from

Maduaka's response that she finds ideas about genetic aptitude more compelling than the role of social forces. It matters little that Maduaka presents caveats to her own arguments, since the strength of her beliefs are undisturbed by isolated contradictions. Furthermore, her views are endorsed by black colleagues who have become accustomed to racing against top-class sprinters who look like themselves. Consider also the following quote from Ian Mackie, a (white) UK international 100 metre sprinter:

> I've got muscles that are not normal for a white person. White peo-
> ple have got long calf muscles that stretch from their knee right
> down to their ankles. I've just got ones that are like big clumps at the
> very top. And I've got big hamstrings. Colin Jackson sometimes says:
> 'I think you're the wrong skin colour, the way you're made.'
>
> (Cited in Mott, 1998, p. 7)

The 'plasticity' of race means that when contradictions occur, these can be accommodated by reference to 'exceptions', or 'freaks of nature'. Mackie's black colleague tells him that his physiognomy does not match his skin colour. To Jackson, and doubtless other black *and* white athletes, there are certain physical characteristics which are recognised as 'belonging' to different racial groups.

The perpetuation of classic ideas has consequences for the plausibility of 'new' developments. So the fact that a Sri Lankan athlete 'emerges' from nowhere is questioned. The fitness levels, technical abilities and physical strength of the Korean national side in the 2002 football World Cup also disturbed traditional ideas about Asian aptitudes and tempera- ment; and precipitated a whispering campaign about performance- enhancing drugs, corruption and bribery.

In Part I, we saw how black sporting limitations have been explained in psychological rather than physical terms – black people have a 'sus- pect temperament', 'no technical grasp', and so on. Maduaka reflected on these ideas, recounting her own personal experience. In her view, the media and other sources:

> . . . *run around thinking we're all [black women] aggressive and all the
> rest of it. You know, the usual crap: like ideas about black women being
> very argumentative and like big-mouthed. Years ago, my grandmother
> died. Admittedly, I'd only met her once. But it still did upset me,
> because it was like the only grandparent I'd ever met. We had a*

competition, and the team manager at the time knew that I didn't like to fly. My grandmother had died on the Tuesday, and I was travelling on the Thursday to go to this competition. This man got me on an Aeroflot flight, which is not like the best airline to be on anyway. I got there, unpacked my case, and then he said to me 'oh you're not running, you're the reserve.' And because there were so much other things going on in my mind, I just walked away, walked away and went to the guys' room and started crying. I was just thinking: 'this is ridiculous, why the hell am I here? If he knew I wasn't running, he could have left my arse at home'. And I remember [athlete] Darren Campbell going down to his room and saying to him: 'look, you can't tell the girl she's not running and not tell her why.' And he said, 'if I approach her, she might [physically] attack me, so if she wants an answer she has to come to me.' And to this day he's obviously still waiting for me to go and ask him why he never let me run . . . why am I going to attack somebody because they told me I wasn't running? . . . you know, they wouldn't use that kind of language if it was about a white girl. They'd probably be sitting down trying to console her because she was in tears but this manager's just let me walk away.

Maduaka appears more comfortable with stereotypes about black physical prowess than about the temperament of black women. Perhaps this is because she interprets 'prowess' positively. Whereas to be aggressive and a *woman* contravenes dominant ideas about femininity, and therefore has limited value outside of sport. Maduaka's reflections are about nebulous, unsubstantiated *feelings* which, as we saw in Chapter 4, are difficult to measure. Maduaka may have communicated her distress to her coach through her 'body language'. But in her view, he employed a racialised filter to ignore her distress, and to resurrect the aggressive, in-yer-face black woman of classic folklore.

Advertising and sponsorship

'If I had blonde hair and blue eyes, they would love me . . .'

Maduaka also has quite definite views on the media coverage received by black and white athletes. In her view:

You can't really talk about it without it sounding like you're really bitter and twisted. But you know, it's like they're out there looking for the great white hope in every event and the white athlete that runs quicker than the black athlete is always going to get the publicity, we know that. Why, we don't know. But as soon as they [white athletes] excel, they're out there backing them to the hilt. If I had blonde hair and blue eyes they would love me . . . When my [white] training partner was running around, suddenly her face was put everywhere . . . and you're thinking, yeah . . . you know why, because everybody wants a white girl who can run, that's the long and short of it. And please don't think you're gonna use me to run alongside her and train to get her to that level [and then leave me behind] . . . it's the same with [Mr X – a British sprinter]. When he won, all of a sudden he was the best thing since whatever. But there were black guys running quicker than him. Darren Campbell was running quicker than him at the time but all of a sudden he [Mr X] gets the Mizuno [sports shoe manufacturer] contract, you know, four-year deal or however many years the contract is for. And the black athletes, they're thinking it's all a fluke; or maybe the sponsors are thinking that he won't last long, that there'll be another black guy come through next year so you know we're not gonna have to invest too much in this white face. I'm not bitter about it, it's the way it is.

Maduaka's reflections are similar in tone and sentiment to those of Sean Viera (Chapter 4). Did the advertiser's need to exploit a 'niche' in the market explain the more aggressive promotion of white sprinters – in the way it might if *black* athletes were a visible minority in particular sports? Maduaka rejected a part of this argument, pointing to the apparently 'negative' coverage of Soraya Bonaly, one of the very few black ice-skaters. Similarly, black tennis stars Venus and Serena Williams have sometimes had their performances subjected to quite puerile copy, which has relied on racist stereotypes (see for example Henderson, 2002).

Maduaka (and perhaps also her colleagues, given her use of 'we') suggests that black athletes are treated like an expendable, faceless, mass commodity. This view was also conveyed through a certain frustration about British (rather than European) announcers who, until recently, persisted in mispronouncing her name at race meetings. Fame has corrected this oversight. But Maduaka still believes that recognition of black success is grudging, and that the British media, advertisers and sponsors lack the political will to promote and support black athletes. By contrast, the same athlete (Mr X) is cited by both Maduaka and Jason Gardener (Chapter 4) as an example of someone receiving unfair levels of sponsorship. This not only points to the existence of underlying racial tensions in the Great Britain squad; but to a coherent body of ideas circulating in the 'athletes' village'.

Maduaka's own sponsorship arrangements (as they stood prior to the time of interview) perhaps support her scepticism. Although she has been Britain's number one sprinter for the past two years, she had no sponsorship commitments, and did not receive a retainer. Sponsorship by her sports manufacturer simply meant free kit, and the odd bonus payment. The relatively limited exposure that Maduaka had, was invariably in specialist magazines like *Athletics Weekly*. The above sponsorship arrangement prompted Maduaka to think about extending her media profile:

> *I decided to approach the advertising agency I'm now with. The guy turned around and said to me: 'you know that little girl on Blind Date that refused to get into the swimming pool? She's more famous than you, people know of her, they don't know you, and look at all the things you've achieved.' I thought, well, these are the people to obviously be around. And in some ways, I think I've given up with national press and stuff like that, and am just targeting the black community. At the end of the day, I think that they're more important than anybody else out there . . . I mean, if people pick up a* Pride *magazine and see me in it, I'm happy. Especially if black people approach telling me like: 'well done, it's really great what you're doing'.*

It is plain that advertising, sponsorship and marketing are essential supporting elements in any athletics career. Maduaka's awareness of her behaviour on and off the track, and its implications for black people, may *appear* incidental to the act of running, but are also no less important. The interview concludes with Maduaka's reflections about culture and politics.

Culture and politics

> '. . . I would like to do something about all the racism in society . . .'

The importance of these issues is reflected both in terms of Maduaka's sartorial style, and her desire for political engagement. On the first point, Maduaka states that:

> *. . . my friends don't do track and field, and if you sit down and hear the things that they're more interested in, they aren't watching athletics for who came first. My friends personally will sit down and have a good laugh*

about a certain person's hairstyle, or did you see her lipstick, and did you see how dry her knees were . . . so I find myself making an effort to grease up my knees and tong my hair and make sure that everything's in place, and that I'm not looking too sweaty because like they all laugh at you about stuff like that. Whereas the white people watching you won't even have a clue that you've got dry ashy knees or anything . . . when I was at the World Trials it was so hot out there I couldn't be bothered to tong my hair. It was just so hot that I had my hair straight. And I remember my best friend said: 'Joice, what happened? Did your tongs break or something?' And I was like: 'no, I just didn't want to tong my hair.' And she said: 'in future, I suggest you tong them.' She couldn't tell me how I'd done or what time I'd run, but she could tell me that I hadn't tonged my hair and that I looked really sweaty . . . that's just my female friends, whereas your male friends tell you: 'we saw your knickers go up your arse.' So it's like, when you're crossing the line, you're pulling them out as quickly as possible. And when you see the camera coming . . . you're fixing yourself, sucking your stomach in, trying to look as good as possible . . .

It was noted in Chapter 4 that cultural style 'over-determines' black subjectivity so that, for some writers, it appears to lack any 'concrete' substance. By contrast, Mercer argues that 'style can be seen as a medium for expressing the aspirations of black people historically excluded from access to official social institutions of representation and legitimation in urban, industrialized societies of the capitalist First World' (1994, p. 100). In other words, the expression of an overt *cultural* style is a political statement in itself. And because expressing this style does not preclude a more 'conventional' vision to challenge existing power structures, Maduaka would welcome the opportunity to exercise political freedom in other ways. We have seen how certain, informal codes of behaviour (Chapter 1) can limit the purposeful action of black sportsmen. Maduaka feels constrained by similar codes, and had this to say on the issue of addressing racism in her sport. Her answer is surprisingly frank, given its concluding sentence.

. . . I would like to do something about all the racism in society, but I'm in a sport where, yes, the person who crosses the line first is the winner, but not necessarily the person on the plane going to the Olympics. There are selectors that select you so I mean unless you're head and shoulders in front of somebody, if there's somebody out there running the same time as you they could choose between you and another person. And if you've been running around shouting your mouth off, you never know what could

happen. So it's not like you're doing yourself any favours by doing something about it . . . and if you're running around like somebody that doesn't know how to hold their tongue, kit sponsors are never sure what you're gonna say or when you're gonna say it. If you give people ammunition to hurt you they will eventually. I keep my mouth shut and say nothing.

Maduaka's political agenda would also include making visits to community centres, and organising training sessions for under-privileged children: except that she is rarely asked. She nonetheless recalls:

I did a coaching session a couple of weeks ago and that was for a friend from work, with a group of six year olds in Essex. There was one black child in this class, and this child, her eyes lit up just to see somebody black that was actually doing something.

Azmina Mitha

Starting out

'. . . you're a young Asian girl, be feminine!'

Figure 6.2   Azmina Mitha, left

Azmina Mitha has had a committed interest in martial art 'contact' sports from an early age. Reflecting on her opportunities for participation, she explained:

> *I always wanted to do karate, and kick boxing as well, when I was younger. In the Asian community there were only lessons for men, but I still went to this Bangladeshi group, and I was the only girl. I'm not Bangladeshi, and they were all between the ages of four up until twenty-six. When I came in the room they were like, 'Oh, my god . . . what's she doing here?' Maybe because I was a girl they felt embarrassed. Maybe they didn't want to show themselves up, guys being guys . . . And another thing was that maybe they didn't want girls kicking them . . . I think gender did make a difference both ways . . . from a girl's point of view, I didn't want them to know that they were a problem to me . . . I thought: 'I can show them!' I was better than some of them but they couldn't handle it. I didn't want to stop going because I didn't want to be bullied out of it. But I stopped because there were situations where if you are kicking up high, traditional dress isn't suitable. We had to have a lot of physical contact and I wasn't feeling comfortable with it so I tried a girls' group instead . . . the instructor was male as well, he was Asian . . . everyone within the group knew each other, knew my father and stuff so eventually I didn't want to continue there either. And in school as well, because I went to a girls' school we weren't really into basketball because it was too physical and we had horse riding . . . it didn't really satisfy me as the sport I like is, like, vigorous . . . guys' stuff.*

Traditional ideas concerning Asian women, femininity and modesty (Chapter 5) had to be abided by, and constrained Mitha's 'inappropriate' displays of sporting behaviour, whilst the threat to her family of local community censure loomed as a further consequence of not doing so.

  Mitha's family background, like the majority of the interviewees in this study, could be described as working class. She nonetheless attended a fee-paying private school. This environment provided a greater range of sports than those available at inner-city state schools, but her aptitude for sport was not particularly encouraged here. She explained that: 'the Asian girls and the African-Caribbean girls were the best in sports in that school. But I can't say that the teachers respected this or anything, because sport was not a very important subject.' Undeterred, Mitha sought more 'liberating' models of sports involvement. These were available outside of school, and enabled her to express her sporting instincts and aptitudes, whilst indulging her passion for more 'vigorous' sports. She explains:

> . . . I went to [an Asian] Saturday school, every Saturday for six years. We had sports lessons, and I started playing basketball. When the guys played football, the reason why they didn't want girls on their team was because the girls weren't that good . . . but because I was a fast girl I used to be on their team. I loved it! In my [Secondary] school we didn't have basketball or football. I used to love football and at [Saturday school] gender didn't make any difference whatsoever. The boys were my age and they were my friends. It was different, and that encouraged me. And being at an Asian-based [Saturday] school, the girls were encouraged to be more fit because our diets are not that healthy with the curries, and its good to have sport . . . they really did encourage that . . . all the teachers were male . . . from then on I wanted to be a sports teacher but I didn't go into that.

Mitha's parents were born and raised in Kenya. They came to this country as part of an exodus of 27,000 African-Asian refugees fleeing Kenya, Uganda and Malawi in 1972. To what extent have they influenced her attitude to physical activity? Reflecting on this enquiry, she claimed:

> I think because my father didn't have any sons, I was like the son . . . He's a typical Asian guy. He loves cricket and he loves football and he would always tell us stories about when he was younger . . . he used to be in a volleyball team in Kenya, and he used to play football. Maybe he wanted his children to do that as well . . . I used to watch cricket with him and I like to watch football matches with him . . . so he has given me lots. I used to ask my mum about sport. She used to be good at running and things 'cos in Kenya, sport was very important. All my aunties, all my Dad's sisters that live in Kenya, you know they're really athletic. You can tell that they were athletic and they were fit but I think that once they have got married, it stopped for them. But mum encouraged me. I used to get a lift after school, to Regency Theatre, and I went to school half an hour from home, and after school one night I'd have netball practice, the other country dancing, and one night gymnastics at Regency. She's the one that forced my dad to pick me up and drop me at night . . . She has encouraged us with all aspects of what we were interested in, and sports was one of those.

Not unlike Zia Haque in Part I, Mitha's parents seem to have been part of a vibrant, *recreational* sporting culture in Africa. But these experiences did not set the tone, as it were, for Mitha's own development as a 'sporting female' (cf. Hargreaves, 1994). In fact, she conveys a sense in which cultural expectations – from her parents, her male peers and other community members – of British Asian women were regressive in a sporting sense. The symbolic 'point' at which Mitha transformed from being a girl to being a woman, had a profound impact on her sports participation, and career aspirations.

> *. . . once I got mature, like when I was thirteen, I still wanted to play with boys outside and hang around with them. At that age, they were my best friends, I always got on with boys more than girls. But then their parents and my parents said: 'Oh you're a girl, now start playing with dolls. Go inside and watch TV. Don't hang around outside.' I didn't understand the logic of that. Why should I do that? They said that: 'The reason why is because you're a young Asian girl, be feminine!' Because I used to never wear dresses or anything and they were all getting worried about me, that's why my parents sent me to an all-girls school. When they started growing up, some of the boys in my area started hanging around boys from other areas, and were influenced into saying: 'What's she doing here?' And you know, I got a bit disappointed with that. And even men, Asian taxi drivers, when they saw me hanging around with boys and playing with them, said: 'What does she think she's doing?' They were worried that lots of Asian girls get pregnant and stuff, so you should divide [boys from girls]. And that dividing thing changed my life really because at that stage I stopped playing sports, I just wasn't interested . . .*

Although her parents were supportive of Mitha's interests, cultural ideas about femininity and womanhood were difficult to reconcile with sport. Defining gender roles meant appropriating obvious 'symbols' of difference, such as dolls and dresses. And as Mitha confirmed herself, pressure to conform to behaviour expected of an Asian woman was more acute, given her status as a Muslim female. But 'feminine' sporting activity is no guarantee that important religious and cultural concerns can be reconciled. As a more 'acceptable' alternative to vigorous contact sports, Mitha seriously considered a dancing career. Furthermore, the aesthetic of Western dancing clashed with traditional ideas, therefore also making it an inappropriate career choice. In Mitha's words:

> *I love dancing, any kind of dancing. I started developing my ability and I just wanted to be a professional dancer. But being an Asian girl, it's not good to do that. Because of religious reasons, you can't wear shorts, or*

clothes which hug your body figure, so figure dancing was totally out of the question. But I think every girl does want to be a good dancer because in our culture you watch Asian films, you see your role models are beautiful young ladies that dance beautifully . . .

Perhaps these experiences explain why Mitha has pursued her sporting dream in ways which provide her with an enhanced degree of self-autonomy and control. Mitha obtained a university degree in Business Management, rapidly followed by short courses in English Language Teaching, and Leisure Studies. It was during her university degree (aged 19), that she started working on a part-time basis at Awaz Utaoh (see below). Whilst it is true that Mitha has not been able to participate in sports on her own 'ideal' terms, she has a sporting identity closely bound to her work. Given her background, it seems appropriate that Mitha found a career in which her 'success' depends on her ability to adapt to the limits of structure, rather than submit to them. The next section will briefly outline the aims and objectives of Awaz Utaoh, and look at how the environment, and Mitha's own experiences, shape the strategies she employs to promote exercise and sport among Asian women.

Awaz Utaoh

By way of background, Awaz Utaoh (which literally means 'raise your voice') was formed in 1996 to tackle concerns specific to local Asian community groups in Bristol. In the main, the centre seeks to help Asian people affected by issues which can be exacerbated in areas of social and economic deprivation: such as crime, drug abuse, racism and domestic abuse. In recent years, drug abuse among Asian youth and instances of domestic violence in Asian families have increased in Bristol, and are priorities for the centre. The centre receives funding and vital support from other organisations such as the local constabulary, Bristol City Council, and the Society Against Racist Incidents (or SARI).

  According to the centre's publicity material, its vision and philosophy move beyond a simplistic approach to dealing with the issues mentioned above. Sports activity, in the form of self-defence classes, and women's badminton, swimming and gym classes, is perceived as a key way to ensure that women do not become victims in the first place. As such, Awaz Utaoh's proactive vision is for more vulnerable members of Asian groups to develop their self-confidence and self-awareness through sport. Finally, Awaz Utaoh claims to offer a range of training courses, employment opportunities and attractions to encourage the community to make the most of their time and skills.

Mitha is employed as a (qualified) fitness and self-defence instructor for the Asian women and girls who attend the centre. How has her practice sought to reconcile Asian women with physical activity, given ideas about gender, culture and religion that are prevalent amongst Asian groups? It is relevant to 'proceed' from the question of biological attributes, since these determine the construction of ideas about gender.

Asian women and sport: ideas, strategies, practice

'I think a lot of people have an image of Asian men keeping their wives locked up at home.'

'. . . we teach them the techniques and they can go home and practice that at home . . . that's how we get away with no physical contact.'

We have seen that debates on the relationship between race and sport focus on the physical aptitudes and mental temperaments of black and Asian groups. Mitha considers the importance of 'race' in terms of sporting 'strengths' and 'weaknesses'. In her view:

. . . whenever you watch TV with fast 100 metres and stuff like that, you always think why do black people always win? . . . generally speaking, in schools and when I do youth groups and things, I see that African-Caribbean guys are so much fitter. Maybe because of their physique, but maybe because of their culture as well and within their families . . . the way of life, the parents, are really sporty. When I use the gym I see a lot of black parents with their children . . . I hardly see Asian dads or Asian young boys. I see guys, dads with big muscles and their sons with big muscles . . . they have someone to look up to. And maybe Asian taxi drivers or a lot of Asian doctors I know, they're very into their education. I know a lot of boys who are Asian, and my uncles, and they are more into education. They want their sons to follow in their footsteps and develop themselves. And its similar with black people, because maybe there are doctors who are black or whatever but still in their culture I've seen them be more into sport . . . like, go to the gym and be fit. Same with the women as well. Asian women only go to the gym if there's like a group going there. You see black girls with their parents and women of any age going to the gym in cycling shorts and whatever. Asian women might see that as wrong, so they don't go because it's a mixed arena.

Mitha's assessment of sporting prowess is less 'biologically reductionist' than a number of the male athletes in Part I, or indeed Joice Maduaka (see above). For Mitha, the influence of culture is more compelling, and explains differences in approach and commitment to sport between black and Asian groups. Mitha reveals more definite ideas about the ways that uneven gender relations shape questions of culture and tradition, and thereby affect Asian women's participation in sport:

I wanted to be a fitness instructor, and I teach women of eighty and six . . . the whole range . . . it's really enjoyable. I don't think they [men] mind women doing sport in a place like Awaz Utaoh, because there are no other men there . . . as long as the women are modestly dressed. They do encourage their wives to come to places like this and do sports, to keep in trim . . . to look good. They don't want their wives to be at home and look horrible . . . I think a lot of people have an image of Asian men keeping their wives locked up at home. It's not really like that. I work with and know about Asian people . . . I know that the men don't want their wives to stay at home, they want them to go out, they want them to meet friends. But I don't think they would want their wives to play football . . . they play badminton . . . you know, feminine kind of games . . . I think games like badminton and aerobics, if you call that a sport, and volleyball, where there are two teams. They take up bowling, something that is easy and not too vigorous. It's important for Asian men that women are in Asian clothes most of the time, and so sport's not really practical. We need sport with a minimum of moving . . . The older generation, they are really starting to do sports together. I think the stage of life you are at depends on if you can change. When we go out with our family, even the ladies will join the rounders . . . we get our grandmother to play as well. When we start playing football or cricket she'll stay and watch.

Although Mitha recognises a generational shift in attitudes, she is conscious of the continuing influence of traditional ideas about modesty, femininity and appropriateness on Asian women's sport. It is important, therefore, that she develops strategies that maximise the value Asian women gain from sport. With this in mind, she explains that:

A lot of Asian women I meet want to exercise . . . but because of the clothes and the women shaking, and the private parts shaking, its not nice for them, they don't feel comfortable doing aerobics. They have to be covered up all the time and be more respectful. And doing aerobics and stuff, they don't feel comfortable because they haven't done it before . . . they can't come and do that in a mixed area, but they do want to do sports. Because of eating curries, they do need to lose a bit of weight for health reasons. Most of them do want to trim up, so we have bought a lot of exercising machines from a gym that's closing down, so we do have facilities here. We even go swimming now. Asian women go swimming on Sunday in Bristol now, because, about six years ago, we got up a petition to use a local sports centre which is in the heart of the community. And they [Bristol City Council] give us two hours every Sunday, when we have swimming lessons and classes. They teach us swimming and they give us . . . no male life-guards . . . you have to respect religion and culture as well and also think about our best ways for participation.

Fitness instruction is one thing. Self-defence is quite another. The practical mechanics of self-defence for very real, threatening situations also have to be 'meshed' with traditional ideas about the appropriateness of 'touch', and femininity. In this way, Mitha explains that:

We do have Asian defence instructors and aerobics instructors who can speak to them in their language and can encourage them . . . A lot of Asian women wear a lot of gold. These women had on about a thousand pounds [worth], and there were five of them. Because they wear it all the time, we give them classes in awareness, of how much eye contact you should have and how much you should not have when walking down the street. Our self-defence classes are also aimed at how to avoid situations where you might get attacked. But if you do get attacked it's important for us to show them and still remember about Asian women not wanting any physical contact . . . so two instructors [demonstrate on] each other . . . if the women like to try on each other, then they will. And while doing the course we've changed it into our own . . . we've started our own techniques . . . we've made them up . . . Asian women wear trousers . . . how they actually get mugged is when the attacker puts their hands in the trouser pockets and pulls them down [to distract them whilst purses are stolen]. This is easy, because we wear elastic waistbands . . . we also wear scarves around our necks, and may get strangled as well. So, we teach them the techniques and they can go home and practice that at home . . . that's how we get away with no physical contact. And because everything is confidential, we do not make someone's personal difficulties and issues obvious to the whole of the class . . . But we tell everyone in advance if you don't feel comfortable doing this exercise sit on the side.

As Chapter 5 has noted, defining 'Asian' women's participation in sport is complicated by the attitudes that different religions have to the notion of mixed sport, and by what constitutes 'appropriate' attire. Mitha confirms this added dimension to sports provision when she claims that:

They are mostly Muslim women at Awaz Utaoh . . . but even though Awaz Utaoh is not a religious group, religious groups of Muslims for example are very into sports. They have their sports days for children, sports days for parents. But in Islam, women and men are segregated. Within the segregation, guys will play football with their dads and brothers outside, and women will be playing football inside. Religion [determines] what you can do and what you can't do. I think that within the religious groups there is a lot of active sports happening but it isn't mixed . . . Sikh women are not like Muslim women . . . Sikh women are more open . . . they don't have to wear head scarves, they wear short dresses, short sleeves. And also Asian women in general are more into the family and family games . . . and I think the Hindus have their own way of life. Islam for Muslims is a way of life, so what they do in their life is based on their religion.

What of the later generations: the younger, British-born descendants of Asian forebears? As Chapter 3 indicated, traditional ideas about Asian family/kinship systems present an image of inter-generational conflict, with the permissive mores of the West clashing with Asian hierarchical family structures, and authoritarian parental attitudes. Strategies to facilitate participation are less involved, since:

It is not the same for the young girls. They do games and whatever at school, so they are comfortable with it, because that's the way they've been brought up. My cousins go to the gym together . . . But the parents are different. I co-ordinate our youth group, and within the youth group we had a lot of Asian girls that wanted to do sports on a Sunday, or a Saturday, or Friday afternoon . . . we hired out a hall for them where they could play sports . . . but with Asian parents, they won't let their girls out after a certain time . . . they are afraid that their children might start smoking or, you know, they just worry about them. So, if they come to an Asian organisation, then they are safe and that's the way of getting them out of the house after a certain time and playing sports. I think Asian parents prefer their children to hang around Asian girls so they have a cultural awareness as well. When they are here they talk about [popular music] and whatever, but the parents are also there, talking about Asian music. Asian parents would and do encourage the girls to come and play sports when they know where they are.

The purchase of gym equipment, organising women-only swimming sessions, and hiring church halls for sports have been recognised by the local council and other organisations as significantly contributing to community sport for Asian women. At a wider level, Mitha's efforts as a self-defence instructor have received recognition in the local media. Mitha finishes the interview, explaining that:

> ... *self-defence was a very good thing we started and, nationally, we are the first people to make a video and a booklet in four different languages. Although it's called self-defence, there is also a lot of aerobics included. We do bhangra [fusion of Punjabi and Western pop music] aerobics, which is with Asian music and basically dancing. But we do it with aerobic exercise and we have a teacher who is qualified and knows what she's doing. So they are dancing but they are losing calories ... a lot of people were interested in what we were doing and through that we had a lot of contacts to teach in other places like in surrounding Bristol areas, in Cheltenham and places like that where there are Asian people but no groups there ...*

Once again, programmes of exercise are mindful of culture and tradition, as the best way to promote user self-empowerment.

Ivy Alexander

Starting out

> '. . . my mother thought I shouldn't have an interest in football . . . because it's a boy's sport.'

Ivy Alexander was born and raised in Leeds. The aptitude she showed for football in her early years was hampered by stereotyped ideas about 'women's sports'; and a lack of available resources. She explains:

> *I probably became interested in football when I was about twelve. But I went to an all-girls school, and the main game there was netball. I used to bring a football to school, and we used to play at lunch time and things like that. I used to be a mad Leeds [United Football Club] supporter at the time, but it wasn't encouraged at all: only for the boys, I suppose. Anyway, most of the girls I hung around with, a lot of them liked football. A lot of them liked sports in general or were into games, so those were the people who I mainly hung around at school with. But because I went to an all-girls school, they were just basically geared towards girls sports. In the last*

Figure 6.3   Ivy Alexander

year before I left there we joined up with the boys' school. I remember there was a PE teacher, because I was quite good at tennis at the time. And he used to encourage that but not in a big way . . .

Although Alexander had sporting peers with whom she could share her enthusiasm for football, there were no real inspirations outside of her own age group; or in more formal school or club settings. In addition, her parents were fairly unenthusiastic about her sporting interests. Alexander confirms that:

They were discouraging, individually . . . sport was never encouraged for me. It was for my brother, though. My older brother's about a year and a bit older than me. He was into football, and that was encouraged. Whereas the girls weren't encouraged to think about sports. There were no actual reasons given; it just happened and you just accepted it. I must admit, though, that within the black community, there's a stereotype about women not going into football or women watching football . . . because I know when I was growing up my mother thought I shouldn't have an interest in football. My brother could but I shouldn't, because it's a boy's sport. And I think it's still around today. I've got a daughter and I've got a son, my son likes football . . . my daughter doesn't. Is she that way because society deems it's a boy's sport? I think in the black community it's probably . . . it's probably more objectionable and I think because black people's history and what they view as . . . a certain image is so concrete within their culture that . . . irrespective of all the changes which take place in society, attitudes continue with football, and how women should behave differently to men.

Alexander alludes to the different ways in which sport can act as a socialisation agent for girls and boys; and of how the effects of socialisation can vary in intensity, depending on the cultural context. Boys and girls learn patterns of behaviour appropriate for their culture, internalising 'social rules' (Horne *et al.*, 2000). These rules mean that boys are positively encouraged to develop an interest in sports like football; whilst any interest that girls have in sport will, at best, be channelled into more 'feminine' forms. In Alexander's view, these trends are exacerbated in West Indian cultures; a view also supported by Hope Powell, the England women's football coach. In an interview with the Kick It Out organisation, Powell claimed that: 'My mother is West Indian and there's a very different culture there so it was a bit difficult for her to understand why a girl would want to play football. It doesn't happen in Jamaica' (taken from the Kick It Out website, April 2002).

By contrast, research cited elsewhere (Chapter 5) suggested that the potential for African-Caribbean women to show more physical aggression in sports was greater than for other women's groups; due to their independent status, and equality within the family. So perhaps it is possible to see the testimonies of both Alexander and Powell as highlighting the *conditional* nature of enhanced involvement. In other words, qualities like aggression, when exhibited in traditionally 'masculine' sports, can present an unacceptable challenge to notions of male identity. As a consequence, they would be acceptable only in certain 'feminine' sports like gymnastics. In this case, the effects of gender socialisation are far more uniformly distributed, shaping sports participation for black women in similar ways to other ethnic and racial groups (see also hooks, 1981).

By 1973, a hitherto barren search for women's football finally led 17 year-old Alexander to place an advert in a local Leeds newspaper, appealing for players to start her own women's team. She was, by this time, 'getting very frustrated'. This enquiry also proved fruitless. Not surprisingly, Alexander felt there were no opportunities for her to pursue a serious interest, or possibly even a career, in football. It was at this stage that a number of other career choices crystallised in Alexander's mind. She states:

> *I thought about becoming a PT [physical training] instructor, because of the sport. But I also wanted to be a pilot. A pilot's something I've always wanted to do since I was very young . . . it used to be a barrister . . . What stopped me? Family pressure. But I could also say role models . . . I went into nursing because there were more black people in nursing and it felt safer; and because my parents felt it was the right thing to do . . . I didn't know anyone who was a barrister . . . there was no significant other black person that I could think: 'well, that person's done it, I could do it as a career' . . . I think that's what stopped me.*

The presence (or absence) of other black people emerges as an important consideration, structuring most of Alexander's sporting and work choices. This priority is reflected in her choice of sporting 'role model', and her allegiances as a football supporter. Reflecting on these issues, she also reveals how racism can challenge traditional ideas about sporting loyalty; and help to establish diasporic connections.

Struggling to stake a claim
'. . . never quite feeling English enough'

Who were Alexander's sporting inspirations? She states that:

> *. . . there was a woman who was brought up here. She was an athlete, a 400 metres runner. She was brought up here, but she wanted to represent Jamaica. I think it was during the Commonwealth Games that she had to go back to reside in Jamaica for a number of years, before she could represent them. She eventually won a gold medal in the Commonwealth Games . . . it was going back quite a few years. I think I'd actually like to do the same, especially when this woman, I can't remember her name, got the Gold medal for Jamaica and all . . .*

Alexander refers to an athlete who was born in Britain, but chose to represent the country of her forebears. Her desire to do the same was motivated by her 'never quite feeling English enough', and reinforces the impression that she found it difficult reconciling her nationality by birth, with being black. It is clear from Alexander's testimony that her desire to compete for Jamaica was not motivated by financial gain and professional advancement, as has been suggested when Zola Budd (South Africa) and Greg Rusedski (Canada) changed nationality to compete for Britain (athletics and tennis respectively). Instead there is a need, first noted in Chapter 4, for research to reconsider how and why allegiances are formed in sport. The choices Alexander made as a football supporter further exemplified her struggle to belong:

I remember when I was younger and I used to start supporting Leeds . . . I was mad about them! But one of the things about being a supporter at the club was that there was a lot of racism. So, a lot of Black people didn't want to go to Elland Road [Leeds football stadium], even though they supported Leeds, and I often used to think about that. Now I support Arsenal, and the reason I do is because there was . . . an acceptance of black players and supporters . . . that's actually been seen. There's more black supporters going to the club and the more black supporters you get in the club, the less likely that you're going to get people chanting racist comments. So it makes sense that Arsenal seems to attract more black supporters than the other clubs. But the whole issue about racism in sport is there, it's there all the time. For instance, I'll go to Highbury [Arsenal football stadium]. It's one of the grounds I feel quite comfortable at, but I still would prefer to be in groups where there is other black supporters, you know? I think the racism on the pitch is in the terrace and I think it's all the way down the line in terms of management and black ex-players getting into management. You see that reflected . . . if, say, John Barnes is going to set up a team, I think he is more scrutinised because he's a black manager going to a big club than a white manager who had limited experience also going to a club . . . so I think its there, its there actually . . . racism in sport.

In the 1970s and early 1980s, Leeds United's Elland Road stadium had a reputation as a recruitment site for far-right organisations. Since that time the club, and supporters organisations (see Chapter 2) have made stringent efforts to encourage local community groups to feel that they have a 'stake', and can attend matches without fear of racist abuse. Unfortunately a recent, high-profile case involving Leeds United players accused of an attack on Asian student, has reaffirmed the club's racist credentials in the eyes of some observers. By contrast, Alexander's observation about Arsenal Football Club was confirmed by a recent study of the premier league (cited in Nichols, 1998). The study found that the club has the highest number of minority ethnic season-ticket holders of any premier league club in the country, and is also one of the places you are least likely to hear racist abuse directed at players and other supporters. Alexander's sporting loyalty to Leeds was eventually eroded by her perception of racism; and illustrates how the *whiteness* of supporting cultures can prove prohibitive for minority ethnic groups, and their willingness to lay claim to their local club (see also Hill, 2001). The fear of racism proved of greater concern to Alexander than her safety as a woman in these predominantly male sites.

Alexander went to live and work in London in 1986, having spent the previous 13 years as a nurse in Leeds. Between 1986 and 1997, she played at a serious amateur level for a number of women's teams, and was also involved in football coaching. The extent to which sexuality interweaves with race and gender as a consideration in her sport is relevant at this stage. Alexander strongly identifies as a 'black gay female', and her experiences in 'ordinary, heterosexual, women's football leagues' provided the motivation to choose a gay team (see below). She detailed one example:

> *I did actually for a time train with QPR [Queens Park Rangers] . . . there were two other lesbian women who played, both were white women . . . so the majority of them were straight women anyway . . . and one of the coaches was male, and I must admit I stopped playing with them because of the fact that there was a relationship between what was happening, and the way he was talking to us . . . there was just too much stereotyping . . . I'll explain that. The coach used to say: 'come on lovely', and: 'come on love', and comments about butch lesbians on the other teams. Stuff like that which I thought wasn't on really. And then secondly, moving to Hackney, it didn't matter that I was a gay woman. In fact, it just complemented you as a person, complemented you being in the football team. But at QPR, you had to keep that [your sexuality] to yourself . . . you felt that way.*

A lesbian identity in sport (and indeed other spheres of social life) can carry significant personal and professional cost to athletes who are 'exposed'. As Hargreaves (1994) confirms, homophobia is an integral part of heterosexual sports cultures, consolidated and reproduced through sexist jokes and attitudes, and reflected in anti-lesbian discrimination (see also Cauldwell, 1999). As a result, gay sportswomen often

hide their true sexual identity, and behave in ways that celebrate a patriarchal heterosexuality. Alexander felt alienated at QPR by the attitudes
and behaviour of the 'straight women' and the male coach, who sought
to motivate the team by castigating the 'butch lesbian' opposition. As a
result of her experiences in apparently heterosexual teams, Alexander
joined a 'gay women's football club' (which will be referred to as
'The Women's Football Club', or TWFC) in 1997. TWFC is based in
North East London, and is affiliated to the national football league.

The Women's Football Club

> 'I thought there would be a significant number of players
> who would be black.'

Alexander referred to other factors which attracted her to this particular
club:

> *... at the time, I was working in [North London] and I wanted something
> local, so that's why I joined [The] Women's Football Club ... when I got
> there, I actually thought that a team in [North London] would have a lot of
> black players ... obviously with the black population in [North London],
> I thought there would be a significant number of players who would be black.
> I certainly would have expected that in that part of the country. In fact I was
> the only black player in the team, for about six months. So that was quite
> surprising ... I was quite keen for other young black women to start play-
> ing football, and I was actually going to put an advert in* The Voice, *the
> black newspaper, to get more women to come and join.*

In trying to account for why no black players were part of the team
when she first arrived, Alexander stated that:

> *... I think part of it is the fact that like seems to attract like, I'm not quite
> sure ... when I went there, I felt that ... while the white players were
> saying there weren't more black players, they weren't able to transfer that
> to encourage black players to join the club. And also I think as a black
> player you join a club, you don't actually want to be treated any different,
> or given any extra treatment. You want to feel you're treated the same, you
> know? I felt, sometimes, that wasn't the case.*

In Alexander's view, a culture of dissuasion was institutionalised in the
clubs practices: in similar ways, perhaps, to those uncovered by Back

and associates in their study of English football (2001). By its very nature, TWFC is perceived as *white* because there are no black members. And welcoming noises on inclusion are actualised in ways which alienate the people they are meant to be encouraging, so that Alexander does not want to be 'singled out', and treated differently, because of her colour. In spite of her desire to 'blend in', the fact remains that Alexander's colour did single her out as different from her team-mates. Did her team-mates express specific views about a link between race, gender and performance in sport? Does Alexander have a strong opinion about this issue herself? Interestingly, she had no comment to make about how difference may have been expressed in ideas about aptitude and temperament. Instead, she chose to reflect on how her presence as a black gay woman has been received by spectators, opposing players and her team mates.

During her time with TWFC, Alexander has experienced negative verbal reactions. She claimed that:

> *I have, from other players . . . I think that when you're in a team which is predominantly white anyway . . . there are certain things that, if they [white team members] start applying to other people, you think apply to yourself. There was one game when we played against this Germany team . . . one of the players in our team started shouting: 'the referee's a Nazi'; no: 'the referee's a German'. And given that comment, I thought: 'how do I fit into this group?' Would colour be mentioned if there were no black players in our team, and there was a black player in the German team? Does that make sense? . . . I can't say I've ever recognised racism directed at myself though, but sexism yes . . . I think with the supporters who watch women's football or walk past a group of women playing football, there are normally derogatory comments about women playing football in general. So, I can't say me myself have actually had comments or felt an intent towards racism. I'm not saying it's not there . . . You see, I tend to think the football crowd is more racist than say rugby and cricket . . . I would think that white people who play and watch football are more racist than supporters of other sports.*

A latent potential for racist insults looms in the background; whilst male spectator antipathy to women playing football reinforces hegemonic gender relations. Although TWFC was formed as a result of the prejudice and sense of alienation its members felt in mainstream sports, the team play 'in an ordinary [heterosexual] women's league'. Would the strength in combination of an all-gay team resist the 'compulsory heterosexuality' (cf. Hargreaves, 1994) of women's football? Alexander claimed that:

Other teams, most of the teams we play now, would actually think straightaway that ours was a gay team . . . possibly because I think the relationship among the gay women is a bit different than a straight team, and most of the women in the gay team did look as if they were lesbian anyway . . . they were all quite gay in appearance. They looked that way so that would be picked up quite quickly. Because of this, I mean comments used to be made . . . negative comments . . . and we used to give as good as we got. But I can't personally recall any comments being made directly to me. But I can recall comments being made to other people around their sexuality . . . but for me no.

The Gay Games
'. . . I felt there was a connection there with the other black people.'

It is partly as a result of these and other negative experiences that the team chooses to compete in the Gay Games. The year after Alexander joined TWFC, Gay Games V were held in Amsterdam.

The Gay Games are an international sporting and cultural festival which takes place every four years. First held in San Francisco in 1982, the festival has rapidly grown into the largest sporting event in the world. The games' essential guiding principles are participation, inclusion and personal best. These principles are reflected by its claim to have no minimum standard; and to be open to anyone regardless of sexuality, ability, HIV status, age, gender, race/ethnic background, or financial means. The popularity of the 1998 Amsterdam Games could be gauged from the large number of athletes who participated in it. Badminton, cycling, dancing, judo, field hockey, football and touch rugby (among other sports events) attracted 15,000 athletes from five continents and 68 countries. A higher proportion (42 per cent) of women competed here than at the Olympic Games held two years previously.

TWFC submitted their team for the amateur football competition, and sought to raise sponsorship to attend the games. Sponsorship was not forthcoming, and so club members paid their own fares. Alexander's interactions with other black players at the games left an indelible impression on her:

... there was other black players from other countries. They were mainly poor African ones, and their poverty showed. And even though you were from miles apart, meeting them, socialising, talking to them, I felt there was a connection there with the other black people. You know, the black teams, or the other black players in teams on the field. I can't really explain why that was. I don't know.

Alexander could not find words to describe this connection (in terms of its basis, meaning, and significance); but she claimed to be profoundly convinced of its existence nonetheless. In the space that her silence leaves, it is perhaps worth hypothesising about the political character of this diasporic connection. Alexander would be all too aware of the potential for ethnic and racial solidarity in these situations. Poorer nations have access to inferior resources and facilities in sport, and this is symptomatic of uneven power relations (see for example Jarvie, 1995). A political 'connection' not only encompasses shared experiences of racism, but a recognition of continuing relations of domination and subordination in the post-colonial world. As such, David Lawrence may have bemoaned the fact that black, British-born youth cheered for the West Indies cricket team, rather than England: but he understood *why* they did. And, at the height of apartheid, Sean Viera tried that much harder to defeat the white South African opponents put before him (both Chapter 4).

Alexander finished the interview by considering whether media coverage of black women in sport is racialised, and subject to gender bias. She described her own media coverage, in the local press, as 'satisfactory'. But in her view, a career in the media would be 'very difficult' to realise because:

I think the exposure of women's sports is so minute ... and even though the exposure is minute, a lot of those commentary jobs are taken up by men ... The interest of the media is to retain the men's sports on television ... and they can't afford to give up any of that exposure to women's sport in case the ratings fall, and that's why women's sport is where it is. I mean you only have to look at something like the tennis every year ... the men's final is given priority over the women's and I just think, you know, it's in the interests of the media, and will remain so for many, many years ... I think the press are biased against black players ... you can see it for example with someone like Patrick Viera as opposed to David Beckham ... and I think part of that is obviously how the press write from a racist perspective anyway, and so this affects how black players are treated by the crowds ... you see it in the press every day.

Alexander identifies a racialised agenda in media coverage of black sportsmen (Chapter 4); and a gender-marking of women's sports events that has been noted in Chapter 5. She continued with this theme of differential coverage of women's sport, and its role in reinforcing negative perceptions:

> ... there is still a certain amount of hostility about women's football ... if, for instance in men's football, a mistake is made by a player, it's just seen as a mistake ... but when it's in women's football, the emphasis is put more on poor play ... it gives it a sense that women's football is not real, not professional enough, are you with me? It doesn't give it that reality, certainly on the TV it doesn't. That kind of commentary is harmful. When you watch men's football, and a goal is scored, there is a heightened sense of the commentator's voice, and you can see it in the crowd when that happens ... with women's football the commentator doesn't get as excited, you don't get that sense of interest ... men's football presents an image of 'macho-ness' and I think that puts women off from playing.

Alexander has striven to participate in a sport which she feels has a masculine, heterosexual character, and which continues to undermine the credibility and seriousness of women players. There is a tangible echo of Imran Khan's earlier remarks (see Chapter 2) in Alexander's comments. Both convey a sense that differences of interpretation and emphasis (in Khan's case, concerning the way that poor umpiring decisions from Asian officials were evidence of 'cheating', rather than genuine 'mistakes') reflect an unconscious agenda to promote the superiority of male, English sport.

Myra Barretto

Starting out: school and the family
'... I was the sporty one out of the girls.'

Choi (2000) has suggested that if a positive commitment to sport is forthcoming in an individual's early years, it is likely to be maintained throughout their lifetime. In common with the other interviewees, Barretto showed intense early interest in, and promise for, school sport. As she explains:

Figure 6.4   Myra Barretto

. . . when I was eight or nine I started to take an interest in swimming, and I joined a swimming club. I was there until about sixteen, swimming competitively. Alongside the swimming there was netball, which was all that was available at junior school . . . obviously, netball is a girls' sport, but swimming has quite an equal representation of boys and girls who get interested . . . so I was lucky that it didn't seem to be one or the other sport that I was allowed to do.

An 'anti-sport' culture of femininity, seen to be so important to school-girls (Chapter 5; see also Scraton, 1992) does not seem to have impeded Barretto's involvement with sport. She is also aware that her favourite sport (swimming) escaped the restrictions imposed by gender socialisation. But whilst Barretto's interest in sport was expressed at school, it was not particularly encouraged by her teachers. Instead, she credits her parents with sustaining and nurturing her commitment, referring to them at some length in this regard:

My parents were really, really positive, both loved sports. I went to a convent school, and the nuns weren't particularly good at teaching sport. It wasn't a particularly sporty school. It was a convent which did sports as a matter of course. My mum used to play when she was at school, and so when parents were asked to get involved I asked my mum to come and she came and ran the netball team; which she did for about ten years actually. So, she started when I was in the junior school, and carried on for the next ten years and really enjoyed that. Eventually, I played for the netball team in tournaments . . . My dad loves sport as well. He's hot on cricket, so he played cricket for his town and goes to Trent Bridge regularly to see international matches. And my parents are also part of a tennis club . . . My dad encouraged me to go for tennis coaching so I was the one that went for tennis coaching after my siblings . . . and my Dad really got me into the swimming. Once I expressed an interest in it, he was the one who came along to the swimming club . . . and was my greatest influence there.

Up to the age of 16, school-based sports activities were convenient, because of the close proximity between Barretto's home and school. If Barretto were to have a more serious commitment after this age, her parents needed to prove particularly enthusiastic and supportive. As she explains:

Once I was at my new school's swimming club . . . the problem was that I lived fifteen miles away from the school, so I found it quite difficult attending training sessions. It was also a big effort to take part in hockey and netball team events, but I did. That really did hinder my sport at my new secondary school. Eventually, a couple of parents got together and we all supported each other's families because it was fifteen miles away. My parents did their best to do things and support me. They took me to wherever . . . supported me so far as taking me abroad for swimming competitions . . . we went on trips to the Netherlands and the Channel Islands. They paid for that and they weren't rich people by any means, and so that was a big influence. They also saved up for me to go on swimming trips on my own, when we all couldn't afford to go . . .

To some extent, Barretto conveys a sense that the support and encouragement of her family were due to her status as the most 'characteristically male' sibling:

. . . my older sister wasn't interested in anything. She sort of opted out of things. My younger sister, she did go to swimming club, but she had a different physique to me. Both of my sisters are very tall and very, very slim, and not quite as much muscle tone. So, I think my parents encouraged me, they thought I was more muscular, more athletic, determined and competitive. One sister was more artistic, and the other one was not sporty. So, I think it was my parents' preconceptions as well . . . I think the big thing there is that we're a family of girls . . . and I was the sporty one out of those girls. So, it seemed right that I should follow the sport whereas my other sisters didn't so much.

In a family of three girls, gender differences were symbolically 'played out' around sport. Myra was perceived as having more sports-appropriate physical and mental attributes and this, combined with her sisters' lack of interest, enabled her to participate more freely in sports.

With such an *empressement* for sport, it seemed feasible that Barretto would opt for a professional sports career. At 16, she joined her local town's netball club, before playing for her university team at 18, and for Bath Ladies Netball Club at 21. However, her desire to be a schoolteacher, and an equal commitment to music, ensured that she could not give sport the time required of a professional aspirant. Barretto provides a flavour of the scale of these other commitments:

. . . for the last two years, I've been a part-time teacher: I'm down to three days a week, in an effort to pursue my other musical interests which are composing . . . I compose musicals for children. I run choirs, I run the Bath

Society for Young Musicians. I've played base guitar in bands. I work as a part-time lecturer, and I also do some work for the Arts Council as an assessor.

Barretto's decision to pursue a vocational career was supported by her parents and seemed sensible in hindsight, given a catalogue of injury problems. It was during her ten-year stay with Bath Ladies Netball Club that she developed the back injury that has since limited her sports participation. Her subsequent, frustrated attempts to engage in sport at a relatively less competitive level, have made her consider broader questions about women and participation.

Gender divisions
'I would like to be a man because I like football . . .'

Barretto states:

When I was at my most serious competitively . . . competing in netball for ten years, it was a night of training, and the Saturday away somewhere at competition. And also with tennis, it was the odd weekend away, and a couple of club nights. But now I take the pace easier. I regularly swim, and there have been a couple of other things. But I still really wanted to compete though, to try different things. So, last year about this time, I did a term of water polo. Bath University were trying to get a women's team together, and only about half a dozen women turned up and . . . maybe because it can be an aggressive contact sport . . . it's quite interesting really . . . after about three weeks there was only me left! And because I paid, I carried on the next six weeks on my own. But it's really a contact sport . . . I did all the training with the instructors, and ploughed up and down and did all the skills. But then when it came to the last twenty minutes playing a game, I had to just sit out and watch . . . It was very frustrating. It was hoped that they [South West counties] would get a women's team together, but I'll have to travel to Bristol [17 miles] to do that . . . and I just wasn't quite prepared to do that. If it was in Bath I'd do it, but I don't want to go to Bristol one or two evenings a week . . .

In general, women's sports participation is increasing, but is concentrated in more 'feminine appropriate' sports such as aerobics, which emphasise aesthetics and grace over strength and speed (Chapter 5). Barretto hoped to compete with more 'recreation-minded' colleagues:

but her frustrations are rooted in this gendered pattern of participation, and its implications for women engaging in sports like water polo. Referring to her female friends, Barretto states:

> . . . there are very few of them who are into sport, who are into fitness, and who go to aerobics, to pilates [muscle strengthening exercise classes], stuff like that. That has really made me aware of myself as a woman who likes and is good at sport. There are very, very few people. When I looked around to my other female friends to say: 'who could come to play water polo?' I really had to think. You know . . . who could swim and had ball skills? There was really no one else I could think of. I thought that was a bit sad really, and I went on my own . . . Whether it's me in my mid-thirties, and a lot of women have started families, and they just don't feel that they're able to commit time. But also it's quite strenuous. You have to be a good swimmer, and you also have to have ball skills. You are combining two things there. I think they're the main reasons really.

Patriarchal ideas about women impose a beauty aesthetic on their fitness and exercise. An over-emphasis on youth, beauty, and an 'ideal type' shape makes it increasingly difficult for women to publicly engage in exercise as they get older (see for example Choi, 2000). As a result, only the most determined women athletes show a serious commitment to sport as they advance through the life course. Barretto endorses the view that hegemonic relations of power also 'show themselves' in other ways. As she eagerly confirmed:

> . . . they do, most definitely, and I don't know why that is. But I think things might change. It's only in the last 20 or 30 years that women have started to get into sports more seriously . . . at the moment, it's so difficult to catch up, because the amount of money that's pumped into certain sports is incredible compared to other sports. And it was always a bugbear really. I really enjoyed netball, but it just seemed like a second-class sport. It wasn't even mentioned in the local paper when we [netball and swimming teams] had a great win against somebody, it was hardly ever mentioned. Whereas all the local men's teams fixtures were put up there, their divisions were there . . . so, speaking metaphorically, it seems like you're playing for a 'B' team all the time.

The status of women's sport, and the types of sports women participate in, leads Barretto to consider the greater potential for agency in men's sport. In her view:

I'm so very aware of being female rather than male . . . especially in a sports context. I would like to be a man because I like football, I would like to be good at football, and I like the whole thing around that, or even rugby, and I don't think netball quite satisfied that . . . that's why I went to go and play water polo. I quite like that intensity you find in men's sport . . . and the attention it gets.

The tone and sentiment of Barretto's reflections echo those of Azmina Mitha (see above), concerning the latter's desire to take part in martial art contact sports. Both women sought to escape the restrictions of gender socialisation, and to participate on their own terms. To promote a comparison still further, it is relevant to consider whether concerns around 'race', religion and culture have also restricted Barretto's freedom in sport.

'Race', religion and culture

'. . . I don't think there have been many doors that have been shut, because of the way that I look.'

Research suggests that schoolteachers can sometimes steer African-Caribbean children into sports, in the belief that they have an aptitude for them; whereas dominant ideas about Asian girls lead to quite different suppositions. Barretto herself has an Italian mother and an Indian father, both of whom are Catholics. Although she makes strong claims about her Asian identity, Barretto is conscious of how her physical appearance presents a contradiction to dominant ideas and presumptions about same. Addressing the first issue of teacher expectations, Barretto states that:

I don't think I was steered into or away from sport because of my ethnicity, maybe because I don't look as if I've got any Indian background. And it was a Catholic school, so there were lots of Italians and, you know, I could well have been Spanish or Italian. So, I don't think that made any difference.

Barretto provides the first indication of how her self-identity as 'an Asian woman of dual-heritage' has been effectively negated in the 'public sphere' outside of the home. As such, she claims not to have been a victim of racist discrimination whilst playing sport, or indeed at other times. However, there is one sporting experience she does recount that marked her out as 'different', and rendered her identity as problematic. She states that:

. . . the only time that I've felt a bit uncomfortable with things was . . . when we went on a sports trip to Holland. I was eight, and I remember my dad coming through the coach station, but they wouldn't let him get back on the coach straightaway . . . he was the only one without a British passport . . . And . . . so the coach went through, and my dad had to go off into a little room with a couple of men and I was on my own on the bus with people. We were delayed by about half-an-hour while immigration checked him out and everything. I remember sitting next to a friend. When the business with my dad was going on, her mum, who was there, took her from sitting next to me; and I was sitting on my own for that half-an-hour. I remember that, and thinking there's nobody really coming to chat to me and they were worried that we were holding the bus up . . . so, that was the only real negative thing that stands out.

The above incident aside, Barretto claims that people are not immediately aware of her part-Asian heritage, and are surprised by this. As a consequence, she seeks to emphasise her Asian identity, to counterpoise other people's perception that she does not 'look' Asian. In this respect, she claims that:

. . . I always try and mention it. So, when I joined my tennis club in Bath, I made sure within the first . . . I don't know . . . within the first few weeks of joining, that people knew that my dad was Indian. Because there were no other Asian, Black Caribbean people there at all, so I wanted to make my mark and say well, you know, this is who I am . . . I want to tell them who I am, and also show them that I'm somebody different because they don't have anybody like me up there . . . and are they aware of it? . . . I'm aware that in the past tennis clubs can be kind of white-middle-class, and you know I just want to make them aware of it. My ethnicity is very important to me. And I wouldn't be without it. And I make a point of telling people who say: 'Who are you? What are you? What job do you do?' I always weave into the conversation that my dad's Indian, and that I've got this whole side of me that probably isn't apparent.

Research suggests that British society's narrow classifications of racial identities as 'black', 'white', 'Asian' or 'Other' are unsatisfactory and exclusive of 'mixed-race' groups (see for example Alibhai-Brown, 2001). By emphasising her Asian heritage in a 'white-middle-class' context, Barretto appears to be challenging these hierarchies based on traditional ideas. And as Chapter 2 indicated, these same ideas meant that the successes of 'Anglo-Asian' sportsmen like Ricky Heppolate and Paul Wilson were not credited as 'Asian' achievements. By contrast, Azmina Mitha's claims to an Asian identity are seen as less ambiguous and more 'real'. Not only is she recognisably Asian, but she could face racist reactions in the same tennis context that Barretto has not.

And in spite of an eagerness to take part in this study, Barretto's 'ethnic invisibility' led her to question her applicability for it. In her view:

> *I probably feel a bit fraudulent doing this interview . . . I don't think I've had the experiences that some other people have had, I don't think there have been many doors that have been shut, because of the way that I look. And I know that doors are shut, and things are much more difficult for certain people, so I felt doing this . . . am I the right person to be interviewed? I know I've got an ethnic background that's different to other people, but I don't feel that other people feel that way. So . . . my answers might not be as revealing as other people's.*

Barretto's tentative enquiry perhaps highlights the problem-centred nature of an epistemology of race and sport: with its focus on restricted access and participation, stereotyping, overt racism, and so on. Such a focus unwittingly obscures the strength of agency that certain groups have in sport, as well as denying the space for people to express more complex self-identities. It has become plain that the effects of gender socialisation in sport are more repressive to Barretto than her ethnicity. But a limited experience of racist reaction has nonetheless led Barretto to consider stereotyped ideas about 'racial' groups. Reflecting on the reasons why certain sports are popular with black people, Barretto states:

> *. . . In my mind, I'm running through images of groups of teams of people, and I can see more black faces in proportion, yes . . . As a teacher, I think it could be very easy to push people in a certain direction, and to have your preconceived ideas about what people are like. Whatever came first, the chicken or the egg? You can see a lot of black faces in athletics or football, then who knows what your mind does, or what you try and do, whether its consciously or sub-consciously? I think I'm quite aware of that [the dangers of stereotyping] . . . but I can imagine that, in certain schools with more traditional teachers, that that could well happen.*

Barretto claims to be 'quite aware' of the potential for teacher stereotyping of black and Asian schoolchildren, but asks the question: 'Whatever came first: the chicken or the egg?' The question really asks whether teacher steering of black children into sport stimulated their aptitude and interest for it; or whether this was already present, and endorsed by the children themselves. As such, it is an oblique reference to the 'nature versus nurture' debate that is consistently raised in a consideration of race and sport performance. Barretto also considers why more Asian women are not attracted to sport. In her view:

> It's quite difficult for me to answer that because my Asian family all live in India, there's nobody that lives here. And certainly in India there are certain roles, family roles, and it is still quite traditional there . . . so, it's more difficult for me to say because we don't really belong to a community here. I just see myself as part of a family, quite a tight unit . . . which doesn't have a community back in my home town. But . . . I'm thinking about my home town now. There weren't that many Asian families, less than half-a-dozen families. But there were a few Asian families who came from Leicester . . . My dad was the only Catholic Indian in town, and I think that might have made a difference . . . there are still very, very few Indian people there. But the whole atmosphere of joining a sports club and going into a communal area, and getting changed and mixing with other people and even families mixing . . . I do sense that it might have been more difficult for my dad to get involved in the swimming club with me because of his background . . . It's a feeling I had at the time. Whether it was me being seven or eight, and realising that I came from a slightly different background to other people, and I hadn't really realised it before. It didn't seem to come across at school, but it seemed to come across when I saw a big group of people who weren't in a school context, in fact a family . . . it was people from all walks of life and still my dad had the only black face there. And I realised I was slightly, slightly different and it was probably realisation time. And I sort of half sense that that probably was the case.

Again, race 'difference' is experienced vicariously for Barretto, through her father. But a sense of cultural difference can be directly inferred from her response. 'The whole atmosphere of joining a sports club and going into a communal area, and getting changed' has also been more forcefully expressed as a problem for Azmina Mitha. Mitha's more definite statements on the subject are not surprising, given her closer proximity to the issues.

Conclusion

This study has shown that sport is an area where the boundaries of 'commonsense' historical 'truths' about race have been re-drawn, rather than erased. In terms of population, goods and information movements, the world has never been more navigable. But marked public anxiety over the consequences of 'race' in shared social contexts has led to a retreat into the particularities of ethnic difference, and the biological assumptions that underlie them. As we begin the twenty-first century, 'new' forms of racism have been inspired by genetics-based research, and social circumstances. It is therefore pertinent to ask about the personal cost to minority ethnic groups of persistent discourses about 'race' in sport, and of racist practices and processes. Do these groups have a sporting chance?

In his award-winning book *The Metaphysical Club*, Louis Menand (2001, p. 396) remarked:

> if groups define themselves by their difference from other groups, a change in the status of one group affects every group that defines itself in relation to it. To the degree that black identity becomes more like white identity ... it is not only blackness that changes. Whiteness changes as well.

This quote emphasises that an analysis of racism should consider how particular ideologies owe their existence to deep-rooted issues of power. Whiteness, in the sense used in this study, drags blackness (and Asianness) along in a dominant–subordinate, and inter-dependent sporting relationship. Given that these constraints produce uneven access to opportunities, positions of power in sport, and so on, whiteness has a vested interest in perpetuating racial division.

Sport is a site where the dissolution of constraining old stereotypes can obscure other forms of restrictive prejudice in sport, and exaggerate the *real* extent of change. In this vein, the majority of the respondents believe that black and Asian people are shifting some, but not all, ideas about their temperament and aptitude in sport, which have been *imposed on them* by white discourses. But one feature of the aforementioned imbalance is the way that individual change is popularly interpreted as evidence of broader structural change. A number of this study's interviewees have benefited from and been rewarded by sport at the highest levels. For Viv Anderson, Paul Hull and Chris Sanigar, individual change has perhaps obscured the operation of racist structures and processes in sport. This comment is not meant as a criticism, or call for them to develop a radical political consciousness. Instead, it is a recognition of how endorsing sport as a realm free of racism, is also integral to survival and success at the élite levels. Acceptance into certain sporting cultures often means abiding by normative codes of behaviour, and (as these sportsmen have done) *interpreting* sports relations using a conformist vocabulary.

Black and Asian Atheletes has indicated that discourses concerning race and sport create artificial divisions between the physical prowess of the body, and the workings of the mind. For 'race realists' like Entine (cf. Back *et al.*, 2001), the 'superior' physiology of black athletes is the start point of their treatises. The reflections of Jason Gardener, David Lawrence and Garth Crooks confirmed that mental acuity is so much more difficult to 'see' when it is assumed that black people are limited intellectually, and have natural physical attributes which will 'carry them through' in athletic competition. I believe that stereotypes in sport are harder to overcome in situations where the separation of body and mind is apparently clearer. The athleticism of black men has led to their eventual acceptance as full-backs and centres in rugby, or as defenders and midfielders in football. Racial stereotyping accommodates such changes because players in these influential positions are getting larger and stronger to cope with the demands of the modern game. Whereas popular stereotypes about the more 'cerebral', tactical qualities required for management and coaching positions make these roles harder for black athletes to obtain or aspire to (see also Jones, 2002).

This feature of uneven relations in sport explains why Jon Entine's *Taboo* (Chapter 1) is more than just an attempt to get at the 'truth'. In its tortuous, overly involved attempts to identify black male sporting characteristics by 'population group', Entine's polemic shows how the popularity of some ideas resist all challenge to what they are implicitly saying: black people are good at certain sports, the gap between black and white is widening, and white people are better at organising, controlling and leading.

In short, a position of normative privilege in sport is based on the meanings and significance attached to 'race'. We have seen that commonsense thinking about the existence of all-Asian recreational leagues, in sports like football and cricket, is testament to the ways that culture racialises practices and norms. The role of racism is obscured, and so we fail to gain a true understanding of why these leagues were formed in the first place, and the level of frustration felt by Asian men in their pursuit of a professional career. Instead, and despite the efforts of some individuals and organisations, there is a feeling at the grassroots level of mainstream sport that the persistent failure of Asian men to make the grade as professionals is due to their physical frailty, lack of 'bottle', lack of interest, and desire to remain 'separate'. Whilst the perception that Asian women have no real interest in sport also continues apace.

By contrast, and for young black *men* in particular, social and cultural circumstances are understood to be important as 'push' factors. The high rates of exclusion of black boys from inner-city state schools contributes to their academic marginalising; and the relatively high unemployment rates of this group in later years are exacerbated by racism. A number of the interviewees have confirmed the significance of additional factors like low teacher expectation, sport stereotyping in their formative years, and a self-perception about sport as a dominant means of identity. The high incidence of matriarchal one-parent families that still exists among Britain's African-Caribbean groups is a linked continuity in these findings. As well as the more obvious risks of poverty and social isolation, the lack of a guiding patriarchal figure has been cited in previous research as a further spur for black children to take up a sports career. When considered alongside the success of black sportsmen, and the commonsense frames that point to innate aptitudes, it is easy to see sports' appeal.

This study has also shown that there is no single, authentic perspective about 'race' and sport. The diversity of perspectives born out of belonging to a minority ethnic group is reflected in different perceptions about innate biological characteristics. To Martin Offiah, Chris Sanigar and Joice Maduaka, 'race' determines sporting attributes; whilst to Jason Gardener, Garth Crooks and Myra Barretto, the issue of ascribed characteristics is less clear-cut. Representative sport is a clear way of seeing the cultural changes in British society which have been of concern to nationalist and racist organisations. For David

Lawrence, Ivy Alexander and Sean Viera, sporting success is fundamentally driven by a sense of injustice shaped by their relationship to the wider political context of the 1980s and 1990s. The contrasting sense conveyed by Viv Anderson, Paul Hull and Chris Sanigar highlights their conception of the nation as relatively 'free' of racial antagonisms, and shapes their different attitudes to sport and nationhood. Hence unity and diversity exist under the terms 'black' and 'Asian'; both across and within sports.

The less integral and 'intense' relationship that Asian groups have to sport certainly would appear to give Gurbinder Singh a more secure identity within it. One of the most striking elements of his, and Zia Haque's reflections, was a feeling that sport was important, but not *essential* to who they were. By contrast Garth Crooks, a former professional sportsman, brings such an erudite seriousness to his job as reporter and journalist that it has been playfully remarked (especially during the 2002 World Cup) that his questions to managers and players are long-winded, academic and difficult to understand. I believe that Crook's rarefied position as a black man in football's administrative hierarchy, leaves little room for the relaxed frivolity that may characterise the approaches of his white colleagues. In Chapter 4, we saw how the precariousness of his previous position at the PFA took even him by surprise.

Feminist research has shown how the social construction of gender has determined women's relationship to sport. Patriarchal ideas about femininity and womanhood continue to affect how women approach and participate in sport, influencing discourses on 'appropriate' physical size, sexual orientation and age. Guthrie and Castelnuovo (1992) have aptly referred to an oppressive 'movement vocabulary' that is overly concerned with grace, aesthetics and passivity in women's sport. Abidance by these feminised patterns of participation is more likely to lead to the female athlete's reward and acceptance into a system of dominant values, rather than their derision and isolation. But the interviewee testimonies have also confirmed the danger of isolating and over-emphasising the effects of patriarchy. The women in this study highlight the complexity and multi layered nature of sporting biographies.

Joice Maduaka is a professional athlete who articulates an awareness of how commercialism and sporting cultures constrain her 'voice' in sport. For her, 'race' superseded gender as the over-arching frame within which to locate structure and agency in sport. Azmina Mitha's 'natural' inclination led her along an involved path in her attempts to reconcile sport with tradition and culture. At specific, planned 'moments' such as Gay Games V, Ivy Alexander managed to participate on terms which liberated this part of her identity. Otherwise, she highlighted the ways in which 'race' and patriarchy limited her sporting expression. Race and ethnicity imposed fewer limits on Myra Barretto's participation than any other female respondent. Her testimony also highlighted how a 'problem-centred' focus in the academic literature, and the contested nature of the term 'mixed-race', denies her a fuller identity. Barretto does not 'look' Asian, and so the chance to overturn stereotyped ideas about Asian women, and their aptitudes and temperaments for sport, can be missed.

Only when we can fully understand the ways that historical discourses and practices are repeated, and only when it no longer makes sense to repeat them, can we decide that the sporting 'cost' is low enough. Much better odds for a sporting certainty.

Bibliography

Abassi, K. (1999) 'Yorkshire's rhetoric doesn't match the reality', *Guardian*, 22 September: 9–12.

Advisory Group Against Racism and Intimidation (AGARI) (1996) *Alive and Still Kicking: a Report by the Advisory Group Against Racism and Intimidation* (London: Commission for Racial Equality).

Alibhai-Brown, Y. (2001) *Mixed Feelings* (London: The Women's Press).

Andrews, D. (1996) 'The fact(s) of Michael Jordan's blackness: excavating a floating racial signifier', *Sociology of Sport Journal*, 13: 125–8.

Arnot, C. (1998) 'Furd Way Forward', *Guardian*, 6 May: 2–3.

Ashe, A. (1988) *A Hard Road to Glory: a History of the African American Athlete*, Vol. 3 (New York: Warner Books).

Askwith, R. (1998) 'Walter Tull: Britain's forgotten multicultural icon', *Guardian*, 25 March: 6.

Baca Zinn, M. *et al.* (1986) 'The costs of exclusionary practices in women's studies', *Signs: Journal of Women in Culture and Society*, 11: 290–303.

Back, L., Crabbe, T. and Solomos, J. (2001) *The Changing Face of Football* (Oxford: Berg).

Bains, J. (1997) '"Punjabi" Wolves', in C. Ross (ed.) *We Are Wolves* (Sheffield: Juma Trafalgar Works).

Bains, J. and Johal, S. (1998) *Corner Flags and Corner Shops: the Asian Football Experience* (London: Victor Gollancz).

Bains, J. with Patel, R. (1996) *Asians Can't Play Football* (Birmingham: D- zine).

Barthes, R. (1973) *Mythologies* (London: Paladin Books) (originally published in 1957).

Ben-Tovim, G. and Gabriel, J. (1987) 'The politics of race in Britain, 1962–79: a review of the major trends', in C. Husband (ed.) *'Race' in Britain: Continuity and Change* (London: Hutchinson).

Bhat, A., Carr-Hill, R. and Ohri, S. (1993) *Britain's Black Population: a New Perspective* (Aldershot: Ashgate).

Birrell, S. (1989) 'Racial relations theories and sport: suggestions for a more critical analysis', *Sociology of Sport Journal*, 6: 211–17.

—— (1990) 'Women of color, critical autobiography and sport', in M. Messner and D. Sabo (eds) *Sport, Men and the Gender Order* (Illinois: Human Kinetics).

Birrell, S. and Cole, C. L. (eds) (1994) *Women, Sport and Culture* (Champaign: Human Kinetics).

Bose, M. (1996) *The Sporting Alien: English Sport's Lost Camelot* (London: Mainstream).

Bowcott, O. (1998) 'Foot in mouth 1', *Guardian*, 5 January: 2.

Bradbury, S. (2001) *Football Unites, Racism Divides: an Evaluation of the Period 1998–2000* (Leicester: Sir Norman Chester Centre).

Bradford Youth Research Team (BYRT) (1988) *Young People in Bradford Survey 1987* (West Yorkshire: Bradford and Ilkley Community College).

Brower, J. (1972) 'The racial basis of the division of labour among players in the NFL as a function of racial stereotypes', paper presented at Pacific Sociological Association Conference, Portland, Oregon.

Brown, A. (1999) *Political Language of Race and the Politics of Exclusion* (Aldershot: Ashgate).

Brown, C. (1984) *Black and White in Britain* (London: Heinemann).

Brown, P. and Chaudhary, V. (2000) 'Everton fans top racist "league of shame"', *Guardian*, 7 January: 5.

Buruma, I. (2001) 'Why the cricket test fails', *Guardian*, 4 June: 4–5.

Calhoun, D. W. (1987) *Sport, Culture, and Personality* (Champaign: Human Kinetics).

Carby, H. V. (1992a) 'Schooling in Babylon', in CCCS (eds) *The Empire Strikes Back* (London: Routledge & Kegan Paul).

—— (1992b) 'White woman listen! Black feminism and the boundaries of sisterhood', in CCCS (eds) *The Empire Strikes Back* (London: Routledge & Kegan Paul).

Carrington, B. (1986) 'Social mobility, ethnicity and sport', *British Journal of Sociology of Education*, 7(1): 3–18.

Carrington, B. (2000) 'Double consciousness and the black British athlete', in K. Owusu (ed.) *Black British Culture and Society* (London: Routledge).

Carrington, B. and McDonald, I. (2001a) 'Introduction: "race", sport and British society', in B. Carrington and I. McDonald (eds) *'Race', Sport and British Society* (London: Routledge).

—— (2001b) 'Whose game is it anyway? Racism in local league cricket', in B. Carrington and I. McDonald (eds) *'Race', Sport and British Society* (London: Routledge).

Carrington, B. and Wood, E. (1983) 'Body talk: images of sport in a multi-racial school', *Multi-Racial Education*, 11(2): 29–38.

Carrington, B., Chivers, T. and Williams, T. (1987) 'Gender, leisure and sport: a case-study of young people of South Asian descent', *Leisure Studies*, 6: 265–79.

Cashmore, E. (1979) *Rastaman: the Rastafarian Movement in England* (London: Allen & Unwin).

—— (1982) *Black Sportsmen* (London: Routledge & Kegan Paul).

—— (1992) *Making Sense of Sports* (London: Routledge).

Cauldwell, J. (1999) 'Women's football in the United Kingdom: theorizing gender and unpacking the butch lesbian image', *Journal of Sport and Social Issues*, 23(4), November: 390–402.

Chaudhary, V. (1999) 'Asian cricket fans face visa tests', *Guardian*, 18 May: 32.

—— (2002) 'Unbeautiful game', *Guardian*, 16 October: 25.

Choi, P. (2000) *Femininity and the Physically Active Woman* (London: Routledge).

Chu, D. and Seagrave, J. (1983) 'Leadership recruitment and ethnic stratification in basketball', *Journal of Sport and Social Issues*, 5: 13–22.

Coakley, J. (1994) (5th edn) *Sport in Society* (London: Mosby).

Coard, B. (1971) *How the West Indian Child is Made Educationally Subnormal in the British School System* (London: New Beacon).

Cole, C. and Denny, D. (1994) 'Visualising deviance in post-Reagan America: Magic Johnson, AIDS, and the promiscuous world of professional sport', *Critical Sociology*, 20(3): 123–47.

Collins, P. (1991) *Black Feminist Thought: Knowledge, Consciousness, and the Politics of Empowerment* (London: Routledge).

Connell, R. W. (1987) *Gender and Power: Society, the Person and Sexual Politics* (California: Stanford University Press).

Cosgrove, S. (1991) *Hampden Babylon: Sex and Scandal in Scottish Football* (Edinburgh: Canongate).

Costa, D. M. and Guthrie, S. R. (eds) (1994) *Women and Sport: Interdisciplinary Perspectives* (Champaign: Human Kinetics).

Creedon, P. (ed.) (1994) *Women, Media and Sport* (California: Sage).

Critcher, C. (1980) 'Football since the War', in J. Clarke, C. Critcher and R. Johnson (eds) *Working-Class Culture* (London: Hutchinson).

Crossett, T. (1990) 'Masculinity, sexuality, and the development of early modern sport', in M. Messner and D. Sabo (eds) *Sport, Men and the Gender Order* (Illinois: Human Kinetics).

Curry, S. (2002) 'He used his pace . . .', *Daily Mail*, 14 February: 95.

Davis, L. R. and Harris, O. (1998) 'Race and ethnicity in US sports media', in L. A. Wenner (ed.) *MediaSport* (London: Routledge).

Dijk, T. A. (1991) *Racism and the Press* (London: Routledge).

Dimeo, P. and Finn, G. (2001) 'Racism, national identity and Scottish football', in B. Carrington and I. McDonald (eds) *'Race', Sport and British Society* (London: Routledge).

Dobson, R. (2002) 'Racist abuse still rife among footballers and spectators', *Independent on Sunday*, 14 April: 11.

Donovan, J. (1985) *Feminist Theory: the Intellectual Traditions of American Feminism* (New York: Ungar).

Duncan, J. (1998) 'White clubs fear ethnic cricketers', *Guardian*, 8 May: 15.

Duncan, M. E. and Messner, M. A. (1998) 'The media image of sport and gender', in L. A. Wenner (ed.) *MediaSport* (London: Routledge).

Dyson, M. E. (1993) *Reflecting Black* (London: University of Minnesota).

Eboda, M. (1995) 'Frankly speaking, Bruno deserves it', *Weekly Journal*, 7 September: 20.

Edwards, H. (1973) 'The black athletes: twentieth century gladiators for white America', *Psychology Today*, 7: 58–60.

—— (1984) 'The collegiate athletic arms race: origins and implications of the 'Rule 48' controversy', *Journal of Sport and Social Issues*, 8: 4–22.

Entine, J. (2000) *Taboo: Why Black Athletes Dominate Sports and Why we're Afraid to Talk About it* (New York: Public Affairs).

Eysenck, H. J. (1971) *Race, Intelligence and Education* (London: Temple Smith).

Fleming, S. (1995a) 'Sport, schooling and Asian male culture', in G. Jarvie (ed.) *Sport, Racism and Ethnicity* (London: Falmer Press).

—— (1995b) *Home and Away: Sport and South Asian Male Youth* (Aldershot: Avebury).

—— (2001) 'Racial science and South Asian and black physicality', in B. Carrington and I. McDonald (eds) *'Race', Sport and British Society* (London: Routledge).

Flint, R. H. and Rheinberg, N. (1976) *Fair Play: The Story of Women's Cricket* (London: Angus and Roberston).

Football Association (F. A) (n.d) *Women's Football History: Fact Sheet 1* (London: FA).

Frankenberg, R. (1993) *White Women, Race Matters: The Social Construction of Whiteness* (London: Routledge).

Fryer, P. (1991) (5th edn) *Staying Power: the History of Black People in Britain* (London: Pluto Press).

Garland, J. and Rowe, M. (1999) 'Selling the game short: an examination of the role of antiracism in British football', *Sociology of Sport Journal*, 16(1): 35–53.
—— (2001) *Racism and Anti-Racism in Football* (Basingstoke: Palgrave – now Palgrave Macmillan).
Gates, H. (1997) 'Black Flash', *Guardian*, 19 July: 1–2.
George, P. (1998) 'Asians stumped by county cricket clubs', *Independent on Sunday*, 5 April: 4.
Gillan, A. (1999) 'Sex appeal "pays in sport"', *Guardian*, 26 August: 4.
Gillborn, D. (1990) *'Race', Ethnicity and Education* (London: Routledge).
Gillborn, D. and Gipps, C. (1996) *Recent Research on the Achievements of Ethnic Minority Pupils* (London: Office for Standards in Education [OFSTED], HMSO).
Gilroy, P. (1987) *There Ain't No Black in the Union Jack* (London: Hutchinson).
—— (1993) *Small Acts* (London: Serpent's Tail).
Gordon, P. and Rosenberg, D. (1989) *Daily Racism: the Press and Black People in Britain* (London: Runnymede Trust).
Gramsci, A. (1971) *Selections from the Prison Notebooks* (London: Lawrence & Wishart).
Greendorfer, S. L. (1992) 'Sociology of sport and the issue of relevance: implications for physical education', in A. Yiannakis and S. L. Greendorfer (eds) *Applied Sociology of Sport* (Illinois: Human Kinetics).
Griffin, P. D. (1998) *Strong Women, Deep Closets: Lesbians and Homophobia in Sport* (Champaign: Human Kinetics).
Guthrie, S. R. and Castelnuovo, S. (1992) 'Elite women bodybuilders: models of resistance or compliance?', *Play and Culture*, 5: 401–8.
Hall, S. (1998). 'Aspiration and attitude . . . reflections on Black Britain in the nineties', *New Formations*, 33, Spring: 38–46.
Hall, S. *et al.* (1978) *Policing the Crisis: Mugging, the State and Law and Order* (Basingstoke: Macmillan – now Palgrave Macmillan).
Hargreaves, J. (1989) 'The promise and problems of women's leisure and sport', in C. Rojek (ed.) *Leisure for Leisure: Critical Essays* (Basingstoke: Macmillan – now Palgrave Macmillan).
—— (1994) *Sporting Females* (London: Routledge).
—— (1997) 'Women's sport, development, and cultural diversity: the South African experience', *Women's Studies International Forum*, 20(2): 191–209.
Hargreaves, J. A. (1986) *Sport, Power and Culture* (Cambridge: Polity Press).
Harris, H. (2002) 'Mystery star fuels racism concerns', *Daily Express*, 19 November: 67.
Harris, O. (1995) 'Athletics and academics: contrary or complementary activities?', in G. Jarvie (ed.) *Sport, Racism and Ethnicity* (London: Falmer Press).
Hartmann, D. (1996) 'The politics of race and sport: resistance and domination in the 1968 African American Olympic protest movement', *Ethnic and Racial Studies*, July, 19(3): 548–66.
Haworth, D. (1986) *Figures in a Landscape: a Lancashire Childhood* (London: Methuen).
Hayes, S. and Sugden, J. (1999) 'Winning through "naturally" still? An analysis of the perceptions held by physical education teachers towards the performance of black pupils in school sport and in the classroom', *Race, Ethnicity and Education*, 2(1): 93–107.

Hearn, J. (1984) *The Gender of Oppression: Men, Masculinity and the Critique of Marxism* (Brighton: Wheatsheaf).

Henderson, M. (2002) 'The yawn patrol', *Daily Mail*, 5 July: 92.

Henderson, R. (1995) 'Is it in the blood?', *Wisden Cricket Monthly*, 17(2): 9–10.

Hesse, B. *et al.* (1992) *Beneath the Surface: Racial Harassment* (London: Avebury).

Hill, D. (2001) (2nd edn) *Out of his Skin: the John Barnes Phenomenon* (Guildford: WSC Books).

Hill, J. (1995) 'Cricket and the Imperial connection: overseas players in Lancashire in the inter-war years', in J. Bale and J. Maguire (eds) *The Global Sports Arena: Athletic Talent Migration in an Interdependent World* (London: Frank Cass).

Hoberman, J. (1997) *Darwin's Athletes: How Sport Damaged Black America and Preserved the Myth of Race* (Boston: Houghton Mifflin Company).

Holt, R. (1989) *Sport and the British* (Oxford: Clarendon).

Honeyford, R. (1984) 'Education and race – an alternative view', *The Salisbury Review*, Winter: 30–2.

—— (1988) *Integration or Disintegration* (London: Claridge Press).

hooks, b. (1981) *Ain't I a Woman? Black Women and Feminism* (Boston: South End Press).

—— (1989) 'Representing whiteness: seeing wings of desire', *Z*, March, 2: 39.

—— (1994) *Outlaw Culture: Resisting Representations* (London: Routledge).

Hoose, P. M. (1989) *Necessities: Racial Barriers in American Sports* (New York: Random House).

Horne, J., Tomlinson, A. and Whannel, G. (2000) *Understanding Sport* (London: E & FN SPON).

Houlston, D. (1982) 'The occupational mobility of professional athletes', *International Review for the Sociology of Sport*, 17: 15–26.

Howat, G. (1975) *Learie Constantine* (London: George Allen & Unwin).

Husband, C. (1987) *'Race' in Britain: Continuity and Change* (London: Hutchinson).

Ikulayo, P. (1982) 'Physical ability and ethnic link', *British Journal of P.E.*, 13(2): 47.

Jackson, D. Z. (1989) 'Calling the plays in black and white', *Boston Globe*, 22 January: A30, 33.

Jarvie, G. (1995) 'Sport, racism and ethnicity', in G. Jarvie (ed.) *Sport, Racism and Ethnicity* (London: Falmer Press).

Johal, S. (2001) 'Playing their own game: a South Asian football experience', in B. Carrington and I. McDonald (eds) *'Race', Sport and British Society* (London: Routledge).

Jones, R. (2002) 'The black experience within English semiprofessional soccer', *Journal of Sport and Social Issues*, 26(1): 47–65.

Kane, M. (1971) 'An assessment of black is best', *Sports Illustrated*, 34(3): 72–83.

Kane, M. J. and Greendorfer, S. L. (1994) 'The media's role in accommodating and resisting stereotyped images of women in sport', in P. J. Creedon (ed.) *Women, Media and Sport: Challenging Gender Values* (London: Sage).

Keith, M. (1993) *Race, Riots and Policing: Lore and Disorder in a Multi-racist Society* (London: UCL).

Khan, V. (ed.) (1979) *Minority Families in Britain: Support and Stress* (Basingstoke: Macmillan – now Palgrave Macmillan).

Kick It Out (KIO) & Football Unites, Racism Divides (FURD) (2001a) *United Colours of Football 2* (Rochdale: Northstar).

—— (2001*b*) *United Colours of Football 3* (Rochdale: Northstar).

Kitching, A. (1992) '10 ways to pack your lunchbox like Linford', *Sun*, 6 August: 15.

Klam, M. (2000) 'American disgruntlement gene', *Guardian*, 1 July: 5.

Klein, G. (1996) *Recent Research on the Achievement of Ethnic Minority Children* (London: Runnymede Trust Bulletin).

Kohn, R. (1996) *The Race Gallery: the Return of Racial Science* (London: Vintage).

Ladyman, I. (2002) 'Who's next for Sven's boys?', *Daily Mail*, 11 June: 76.

Lane, H. (2000) 'Body politics', *Observer Sport Monthly*, October: 24–31.

Lawrence, E. (1992*a*) 'Just plain common sense: the 'roots' of racism', in Centre for Contemporary Cultural Studies (CCCS) (eds) *The Empire Strikes Back* (London: Routledge).

—— (1992*b*) 'In the abundance of water the fool is thirsty: sociology and black "pathology"', in CCCS (eds) *The Empire Strikes Back* (London: Routledge).

Lewis, T. (1979) 'Ethnic influences on girls' physical education', *British Journal of Physical Education*, September, 10(5): 113.

Lindsey, E. (1997) 'The hateful game in Essex', *Observer*, 23 February: 9.

—— (1999) 'The player', *Observer Weekend*, 7 March: 5.

—— (2000) 'Cashing in on the clamour for glamour', *Observer Weekend*, 9 April: 12.

Long, J. *et al.* (1995) *What's the Difference? A Study of the Nature and Extent of Racism in Rugby League* (School of Leisure and Sports Studies: Leeds Metropolitan University).

Long, J. *et al.* (1997) *Crossing the Boundary: a Study of the Nature and Extent of Racism in Local League Cricket* (Leeds: Leeds Metropolitan University).

Lopez, S. (1997) *Women on the Ball: a Guide to Women's Football* (London: Scarlet Press).

Lovell, T. (1995) 'Sport, racism and young women', in G. Jarvie (ed.) *Sport, Racism and Ethnicity* (London: Falmer Press).

Lyons, A. (1988) *Asian Women and Sport* (West Midlands: Sports Council).

MacDonald, M. (1995) *Representing Women* (London: Edward Arnold).

Mackay, D. (1998) 'Starting blocks for equality', *Guardian Sport*, 8 May: 2.

Maguire, J. (1995) 'Sport, racism and British society', in G. Jarvie, (ed.) *Sport, Racism and Ethnicity* (London: Falmer Press).

Maguire, J. and Stead, D. (1996), 'Far pavillions?: cricket migrants, foreign sojourns and contested identities', *International Review for the Sociology of Sport*, 31(1): 1–24.

Malcolm, D. (1997) 'Stacking in cricket: a figurational sociological reappraisal of centrality', *Sociology of Sport Journal*, 14(3): 263–82.

Malik, S. (1998) 'The construction of Black and Asian ethnicities in British film and television', in A. Briggs and C. Cobley (eds) *The Media: an Introduction* (Essex: Longman).

Majors, R. (1990) 'Cool pose: black masculinity and sports', in M. Messner and D. Sabo (eds) *Sport, Men and the Gender Order* (Illinois: Human Kinetics).

Marqusee, M. (1995*a*) 'Fear and fervour', *Guardian*, 4 July: 2.

—— (1995*b*) 'Sport and stereotype: from role model to Muhammad Ali', *Race and Class*, 36(4): 1–29.

—— (1998) *Anyone but England: Cricket, Politics and the Fate of the Nation* (London: Two Heads Publishing).

Mason, D. (1996) *Race and Ethnicity in Modern Britain* (Oxford: OUP).

Mason, T. (1988) *Sport in Britain* (London: Faber & Faber).

McDonald, I. and Ugra, S. (1998) *Anyone for Cricket? Equal Opportunities and Changing Cricket Cultures in Essex and East London* (London: Roehampton Institute and the Centre for New Ethnicities Research, University of East London).

McDonald, M. G. (1996) 'Michael Jordan's family values; marketing, meaning, and post-Reagan America', *Sociology of Sport Journal*, 13(4): 344–65.

Medoff, M. (1986) 'Positional segregation and the economic hypothesis', *Sociology of Sport*, 3: 297–304.

Menand, L. (2001) *The Metaphysical Club* (London: HarperCollins).

Mercer, K. (1994) *Welcome to the Jungle* (London: Routledge).

Messner, M., Duncan, M. and Jensen, K. (1993) 'Separating the men from the girls: the gendered language of televised sports', *Gender and Society*, March 7(1): 121–37.

Messner, M. and Sabo, D. (eds) (1990) *Sport, Men and the Gender Order* (Illinois: Human Kinetics).

Millar, B. (2000) 'Factor Phwoar', *Observer Sport Monthly*, December: 20–6.

Mirza, H. (1992) *Young, Female and Black* (London: Routledge).

—— (2000) 'Race, gender and IQ: the social consequence of a pseudo-scientific discourse', in K. Owusu (ed.) *Black British Culture and Society* (London: Routledge).

—— (ed.) (1997) *Black British Feminism: a Reader* (London: Routledge).

Modood, T. (1994) 'Political blackness and British Asians', *Sociology*, 28(4): 859–76.

Modood, T. *et al.* (1998) *Ethnic Minorities in Britain: Diversity and Disadvantage* (London: Policy Studies Institute).

Moore, E. (1998) 'Asians can't play football?', *Guardian*, 2 June: 9.

Mott, S. (1998) 'Mackie sets out on the road to international standing', *Daily Telegraph*, 25 April: 7.

Murdock, G. (1984) 'Reporting the riots: images and impact', in J. Benyon (ed.) *Scarman and After* (London: Pergamon).

Murphy, P., Williams, J. and Dunning, E. (1990) *Football on Trial: Spectator Violence and Development in the Football World* (London: Routledge).

Murray, N. (1986) 'Anti-racists and other demons: the press and ideology in Thatcher's Britain', *Race & Class*, 27(3): 1–20.

Nazroo, J. Y. (2000) 'Understanding the poorer health of black people in Britain', in K. Owusu (ed.) *Black British Culture and Society* (London: Routledge).

Nichols, P. (1998) 'Fans take Mellor to task', *Guardian*, 9 May: 34.

O'Donnell, H. (1994) 'Mapping the mythical: a geopolitics of national sporting stereotypes', *Discourse and Society*, 5(3): 345–80.

Oliver, M. (1980) 'The transmission of sport mobility orientation in the family', *International Review of Sport Sociology*, 2(15): 51–73.

Omi, M. (1989) 'In living color: race and American culture', in I. Angus and S. Jhally (eds) *Cultural Politics in Contemporary America* (London: Routledge).

Pahl, J. (1990) 'Household spending, personal spending and the control of money in marriage', *Sociology*, February, 24(1): 119–38.

Parkinson, E. *et al.* (2001) 'Part and parcel', *When Saturday Comes*, August: 26–8.

Parmar, P. (1995) 'Gender, race and power: the challenge to youth work practice', in C. Critcher, P. Branham and A. Tomlinson (eds) *Sociology of Leisure: a Reader* (London: E & FN SPON).

Parry, J. and Parry, N. (1995) 'Sport and the Black Experience', in G. Jarvie (ed.) *Sport, Racism and Ethnicity* (London: Falmer Press).

Phillips, M. and Phillips, T. (1998) *Windrush: the Irresistible Rise of Multi-Racial Britain* (London: HarperCollins).

Phoenix, A. (1987) *Gender Under Scrutiny* (London: Allen & Unwin).

Polley, M. (1998) *Moving the Goalposts: a History of Sport and Society Since 1945* (London: Routledge).

Powell, J. (2002) 'Shotgun wedding', *Daily Mail*, 27 March: 88.

Pryce, K. (1979) *Endless Pressure* (Harmondsworth: Penguin).

Rattansi, A. (1993) 'Changing the subject? Racism, culture and education', in J. Donald and A. Rattansi (eds) *'Race', Culture and Difference* (London: Sage).

Raval, S. (1989) 'Gender, leisure and sport: a case study of young people of Asian descent – a response', *Leisure Studies*, 8: 237–40.

Reay, D. and Mirza, H. S. (1997) 'Uncovering genealogies of the margins: black supplementary schooling', *British Journal of Sociology of Education*, 18: 477–99.

Roediger, D. (1994) *Towards the Abolition of Whiteness* (London: Verso).

Rose, S., Lewontin, R. C. and Kamin, L. J. (1984) *Not in Our Genes: Biology, Ideology and Human Nature* (London: Penguin Books).

Rosenbaum, R. (1995) 'The revolt of the basketball liberals', *Esquire*, 123(6): 102–6.

Runnymede Trust (1997) *Islamaphobia: a Challenge for Us All* (London: Runnymede Trust).

Saunders, V. (2002) 'No birdies', *Guardian*, 16 July: 2–3.

Scraton, S. (1992) *Shaping up to Womanhood: Women and Girls' Physical Education* (Buckingham: OUP).

—— (2001) 'Reconceptualizing race, gender and sport: the contribution of black feminism', in B. Carrington and I. McDonald (eds) *'Race', Sport and British Society* (London: Routledge).

Searle, C. (1987) 'Your daily dose: racism and the *Sun*', *Race and Class*, 29(1): 55–71.

—— (1996) 'Towards a cricket of the future', *Race and Class*, 37(4): 45–9.

Sewell, T. (1997) *Black Masculinities and Schooling: How Black Boys Survive Modern Schooling* (Chester: Trentham Books).

Sivanandan, A. (1977) 'The liberation of the black intellectual', *Race and Class*, 18(4): 329–43.

Skellington, R. (1996) (2nd edn) *'Race' in Britain Today* (Milton Keynes: Open University Press).

Small, S. (1994) *Racialised Barriers* (London: Routledge).

Smith, D. J. (1977) *Racial Disadvantage in Britain* (London: Penguin).

Strinati, D. (1995) *An Introduction to Theories of Popular Culture* (London: Routledge).

Solomos, J. and Back, L. (1996) *Racism and Society* (Basingstoke: Macmillan – now Palgrave Macmillan).

Speck, I. (2002) 'Tennis sportsmail', *Daily Mail*, 16 May: 77.

Spender, D. (ed.) (1983) *Feminist Theorists: Three Centuries of Key Women Thinkers* (New York: Random House).

Spracklen, K. (2001) '"Black pearl, black diamonds": exploring racial identities in rugby league', in B. Carrington and I. McDonald (eds) *'Race' Sport and British Society* (London: Routledge).

Staples, R. and Jones, T. (1985) 'Culture, ideology and black television images', *Black Scholar*, 16(3): 10–20.

Steen, R. (1999) 'World series with a strawberry flavour', *Guardian*, 23 October: 10.

Stoddart, B. (1988) 'Caribbean cricket: the role of sport in emerging small-nation politics', *International Journal*, 43(4): 618–42.

Szymanski, S. (1997) 'Beaten in the race for the ball', *New Economy*, Winter, 4(4): 212–7.

Talbot, M. (1988) 'Understanding the relationships between women and sport: the contribution of British feminist approaches in leisure and cultural studies', *International Review for the Sociology of Sport*, 23(1): 33–41.

Tennant, I. (1994) *Imran Khan* (London: Gollancz/Witherby).

Theberge, N. (1993) 'The construction of gender in sport: women, coaching and the naturalisation of difference', *Social Problems*, 40(3): 301–13.

Tong, R. (1989) *Feminist Theory: a Comprehensive Introduction* (Colorado: Westview).

Toolis, K. (2001) 'The running mate', *Observer*, 18 February: 9.

Vasili, P. (1998) *The First Black Footballer: Arthur Wharton* (Essex: Frank Cass).

Verma, G. K and Darby, D. S. (1994) *Winners and Losers: Ethnic Minorities in Sport and Recreation* (London: Falmer Press).

Vertinsky, P. and Captain, G. (1998) 'More myth than history: representation of the black female's athletic ability', *Journal of Sport History*, 25(3): 532–61.

Viner, K. (1997) 'Rock bottom', *Guardian*, 30 June: 4–5.

Wainwright, M. (2001) 'Spark that ignited Leeds violence', *Guardian*, 6 June: 9.

Watman, M. (1968) *History of British Athletics* (London: Robert Hale).

Werbner, P. (1996) '"Our blood is green": cricket, identity and social empowerment among British Pakistanis', in J. MacClancy (ed.) *Sport, Identity and Ethnicity* (Oxford: Berg).

Westwood, S. (1990), 'Racism, black masculinity and the politics of space', in J. Hearn and D. Morgan (eds) *Men, Masculinities and Social Theory* (London: Unwin & Hyman).

Whannel, G. (1992) *Fields in Vision* (London: Routledge).

Williams, J. (1992) *Lick My Boots . . . Racism in British Football* (Leicester: Sir Norman Chester School for Football Research).

Williams, J. (2001) *Cricket and Race* (Oxford: Berg).

Williams, R. (2000) 'Time for French lessons', *Guardian*, 22 June: 5.

Wimbush, E. (1986) *Women, Leisure and Well-Being* (Edinburgh: Centre for Leisure Research, Dunfermline College).

Wright, I. (1996) *Mr Wright* (London: Collins Willow).

Wright, J. and Clarke, G. (1999) 'Sport, the media and the construction of compulsory heterosexuality: a case study of women's rugby union', *International Review for the Sociology of Sport*, 34(3), September: 227–43.

Wright, S. (2002) 'Crime exclusive', *Daily Mail*, 12 June: 7.

Young, I. M. (1980) 'Throwing like a girl: a phenomenology of feminine body comportment, motility and spatiality', *Human Studies*, 3: 137–56.

Zaman, H. (1997) 'Islam, wellbeing and physical activity: perceptions of Muslim young women', in G. Clarke and B. Humberstone (eds) *Researching Women and Sport* (London: Macmillan – now Palgrave Macmillan).

Index

Note: the names of athletes interviewed for this book appear in bold type.

Abdullah, Tewfik 24
African-Caribbean *see* black
Akram, Wasim 52
Alexander, Ivy (football) xi, xxi,
    163–73, 186
  Gay Games V 171–2, 186
  experiences racial solidarity 172
  homophobia in football 168–9,
    170–1
  media coverage as racist and
    sexist 172–3
  national identity/belonging
    166–8, 186
  parent's attitudes towards
    sport 164–5
  role models 166–7
  sexism in football 170
  sports experiences in early
    years 163–6
  TWFC 169–71
  see also black girls/women;
    Maduaka, Joice
Amateur Athletics Association
    (AAA) 27
Anderson, Viv (football) x, 31, 34,
    44, 48, 184
  career unimpeded by racism 114,
    184, 186
  enthusiasm for sport 68–9
  family's attitude to sport 83
  management roles in football 104
  racial abuse as a diversionary
    tactic 111–13
  role models 65–7
  teacher expectations of 71–2
anti-racist initiatives 32, 36–7,
    37–9, 42, 50
Armanath, Lala 46
Arsenal FC 168

Ashe, Arthur 66
Asian boys/men
  in cricket 45–6, 47, 49, 51–4
  in football 45, 47–8, 49–51
  history in British sport 45–54
  marginal position in sport 21,
    48, 50
  media representations 47–8,
    53–4, 118–19
  in recreational sport 20–2, 47, 49
  social class in sports 62
  effects of whiteness in sport 20–2
  see also anti-racist initiatives; racial
    abuse; racism; stereotyping
Asian Games 47
Asian girls/women xv, xvii–xviii,
    xix, xx, xxi
  sports participation 133–4, 137
  see also Barretto, Myra; Mitha,
    Azmina
Askwith, R. 25
athletics (track) 27
  see also Gardener, Jason; Maduaka,
    Joice
'Awaz Utaoh' 158–9

Back, Les (*et al.*) xvii, 16, 19, 40,
    104, 111, 121, 169–70
Bains, Jas 49, 50, 64, 134
Barnes, John 34–5, 36, 38, 44, 103
Barretto, Myra (multi-sports) xi,
    134, 173–82
  absence of racism in sport
    179–81
  'Asian' identity 179–81, 187
  enthusiasm for sport in early
    years 173–5
  experience of racism 179–80
  family's attitude to sport 175–6

Barretto, Myra – *continued*
  gender socialisation in
      sport 177–8
  sexism in sport 178–9
  sports participation blighted by
      injury 177
  symbolic gender differences in
      family 176
  teacher expectations 179
  views on sport and race 181–2,
      185
  see also Asian girls/women; Mitha,
      Azmina
Barthes, Roland
  concept of 'myth' 13, 92–3,
      142
Batson, Brendan 31
Bennett, Louise 29
Best, Clyde 31
Birrell, S. 131–2
black boys/men
  in athletics 27
  in boxing 27, 31
  in cricket 26–7, 30, 35–6
  in football 24–6, 27–9, 31–2,
      34–5, 36, 40–1, 44
  history in British sport 24–44
  media representations 32–3,
      115–18
  in rugby league 31, 35
  in rugby union 31
  see also race; racial abuse; racism;
      stereotypes
black girls/women xvii, xx, xxi
  sports participation 134–6
  see also Alexander, Ivy; Maduaka,
      Joice
Blake, Nathan 18
Bonaly, Soraya 151
Boulmerka, Hassiba 131
boxing 27, 31
Bradford City FC 50
British Boxing Board of Control
    (BBBC) 27
Brown, A. 39
Bruno, Frank 33–4, 42–3, 44
Budd, Zola 167
Butcher, Roland 31
Butia, Bhaichung 50

Campanis, Al 7–8
Campbell, Kevin 40
Cantona, Eric 18, 38
Carpenter, Harry 43
Carrington, Ben xvii, 14, 20, 34, 43,
    52, 141–2
Carrington, Bruce 79
Cashmore, Ellis xvi, 49, 71, 79, 116
Castelnuovo, S. 139, 186
Celtic FC 48
Chambers, Dwain xv
Chelsea Ladies FC 137
Choi, Precilla 138–9, 173
Christie, Linford 24, 37, 44, 108,
    116, 120
coaching, sports *see* management
Coakley, Jay 9, 11
Coard, B. 33
Coe, Sebastian 108
Cole, Andy 38, 117
Cole, Ashley 19
Cole, C. 118
Collymore, Stan 18
Commission for Racial Equality
    (CRE) 38
Commonwealth Immigrants Act
    (1962, 1968) 29–30
Connors, Jimmy 66
Constantine, Learie 26, 27
Conteh, John 31
Corner Flags and Corner Shops xvii,
    49, 98
Cother brothers 45
Couch, Jane 137
Cricket 26–7, 30, 35–6, 45–6, 47,
    49, 51–4, 128
  see also Lawrence, David; racial abuse;
      racism; stereotyping; whiteness
Crooks, Garth (football) x, 44
  Asian men and sport 97–8
  contradictions in racial
      abuse 111
  enthusiasm for sport in early
      years 58–9, 68–9
  family's attitude to sport 80
  media coverage of 121–2
  minority ethnic groups and
      media use 123
  PFA Chairman 106–7

role models 66–7
sporting identity 186
sports stereotyping 95–6,
    184, 185
teacher expectations 73
Cunningham, Laurie 31
Curry, Steve 44

Davis, Sharron 138
Deford, Frank 7
Delaphena, Lloyd 28
Denny, D. 118
Dick, Kerr's Ladies FC 128
Dimeo, Paul 16
D'Oliveira, Basil 30
Dosanj, Aman 137
Duleepsinhji, Kumar 46
Dyer, Kieron 19
Dyson, M. E. 65, 100

Earle, Robbie 44
Edward, Harry 27
Edwards, Maxine 137
Engineer, Farouk 47
Entine, Jon 22
    critique of *Taboo* 9–12, 184
Eubank, Chris 43
Eysenck, H. J. 7

FA (Football Association) 24, 29, 39,
    128–9, 137, 138 (*Rule 37*)
families 77–90, 145, 156–7, 162,
    164–5, 175–6
far-right groups 30, 32
    see also anti-racist initiatives;
        racial abuse
Fashanu, John 44
Fashanu, Justin 32
feminisms 129–33, 140
femininity 127–8, 131, 138–9,
    140–2, 150, 154–5, 156–8,
    160–2, 165, 177–9, 186
Ferdinand, Les 38
Ferguson, Sir Alex 17, 18
Finn, Gerry 16
Fleming, S. xvii
football 24–6, 27–9, 31–2, 34–7,
    37–41, 43–5, 47–8, 49–51,
    128–9, 137–8

see also Alexander, Ivy; Anderson,
    Viv; Crooks, Garth; racial
    abuse; racism; Regis, Cyrille;
    stereotypes; whiteness
Football (Offences) Act 1991 38
Football (Offences and Disorder) Act
    1999 38
Football Supporters Association 37
'Football Unites Racism Divides' 38
Foucault, Michel (notion of *power*)
    69–70
'Foxes Against Racism' 50
Fusco, Coco 13

Gardener, Jason (track athletics) x
    absence of racism in sport 107–8
    dissatisfied with black media
        coverage 120, 122
    enthusiasm for sport in early
        years 56–8
    family's attitude to sport 86–7
    father's warning 68
    role model 67, 105–6
    sports stereotyping 94–5, 184, 185
    'stacking' 102–3
    teacher expectations 71–2, 74
Garland, Jon 23, 37
Gay Games V (Amsterdam) 171–2,
    186
George, Paula 137
gender 160, 165, 176, 177–9, 186
    see also femininity; race; sexism
'gender marking' 140, 173
genetics 6–7
    see also 'race'
Giggs, Ryan 38
Gilroy, Paul 6
Gramsci, Antonio 13, 67, 69
    concept of 'hegemony' 13–14, 67,
        69
Griffiths, Peter 30, 47
Guardian 115
Gudjohnsen, Eidur 117
Gullit, Ruud 19, 103
Guscott, Jeremy 31
Guthrie, S. R. 139, 186

Hagler, Marvin 31
Hague, William xiii

Hall, Stuart   7, 32
Hamed, Naseem   53
Hanley, Ellery   35, 37, 121
Hansen, Ashia   135
Haque, Robeel   75–6
Haque, Zia (hockey, badminton)   xi,
    156, 186
  'Asian' business acumen   98
  'Asian' temperament   88–90
  experiences covert racism   108–9
  family's attitude to sport   88
  role models   67
  sport and race   88
  sports opportunities   64
  sport with army career   85
  teacher expectations   71–2, 75–6
      (Robeel's answer)
Hargreaves, Jennifer   xviii, 14, 128,
    138, 168
Harriman, Andrew   31
Harrison, Audley   115
Hasselbaink, Jimmy Floyd   117
Haworth, D.   26
Headley, George   26
Hegazi, Hussein   24
hegemony *see* Gramsci, Antonio
Henderson, Robert   41–2, 51, 114, 122
Heppolate, Ricky   47, 181
Heron, Giles   28
Heskey, Emile   19
Hidegkuti, Nandor   28
Hill, Dave   15, 29, 34–5, 36
Hingis, Martina   141
'Hit Racism for Six'   42
Hoberman, John
  Darwin's Athletes   12
homophobia
  and women's sport   139, 141,
      168–9, 171
hooks, bell   130–1
Houlston, D.   84
Hull, Paul (rugby union)   x, 31
  absence of racism in rugby union
      107–8, 184, 186
  family's attitude to sport   85
  favourable media coverage   119
  sport and social class   101, 119
  sports opportunities   63–4
  'stacking'   101

  teacher expectations   71–2, 76
  sport with RAF career   85
Husband, Charles   xv, 6
Hussain, Nasser   53, 114

Ince, Paul   18, 44, 93
Illingworth, Ray   44
'infantilising'   140
Iqbal, Asif   47
'Islamophobia'   53–4, 133

Jarvie, Grant   xvi–xvii
Jhooti, Permi   137
Johal, S.   21–2, 49, 134
Johanneson, Albert   29
Johnson, Bunny   31
Jordan, Michael   100, 118

Kane, Martin   5
Khan, Iftikhar Ali   46
Khan, Imran   51
Khan, Salim   45
'Kick It Out' (KIO)   39, 165
Kohn, R.   5
Kournikova, Anna   140

Lannaman, Sonia   135
Lawrence, David 'Syd' (cricket)   x,
    172
  abuse from black British
      supporters   114
  abused by spectators   110
  enthusiasm for sport   68
  family's attitude to sport   85–6
  racism in cricket   35–6
  role models   66
  sports stereotyping   94, 184
  teacher expectations   71–3
  and white South African
      cricketers   110, 185–6
Lawrence, Stephen   xiii
Lee, Bruce   66
'Leeds Fans United Against Racism
    and Fascism'   37
Leicester Asian Sports Initiative   21,
    38, 49
Leslie, Jack   25
'Let's Kick Racism out of Football'
    (LKR)   38–9, 50

Lewis, Denise xv, 135, 142
Liverpool FC 15–16
London, Jack 27
Louis, Joe 8
Love Thy Neighbour 66

Macey, Dean 115
Mackie, Ian 149
Maduaka, Joice (track athletics) xi,
135, 143–54, 186
cultural style 152–3
family's attitude to
education 145
introduction to competitive
sport 143–4
media coverage as racist 150–2
race and sports performance
147–9, 185
racism in sport and society 153–4
starts to take sport more seriously
145–7
stereotyping 149–50
see also Alexander, Ivy; black
girls/women
Maguire, J. 41
Majors, R. 71, 100
Malcolm, Dominic 41, 99
Malik, S. 106
management 103–4
Mauresmo, Amelie 141
M'bomba, Patrick 41
McDonald, Ian xvii, 20, 52
McDonald, M. G. 118
MCC (Marylebone Cricket Club) 139
McFarlane, Mike 146
media coverage 19, 32–3, 35, 38, 48,
53–4, 115–23, 139–42, 150–2,
172–3
Menand, Louis 183
Mercer, Kobena 116, 153
Messner, M. A. 129
Midland Asian Sports Forum 50, 75
Minter, Alan 31
Mirza, Heidi 6–7, 78
Mitha, Azmina (martial arts) xi,
134, 154–63, 179
Awaz Utaoh 158–9
community sport 163
early experiences of sport 154–7

gender and sport 160
parent's attitude to sport 157
race and sports performance 159
sports activity outside school
155–6
sports participation and femininity
155, 157–8, 160–2, 186
sports participation for young
people 162–3
see also Asian girls/women; Barretto,
Myra
Motson, John 115, 122–3
'myth' *see* Barthes, Roland

national identity 27, 41–3, 44, 46,
48, 114, 122, 166–8, 186
nationalism 31, 34–5, 35–6, 40–1, 48
Noades, Ron 115–6

Offiah, Martin (rugby union and
league) x, 35
family's attitude to sport 81
race and sports performance 102,
185
racial abuse as diversionary
tactic 113–4
role models 67
sports opportunities 64
'stacking' 102
teacher expectations 71–2, 76
Ollivierre, C. A. 26, 45
Oti, Chris 31

Pakistan cricket team 51–2,
119
Parmar, Arvind xv, 53
Parris, John 25–6
Patel, R. 64
patriarchy 130
Pemberton, John 16
Peters, James 'Darkie' 31
Powell, Enoch
Rivers of Blood speech 30
Powell, Hope 136,
137, 165
Professional Footballer's Association
(PFA) 38, 106

'Quaid-e-Azam' League 49

'race'
  and genetics 6–12
  and media representations 115–23
  resurgence of ideas about 6–9
  and social class in sports 61–4,
    67–9
  social construction of 5–6
  and sports performance xiii–xiv,
    xv–xvi, 5, 7–12, 69–70, 92–8,
    99–103, 147–50, 159, 181–2,
    185
  and teacher expectations 70–7
  vocabulary 7, 9, 115
  and gender in sport 130–6, 137,
    141–2
  see also racial abuse; racism;
    stereotypes; whiteness
racial abuse
  absence in sport 107–10, 114,
    179–81, 184, 186
  as diversionary tactic 111–3
  exacerbated by social events 25,
    29–30, 32–4, 35, 53–4
  as humour 15–16
  media reactions to 19, 36, 38
  by other athletes 20, 29
  overt 20, 25, 27, 29, 34–5, 35–6,
    39–42, 53–4, 110–14, 131–2
  by supporters 17, 18–19, 20, 29,
    111–14
  types of 107
  see also Asian boys/men; black
    boys/men; racism; whiteness
racism 6, 183, 184–5
  covert 179–80, 153–4
  cultural xiii, xiv, 185
  institutional 15–18, 18–19, 27,
    38–9, 46–7, 52–3, 99–103,
    115–23
  and national identity 27, 41–3, 46,
    48, 114, 122, 186
  see also race; racial abuse;
    stereotypes; whiteness
Ramprakash, Mark 53
Ranjitsinhji, K. S. 10, 46
Rastafarianism 32
Regis, Cyrille (football) x, 31
  black men exploding
    stereotypes 119

enthusiasm for sport 57, 68–9
family's attitude to sport 83–4
management roles in football
  103–4
racial abuse as diversionary
  tactic 113
role model 66–7, 105
teacher expectations 71–2
Ricketts, Michael 44
Robinson, Sugar Ray 27
Roediger, David 13
role models 64–7, 104–7, 165–6
Rosenbaum, R. 116
Rowe, Michael 23, 37
rugby league 31, 35
  see also Offiah, Martin
rugby union 31
  see also Hull, Paul
Rusedski, Greg 167
Rushdie, Salman
  The Satanic Verses 53

Sabo, D. 129
Samuel, Mollie 135
Sanderson, Tessa 135
Sanigar, Chris (boxing) x,
    184, 185
  'Asian' business acumen 198
  conflicts in early years 59–60
  race and sports performance 97,
    185
  role models 67
  teacher expectations 71–2, 75
SARI (Society Against Racist Incidents)
    158
Sarwar, Rashid 48
Saunders, Vivien 139
Schmeichel, Peter 18
Scraton, Sheila 138
sexism 127–9, 138–42, 170, 178–9
Sheffield United FC 50
'Show Racism the Red Card' 38
Singh, Amar 46
Singh, Gurbinder (weightlifting) xi
  'Asian' business acumen 98
  Asian identity in sport 106, 186
  enthusiasm for sport 59
  experiences covert racism 109
  family's attitude to sport 87

popularity of sport among Asian
groups 98
role models 67
teacher expectations 71–2,
75, 76
'sledging' 20
Small, Stephen 11, 69, 104, 122
Smethwick (Birmingham) 30, 47
Smith, Jim 92
Smith, Roy 47
Snyder, Jimmy 'the Greek' 7, 8
South Asian *see* Asian
social class 61–4, 67–9, 101, 132,
134, 136
South Africa 30, 46, 109–10, 131,
172, 186
sport
solution to 'race' problems xiii,
5, 33–4, 48–9
and Empire 26, 45
and gender xvii–xviii, xx, xxii,
127–42, 143–82
and identity xv, 21–2, 26–7, 41–3,
44, 46, 106, 114, 122, 166–8,
179–81, 185–7
teacher expectations (school)
70–7, 133, 175, 179, 181
Sports Sponsorship Advisory
Service 141
Spracklen, K. 15, 50
'stacking' 99–103, 148
'St Helen's Ladies' 128
Stead, D. 41
stereotypes 91–2, 184–5
Asian boys/men 50–1, 51–2,
97, 98–9
Asian girls/women 133–4
black boys/men 28–9, 44, 91–7,
119, 184–5
black girls/women 135–6
sexual 127–9, 135
see also gender; race; racism; sexism;
teachers; whiteness
Sterling, Bunny 31
Storer, Bill 27
Strawberry, Darryl 118
Sudan, Amy 118
Sullivan, Clive 31
'symbolic annihilation' 140

'symbolic representation' 140
Szymanski, S. 100

Taylor, Graham 92
teachers (school)
attitudes to minority ethnic pupils
70–7, 133, 175, 179, 181
Tebbit, Norman xiii, 33, 41, 51
Thatcher, Margaret 32, 34
Thomas, Geoff 16
Thompson, Daley 31
Tigana, Jean 104
Tuchman, G. 140
Tull, Walter 25, 41
Turpin, Dick 27
Turpin, Randolph 27
TWFC (The Women's Football Club)
169–71
Tyson, Mike 118

Ubogu, Victor 31
UEFA (Union of European Football
Associations) 40

Vasili, Phil 25, 34
Viera, Sean (martial arts) xi
experiences covert racism 109–10
family's attitude to sport 81–6
rival's media coverage 120–1
sports stereotyping 96–7
'stacking' in martial arts 103
teacher expectations 71–2, 76–7
and white South Africans 109–10,
172, 186

Wenger, Arsene 116–7
Werbner, P. xvii, 53
West Bromwich Albion FC 83
Wharton, Arthur 24–5
whiteness 12–22, 130, 168, 183
see also Barthes, Roland; Gramsci,
Antonio; 'race'; racial abuse;
racism; sexism; stereotypes
Williams, Charlie 28
Williams, Jack 46, 47, 51
Williams, R. 117
Williams, Serena 136, 141, 151
Williams, Venus 136, 141, 151
Wilson, Paul 47, 48, 181

women
    in football   137–8, 139
    in golf   139
    media representations of   139–42
    in tennis   140–1
    in aerobics   142
    in beach volleyball   142
    in bodybuilding   142
    see also sexism; sport. *See under*
        female athletes interviewed

Women's Cricket Association   128
Women's Football
    Association   139
Women's Tennis
    Association   140
Wright, Ian   16, 18, 44

Yorke, Dwight   117
Young, I. M.   138
Younis, Waqar   52